Daniel Reconstructed

Daniel Reconstructed

Reading, Teaching, and Preaching with Fresh Eyes

Jonathan D. Redding

BAYLOR UNIVERSITY PRESS

Cover and book design by Elyxandra Encarnación
Cover illustration by Elyxandra Encarnación

Library of Congress Cataloging-in-Publication Data

Names: Redding, Jonathan D., author.
Title: Daniel reconstructed : reading, teaching, and preaching with fresh eyes / Jonathan D. Redding.
Description: Waco, Texas : Baylor University Press, [2024] | Includes bibliographical references and index. | Summary: "Reconsiders the biblical book of Daniel as a theological and interpretive resource, with attention given to how contemporary Christian readers can responsibly approach Daniel's challenging but compelling messages"-- Provided by publisher.
Identifiers: LCCN 2024004243 (print) | LCCN 2024004244 (ebook) | ISBN 9781481320153 (paperback) | ISBN 9781481320177 (adobe pdf) | ISBN 9781481320160 (epub)
Subjects: LCSH: Bible. Daniel.--Criticism, interpretation, etc. | Christian life.
Classification: LCC BS1555.2 .R534 2024 (print) | LCC BS1555.2 (ebook) | DDC 224/.506--dc23/eng/20240513
LC record available at https://lccn.loc.gov/2024004243
LC ebook record available at https://lccn.loc.gov/2024004244

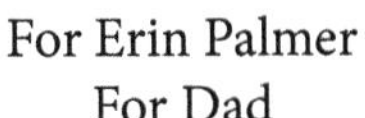

For Erin Palmer
For Dad

Contents

Preface

I was born and raised in the foothills of North Carolina, just along the Appalachian Mountains. My dad was the pastor of a medium-sized Baptist church in one of the little towns nearby, so I grew up going to church all the time. The lingo my fellow preachers' kids and I use to describe ourselves is that we are "church rats," meaning any time the church doors opened we were there. Mom taught Sunday school at the church for many years across all age ranges, from pre-K to young adults. My brothers and I considered that building and accompanying Fellowship Hall a second home. It made me who I am, and I am proud of it. This book's roots stand in that church upbringing.

The rural community near my home built itself on the back of the furniture industry, and everything changed when those factories went overseas. People lost their jobs and homes, and, in many ways, the community is still recovering from that now decades-old economic shift. It was during this time that talk of "the end of the world" ran wild. Historically speaking, in America particularly, cultural and economic shifts make people panic and seek something, anything, for answers. Where I am from, people turn to the Bible for guidance and help through such a shift.

One book that got much traction during this time was the book of Daniel. Suddenly, everyone was an expert on it. Kids my age began coming to elementary school talking about how last night's news made their parents even more sure that Daniel was coming true and that the end was near. Tent revivals popped up, and churches brought in so-called experts to preach Daniel's "prophetic code" and reveal how it applies to the current state of things. Then September 11, 2001, happened, and the apocalyptic rhetoric spun out of control. Many pastors and Christian leaders presented Daniel as pointing to one truth: everyone outside the United States was now just a cog in Daniel's wheel, existing only to usher in the second coming of Jesus.

And yet, Daniel says nothing about the United States or Jesus. Nor does it say anything about Afghanistan, Osama bin Laden, and the price of oil. I dug into the topic and found that my small community's use of Daniel was, oddly, an established, historical practice. In times of perceived crisis, American Christians use Daniel to understand our history, for better or worse.

I found myself wondering about the origins of such readings. Is this the only way to read Daniel? Or are there other possibilities that my fellow Christians and I neglect? I remembered the stories of Daniel and the lions' den, the fiery furnace, and the handwriting on the wall, but that was where every church I attended stopped. This created a gulf between churches that preach and teach Daniel's stories for some kind of moral guidance and churches that use Daniel to strike fear into the hearts of whoever listens. Conversations stopped there. I remember thinking, even at a young age, "There has to be another way . . . Is what I've heard preached and taught all there is to learn about Daniel?"

This book is my attempt to answer that question and offer another voice in how we read Daniel. I wrote it not to claim the conversation starts and stops with what I say. I want the opposite. I want this book to spark conversation and make people not only ask what a biblical text can mean but also consider how people use biblical texts to perpetuate political and social agendas. As you read this, I invite you to join the conversation. Let us reconsider Daniel, shall we?

Acknowledgments

As always, there are far too many people to thank and acknowledge, but here is my feeble attempt. I want to thank four students of mine from Nebraska Wesleyan University: Chandler Smith, Anastasia Popham, Justise Propp, and Camryn Melroy. These four brilliant and talented people were research assistants with me at some point during the project. They chased down obscure books and articles while also having to meet with me to talk through their research at least once a week. There ideas and insights buttress this work, and it is much, much better for it. I also want to thank the Nebraska Wesleyan University students who took Biblical Greek and Biblical Hebrew with me as I translated Daniel. You each gave me the courage to leave the more complicated translation issues on the page so others can join the difficult but beyond worthwhile work that comes from engaging the biblical languages.

I want to thank my graduate school professors, specifically Dr. Neal Walls and the late Dr. Gail O'Day of the Wake Forest University School of Divinity. I had so many questions during my time at Wake, and you each answered them with grace, patience, and honesty. I also want to thank Dr. Fernando Segovia, Dr. Annalisa Azzoni, Dr. Choon-Leong Seow, Dr. Jack Sasson, Dr. Douglas Knight, and Rev. Dr. Herbert Marbury at Vanderbilt University. You each taught me not to shy away from the hard and challenging work of biblical studies. I am thankful for what you taught (and still teach) me.

Dr. Rita Lester at Nebraska Wesleyan University has been the best possible peer, mentor, and friend during this time. Thank you for being a sounding board and for always being honest. It means more than I can ever say.

I very much wanted this work to stay grounded in my love for the church and my faith, and Rev. Brandee Mimitzraiem—my pastor, mentor, and friend—helped me do that. Rev. Mimitzraiem also dared me to push harder and asked deeper theological questions. She told me not to let any idea or challenge raised by the text go unanswered. I did my best to do just that.

My family also played an immeasurable role in keeping my research and writing grounded in the church. My mother and late father were constantly asking how the work was going, and my brothers gave a listening ear when I had questions about the lived realities of Christian life connected to the book of Daniel. Thank you for your love, support, and, most of all, patience.

My final acknowledgments will always go to my partner and spouse, Erin Palmer. I met Erin in a graduate class about the book of Daniel, so it is fitting that we somehow ended up together. Erin, your honesty, scholarly brilliance, friendship, and love make everything I do better. Not every Daniel scholar gets to have dinner each night with a Revelation scholar, do they? Thank you for everything.

Abbreviations

ABD *Anchor Bible Dictionary*. Edited by David Noel Freedman. 6 vols. New York: Doubleday, 1992.

ANF *Ante-Nicene Fathers*

BDB Francis Brown, S. R. Driver, Charles A. Briggs, James Strong, and Wilhelm Gesenius. *The Brown-Driver-Briggs Hebrew and English Lexicon: With an Appendix Containing the Biblical Aramaic: Coded with the Numbering System from Strong's Exhaustive Concordance of the Bible*. Peabody, Mass.: Hendrickson, 1996.

BHS *Biblia Hebraica Stuttgartensia*. Edited by Karl Elliger and Wilhelm Rudolph. Stuttgart: Deutsche Bibelgesellschaft, 1983.

CANE *Civilizations of the Ancient Near East*. Edited by Jack M. Sasson. 4 vols. New York, 1995. Repr. in 2 vols. Peabody, Mass.: Hendrickson, 2006.

CO *Ioannis Calvini Opera Quae Supersunt Omnia*

CSCO Corpus Scriptorum Christianorum Orientalium. Edited by Jean Baptiste Chabot et al. Paris, 1903.

CTS *Calvin's Commentaries*. Calvin Translation Society. Grand Rapids: Baker, 2005.

ESOO Ephrem the Syrian. *Sancti patris nostri Ephraem Syri Opera omnia*. Edited by J. A. Assemani. Rome, 1737.

DDD *Dictionary of Deities and Demons in the Bible*. Edited by Karel van der Toorn, Bob Becking, and Pieter W. van der Horst. Leiden: Brill, 1995. 2nd rev. ed. Grand Rapids: Eerdmans, 1999.

JCD Jerome. *Commentary on Daniel*. Translated by Gleason Archer. Grand Rapids: Baker, 1958.

LW	Martin Luther and Jaroslav Jan Pelikan. *Luther's Works*. Edited by Jaroslav Pelikan, Hilton C. Oswald, Helmut T. Lehmann, Christopher Boyd Brown, Benjamin T. G. Mayes, and James Langebartels. American ed. St. Louis: Concordia, 1955.
OG	Old Greek version
θ	Theodotion Greek Version
Vg	Latin Vulgate
WADB	*D. Martin Luther's Werke: Kritische Gesamtausgabe (Weimarer Ausgabe)*. Weimar: H. Böhlaus Nachfolger, 1883.

Introduction

Reading Daniel Anew

Christians fear the book of Daniel. Maniacal kings, court tricksters, fearsome animals, chaotic primordial seas, and beings fighting across the heavens overwhelm us, prompting even the most studious Christian to avoid it. Scarce congregational and denominational attention stacks the proverbial cards against Daniel, forcing us Christians out of our way just to read it. For example, the 2019–2022 lectionary cycle includes only three Daniel readings, fourteen verses total. This sparse discussion underlines a "canon within the canon" phenomenon, as selected Daniel stories get traction while we cast other chapters and verses aside. Children learn about "Daniel and the Lions' Den" and "The Fiery Furnace." Adults discuss possible end-times scenarios with handpicked verses from Daniel 2 and 7–12 as their guide. Devotional books urge readers to "be like Daniel," cherry-picking verses to reconstruct Daniel in their image. But far too often conversations stop there, leaving Daniel to waste away, hidden in plain sight.

What makes us avoid Daniel? What deters larger Christian audiences from wrestling with it and reading it, and I mean really reading it, leaving ourselves open to the challenges and callings that may lay within? What makes us avoid Daniel's puzzling questions, complex possibilities, and dynamic images? The book's content alone cannot be the issue, because Christian readers are more than comfortable with what the Bible offers. We gravitate toward the biblical prophets despite Ezekiel's fantastical visions. We preach and teach Jeremiah and Isaiah's hyperbolic violence ad nauseam. Church folks use the plagues, death, and destruction in Exodus and Joshua to support sermons and lessons of divine intervention on behalf of God's faithful flock. Like the prophets, Exodus, Joshua, and the rest of the Bible, Daniel itself is innocuous. Its words carry no lethal poison, and its stories yield no dreadful curses. Yet we hide it away and sanitize it as we see fit.

If content is not the problem, what is? The answer is deceptively simple: contemporary Christian audiences avoid Daniel because of what other Christians have done to it. We accept previous readings without question, allowing them to become as sacred as the text itself. Sermons about apocalyptic gloom and doom and needlessly verbose scholarly discussions scare lay audiences away from Daniel. Christians who define their theologies according to pain and suffering allow blusterous and boisterous voices to suffocate readings they deem unworthy. The result is minimal interaction with Daniel, creating an interpretive double-edged sword. On one side, readers never absorb the rich history in and behind Daniel, silencing its stories of success, failure, hope, and sorrow. The other side leaves Daniel to a vocal Christian contingent that creates restrictive dominant hermeneutical narratives; it is quite literally their way or no way. Loud, unchallenged voices make Daniel their destructive tool as the Christians who wield Daniel use it to create a self-reinforcing standard of hellfire, brimstone, and eternal damnation.

As a Baptist raised in the American South, I am no stranger to such readings. Family and friends still send me unsolicited Daniel pamphlets, cards, and other religious artifacts filled with apocalyptic gloom, doom, and despair. Such materials show the vibrant interpretive power Daniel holds among American evangelicals, but these readings are narrow, limited, and relay minimal theological nuance. Billboards, advertisements, and mailings for conferences and sermon series use Daniel to attract, and sometimes scare, the public into believing one way over all other possible readings. They tout "The end is nigh!" and "Learn the truth before it's too late!" to manipulate a captivated audience to accept their reading or else. For example, figure 1 is a mailing shared by a student at the undergraduate institution where I teach.[1]

This mailing came unrequested, appearing one day in this student's mailbox. According to the glossy and color-print card, Daniel is but one of many biblical texts foretelling the doom that will unfold seven years from an undefined date. A striking absence of chronological specifics means the start date of the seven-year clock remains unknown. And yet, those responsible for the mailing in figure 1, InCaseNoOneToldYou.com, feel so impassioned about sharing their interpretation that they paid to disseminate these ideas via the United States Postal Service to complete strangers.

Figure 2 is the front of another mailing, and figure 3 is the back of the same mailing. Like figure 1, the document in figures 2 and 3 arrived via the United States Postal Service unrequested by the receiver.

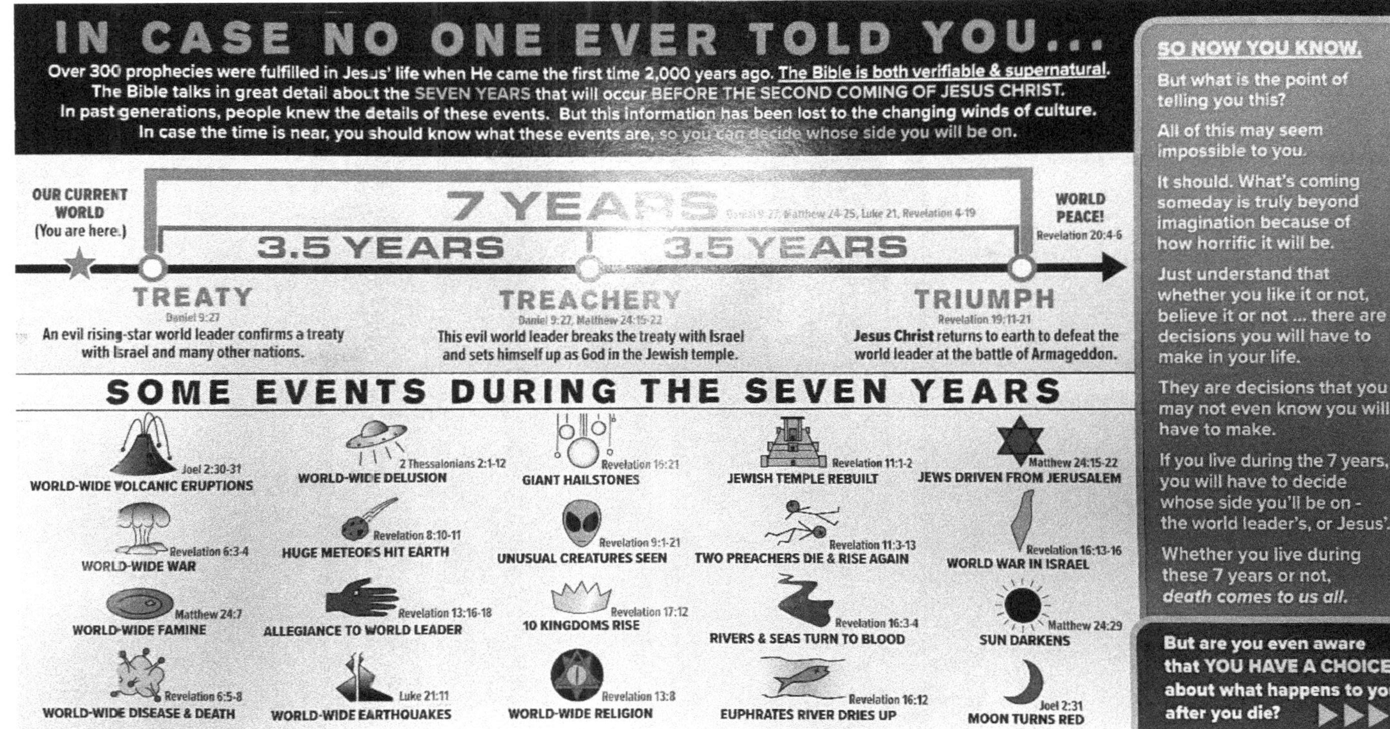
IN CASE NO ONE EVER TOLD YOU...
Over 300 prophecies were fulfilled in Jesus' life when He came the first time 2,000 years ago. The Bible is both verifiable & supernatural.
The Bible talks in great detail about the SEVEN YEARS that will occur BEFORE THE SECOND COMING OF JESUS CHRIST.
In past generations, people knew the details of these events. But this information has been lost to the changing winds of culture.
In case the time is near, you should know what these events are, so you can decide whose side you will be on.
OUR CURRENT WORLD (You are here.)
7 YEARS
Daniel 9:27, Matthew 24-25, Luke 21, Revelation 4-19
3.5 YEARS
3.5 YEARS
WORLD PEACE!
Revelation 20:4-6
TREATY
Daniel 9:27
An evil rising-star world leader confirms a treaty with Israel and many other nations.
TREACHERY
Daniel 9:27, Matthew 24:15-22
This evil world leader breaks the treaty with Israel and sets himself up as God in the Jewish temple.
TRIUMPH
Revelation 19:11-21
Jesus Christ returns to earth to defeat the world leader at the battle of Armageddon.
SOME EVENTS DURING THE SEVEN YEARS
Joel 2:30-31
WORLD-WIDE VOLCANIC ERUPTIONS
2 Thessalonians 2:1-12
WORLD-WIDE DELUSION
Revelation 16:21
GIANT HAILSTONES
Revelation 11:1-2
JEWISH TEMPLE REBUILT
Matthew 24:15-22
JEWS DRIVEN FROM JERUSALEM
Revelation 6:3-4
WORLD-WIDE WAR
Revelation 8:10-11
HUGE METEORS HIT EARTH
Revelation 9:1-21
UNUSUAL CREATURES SEEN
Revelation 11:3-13
TWO PREACHERS DIE & RISE AGAIN
Revelation 16:13-16
WORLD WAR IN ISRAEL
Matthew 24:7
WORLD-WIDE FAMINE
Revelation 13:16-18
ALLEGIANCE TO WORLD LEADER
Revelation 17:12
10 KINGDOMS RISE
Revelation 16:3-4
RIVERS & SEAS TURN TO BLOOD
Matthew 24:29
SUN DARKENS
Revelation 6:5-8
WORLD-WIDE DISEASE & DEATH
Luke 21:11
WORLD-WIDE EARTHQUAKES
Revelation 13:8
WORLD-WIDE RELIGION
Revelation 16:12
EUPHRATES RIVER DRIES UP
Joel 2:31
MOON TURNS RED
SO NOW YOU KNOW.
But what is the point of telling you this?
All of this may seem impossible to you.
It should. What's coming someday is truly beyond imagination because of how horrific it will be.
Just understand that whether you like it or not, believe it or not ... there are decisions you will have to make in your life.
They are decisions that you may not even know you will have to make.
If you live during the 7 years, you will have to decide whose side you'll be on - the world leader's, or Jesus'.
Whether you live during these 7 years or not, death comes to us all.
But are you even aware that YOU HAVE A CHOICE about what happens to you after you die?

Figure 1

Outside of their striking and obvious inaccuracies, the problem with such mailings and interpretations is this: Christians can believe (and historically have believed) such interpretations to the point of extremism, violence, and financial ruin. We get them in the mail and accept them without question thanks to their high production value, color printing, and unquestioned sense of certainty. If what these materials say about Daniel is untrue, why send them?

A most compelling example of the danger such readings can yield stems from the teachings of William Miller. Based heavily on his interpretation of Daniel and Revelation, Miller taught followers that Jesus would return in 1843 CE. He preached throughout the American Northeast,

Figure 2

prompting adherents to sell their homes, abandon their savings, and fully dedicate themselves to his movement. The year 1843 came and passed without Jesus' return, sparking some followers to reject Miller's teachings and return to their old lives. Despite this initial prophetic failure, Miller retooled his reading and argued that Christ would instead return in 1844. Like 1843, 1844 came and went without a single messianic return. This

Figure 3

second failure, known as the Great Disappointment, should have spelled the end of Miller and his movement.[2] And yet, a Methodist preacher named Ellen Gould White picked up after Miller, claiming visions that blend Miller's apocalyptic ideas and that her religious fervor corrected Miller's errors. White used her penchant for auspiciously correct oracles to grow the remaining Millerites into what would become the Seventh-day Adventists. Seventh-day Adventists believe Jesus did return in 1844 but saw far too many Christians worshipping on Sunday instead of Saturday, the date White and her followers deemed the "correct" Sabbath.

White and the birth of Seventh-day Adventists show that ardently apocalyptic readings of Daniel can (and do) take on lives of their own. It completely changed the American religious landscape. Both Miller and White made Daniel fit their respective understandings of history and theology, creating a hermeneutical through line that evangelical Christians still use. Evangelical Christian readings often stifle Daniel's profound and complex messages of hope, courage, and defiance into diluted propaganda, ill-conceived rants, and outright lies. Daniel is a highly politicized book, with prominent Christian evangelists, American politicians, and even sitting presidents making its words harbingers of contemporary world events. Such impassioned readers use Daniel for one reason and one reason only: to justify their own choices. But there is space for another way. Daniel does not have to stay trapped and controlled by those using it for their own ends. Daniel waits for readers to uncover the pieces necessary to liberate its words, wisdom, and theological potential from restrictive interpretive shackles.

This book attempts to do just that: to reconsider and expand how Christians read and interpret Daniel. It does so by offering perspectives and tools to revitalize how Christians preach, teach, talk, and think about Daniel. Reading Daniel with fresh eyes and a renewed sense of what books like Daniel can do in contemporary settings reclaims the interpretive narrative from voices using its beautifully written stories, fantastically described dreams, and bold prophetic sentiment to cause harm or reinforce passive theologies standing out of touch with our world. This book unpacks mainstream Christian interpretations to highlight Daniel's considerable interpretive possibilities to deconstruct said interpretations and reconsider, reconstruct, and renew Daniel.

Rereading Daniel requires no special training or magic, nor does someone need to find "secret knowledge" that will reveal ancient prophetic puzzles to unlock how the world ends. Reconsidering Daniel requires patience and respect for historical contexts that produced it alongside contemporary reading frameworks. Deconstructing to reconstruct does not tell an audience what Daniel (or any text, for that matter) means. Rather, this approach opens interpretive possibilities. It grants opportunities to reconsider what our interpretations say about us as individuals, communities, and people looking to do God's work in the world. This work must begin and end in the same place: the text itself. With that in mind, let us consider two questions. First, what is this book? Second, what is this book not?

What This Book Is

This book takes a text-centric approach to highlight then expand upon Daniel's interpretive possibilities to underscore the considerable theological, political, and interpretive baggage readers project onto its pages. For example, Daniel says nothing about Barack Obama, Donald Trump, or any American president, living or dead. And yet, there seems to be no shortage of readers willing to project political figures onto Daniel's dreams and visions, creating self-reinforcing interpretive loops that make Daniel about their time and their place. History shows such an approach is more a norm than an exception. For example, Christian bastion Protestant reformer Martin Luther zealously (and quite politically) lobbied for reading the anonymous and unknown fourth beast at Daniel 7:7 as Pope Clement VII.[3] Fittingly enough, Christians opposing Luther and supporting Pope Clement VII fired back and declared that Luther was Daniel's fourth beast. Such ping-ponging snared Daniel between the Roman Catholic Church's scramble to maintain power and Luther's political and ecclesial aspirations, with the future of how Christians would read Daniel at stake.

This book's deconstructive approach eschews "either/or" binaries like Luther and Clement VII. Instead of lobbying for "correct" readings over and against all others, this book considers Daniel as a template of possibilities. Deconstruction's critics claim it is nihilistic and done simply to tear the Bible to pieces. That is the opposite of this exercise. This book does not shred Daniel to leave its interpretive fragments ruined; instead, it uses the text to liberate Daniel from confined and contracted receptions. That being said, unilateral deconstruction is an impractical goal, as the Daniel text itself endures across lived religious traditions. Further, Daniel's ongoing canonicity underlines the need to dismantle philosophical, cultural, political, and institutional interpretations that limit how congregations and other active religious communities might use Daniel.[4]

Like all written texts, Daniel carries inherent interpretive flexibility and possibility. No unseen and unknown force guides my work. I also do not claim to be objective and unbiased. I mold this book as a tool to move the Daniel conversation beyond traditional evangelical boundaries. This book contains no sermons or morality plays, nor is it a hit piece tearing Daniel apart, leaving readers nothing to use. I peel back interpretive layers not to show new ways of getting to the text's "one meaning." Instead, I want to create starting points for reading Daniel apart from traditional interpretations. Daniel holds the very pieces necessary to deconstruct old, unquestioned readings and create something vibrant, relevant, and challenging. Biblical interpretive landscapes are deep and wide, and Daniel, with all its complexities, is the perfect book to begin a radical reconsideration of what the Bible can say, do, and be.

What This Book Is Not

Christian interpretations frequently ignore Daniel's Jewish heritage and reconstruct the text's religious language to make it reflect Christian eschatology. We put Jesus into Daniel, but Jesus is not in Daniel. Making Daniel about Jesus is anti-Semitic supersessionism of the highest order, and this book actively avoids it. This is not to say a reconsideration removes concepts like forgiveness, fate, divine sovereignty, love, and hope; Christianity holds no monopoly on such things. Daniel was born from the existential fallout of the Israelite exile, meaning that it can offer hope against overwhelming odds while also challenging us to reconsider our place in the active work of God. It can also challenge preconceived notions of what Scripture is and can be in contemporary religious communities. Just because something mentions hope, resilience, and religious devotion does not make it explicitly Christian. One could argue such qualities reflect a profound sense of humanity woven throughout Daniel, making it far more introspective and interpretively complex than generic, shallow Christian hope.

This book is also no condemnation of Christian hermeneutical practices; such an exercise would be myopic, aimless, and without a discernable purpose. It also would be disingenuous to the book's focus and function, because make no mistake: the work here is profoundly Christian. I, Jonathan Redding, am a Christian. I grew up in a rural Baptist Christian community and am ordained in that tradition; I also teach at a Wesleyan University. To deny evangelical Christianity's influence on my work would be an outright lie. And yet, as a Christian, I want to shed accepted interpretive boundaries and create space to build something new. Growth can be painful but necessary for fruitful and engaging study. Annalisa Azzoni articulates well the need for such interpretational growth:

> In the telling and retelling of these stories the authors knew that for their audiences they must contribute something specific to their own context and use these stories as a means to convey the particular message that was in their intent. They were so sophisticated as to understand that, and if they could understand and handle such multiplicity of texts and complexity of meanings, why can't we?[5]

Azzoni's insight summarizes my intent: texts have multiple voices to hear, and interpreters must let those voices speak. Interpretive polyvalence can unsettle as reading against the grain can take us places we may be unwilling to go. And yet, Daniel's future in Christian circles only stands to benefit from this approach. Stringent limitations disable and hinder Daniel within Christianity's past, present, and future. Moving past traditional interpretations reconsiders everything about Daniel, including and especially the role of history, imperialism, economics, politics, and military power. Daniel engages each with striking consistency, so much so that one must ask what those ideas are doing in Daniel in the first place. With that in mind, the work begins with a question: what history is Daniel telling, and how might that contrast with contemporary understandings of history?

Dating Daniel

Engaging histories in and around Daniel uncovers complex interpretive layers, and from those layers come choices: Which history will you choose as your staring point? Was Daniel written when it says it unfolds, starting with Nebuchadnezzar's siege and capture of Jerusalem? One could start there, but that place is unwieldy. Nebuchadnezzar's Jerusalem siege during the Judean king Jehoiakim's third year opens Daniel 1:1, so somewhere around 606 BCE.[6] However, 2 Kings 24 counters Daniel 1's chronology, saying at verses 8–12 that Nebuchadnezzar conquered Jerusalem during Jehoiachin's reign, thereby situating the Babylonian ruler's reign between 598 and 597 BCE. Further, nonbiblical sources show that, in 606 BCE, Nebuchadnezzar fought in Northern Syria, not Israel.[7] This gaff gets a careful reader's attention as such a glaringly obvious mishap cannot (and should not) go overlooked. So now the question becomes one of resolving the clear chronological tension Daniel 1 presents: Do differing timelines between Daniel 1, 2 Kings, and extrabiblical sources point to a glaring error or different memories of a similar event? Or is this apparent mix-up doing something else from a literary perspective?

If this is the case, Daniel's skewed timeline reorients the book beyond historical recitation and into an overt historiography. To clarify, I use the term historiography here to mean a reconstructed, idealized retelling. This is not to say Daniel then becomes fiction; this would be an oversimplification and a marker of profound disrespect for the people who bare their very souls across its pages. Reading Daniel as historiography makes it a vibrant, living conduit of cultural memory that uses historical figures and events to reconsider a very particular understanding of history to ask whose history Daniel tells, and for what purpose(s). Considering answers to this question leads to another possibility: perhaps Daniel is intentionally ahistorical without abandoning all historical moorings, a move granting it considerable interpretive flexibility without separation from lived histories. This kind of literary brilliance allows Daniel to exist across historical eras as it simultaneously speaks to ancient contexts and presses contemporary audiences to heed, listen, and ask how Daniel still challenges us.

The questions we just considered highlight why scholarly debates about the particulars of Daniel's date of composition persist and recur, with each position seemingly more zealous than the last. For the purposes of this book, Daniel exists in multiple locations at once. On one hand, it exists in the biblical canon here and now, with interpreters staking their claim according to particular theological agendas. On the other hand, Daniel connects to a wide time expanse that begins in the late Persian era and continues into the Hellenistic period. I stop my discussion about dating here because further consideration about "when what verse came in" or "who wrote what story where" avoids pressing questions about what Daniel can say, do, and be now. That being said, the text's histories remain essential. To offer an exaggerated hypothetical example, claiming someone wrote Daniel in the United States in 1935 or Russia during the 1800s would be (and is) disproven by the text. Such an example is intentionally hyperbolic to highlight that this book makes no such claim, as Daniel reflects cultures in and around the Levant between the sixth century BCE and the second century CE.[8] My broad approach to dating Daniel comes from sheer pragmatism, as it places Daniel after the Israelite exile and into the Second Temple period. Further, it lets us move past this proverbial "elephant in the room" to shift our focus onto conversations about what the text can mean without sacrificing valid historical tensions.[9]

Chapter by Chapter, Verse by Verse

Daniel does not lend itself to "cherry-picking" verses for sermons and lessons. No book of the Bible does, for that matter. Reading entire chapters tells a fuller, richer story. For example, one would not select lines from a stanza in a random chapter of a Shakespearian play to understand that play. Nor would anyone watch a five-minute segment from a movie and say they understand said movie. Full literary contexts tell more complete, complex stories that connect chapter to chapter, idea to idea, and interpretation to interpretation. The character Daniel connects disparate stories united around one character (Daniel), so reading Daniel in conversation with itself opens bolder possibilities of what the book can become for individuals, communities, and congregations.

That is why this book starts with Daniel 1 and works through each chapter, verse by verse, like an interconnected scaffold through which ideas and insights grow. As we read Daniel together, I challenge you to challenge yourself, to challenge me, to challenge this very book, because what I write here is meant to start the discussion, not end it. Like the act of interpretation itself, I want to keep conversations around Daniel moving to push back against stalled and stilted readings. Christians entrap and limit Daniel. Instead of asking what Daniel can be, say, and do, we parrot previous receptions, keeping Daniel theologically declawed and stale. A cursory overview of Christian readings, both contemporary and timeworn, illuminates a telling trend. Interpreters make Daniel, a text intended for ancient Israelite and Jewish audiences, into a profoundly Christian ethical and theological manifesto. For Christians to blindly accept such approaches causes considerable damage, making Daniel stilted and anti-Semitic.

Dominant Strains of Christian Receptions

The problem with Christian readings of Daniel presents itself early, often, and with startling consistency: Christian readers are so quick to resolve Daniel's narrative and theological tensions with Jesus that we trample over all other possible interpretive possibilities. Showing the depth of Christian overlays on Daniel underlines the need for this deconstructive reconsideration. One might be quick to think such "Jesus-ification" of Daniel is limited to more fundamentalist Christian circles, but such Christianization is shockingly commonplace across theological spectrums. Regardless of theological orientation, commentaries, books, articles, sermons, and lectures bind Daniel so closely to Christianity that they become seemingly inseparable. It is in citing the need for such separation that Daniel's raw interpretative potential materializes. The following is a bit more of a list than I might like, but, to understand how deep the Christianization of Daniel goes in interpretation, we must work through several examples. With that in mind, the examples here come from world-class, widely read, and academically accepted scholars. Further, their theological orientation ranges from fundamentalist, to conservative, to moderate, to liberal (however crude and inaccurate such politically fueled labels may be).

W. Sibley Towner describes Nebuchadnezzar's pivot toward the faith of Daniel and his friends at Daniel 2:47–49 as "giving expression to Israel's eschatological faith."[10] Towner argues this is the same faith that "Paul exhibits in his own expression of future hope, using the words borrowed from Isaiah 45:23" at Philippians 2:10–11.[11] In short, Towner's reading situates Daniel 2 as a vehicle for the Christian faith and implies that Nebuchadnezzar gives himself over to the faith that would become fulfilled in Jesus. Towner's commentary oozes Christian overlaying, as any semblance of something good or noteworthy becomes a tool to justify inserting Jesus into a book set six hundred years before Jesus' birth.

This kind of "What does Daniel have to say to and for Christians?" reading is paradigmatic, as other commentators and readers take similar paths. Daniel Smith-Christopher makes Daniel 4 Christian-focused with conspicuous calm, reading it as offering Christians instructions about living under imperial authority: "The book of Daniel suggests that the mere fact that Christians may find themselves under the rule of an oppressive state (whether overt or more subtle), does not mean that they need bow to its authority."[12] He continues this Christian bent and ascribes lessons on civic duty upon Daniel 4: "In their involvement in the government of the state, whether it be political office or civil service or some other role, Christians should maintain a sense of the tentativeness of the state's role as a tool of God."[13] Smith-Christopher wraps up his work on Daniel 4 by making Nebuchadnezzar's comeuppance allegorical for Christians trying to understand their place in government systems alongside the ethics of Christians holding political office.

C. L. Seow builds his reading around the Christian theological concept of divine sovereignty.[14] He establishes this paradigm early at Daniel 1:2, saying that God giving Judah into Nebuchadnezzar's hand shows "Israel's God was really in control of the whole operation."[15] Such readings may appear neutral, but Seow cites theological sentiment from John Calvin to support this thematic approach: "Here, as Calvin appropriately observed long ago, [Daniel's] narrator is asserting the providence and judgment of the sovereign God."[16] As this book will show, Seow is not alone in reusing previous Christian readings for contemporary support. Such a practice makes Daniel into a Christian proof text, trapping it in a self-reinforcing Christian-centric hermeneutical loop.[17]

Like Towner and Seow, John Goldingay argues that Daniel's aggressive apocalyptic thought makes "Daniel's focus on God's Kingdom" the "key to the missional implications of the book."[18] Goldingay roots his commentary in sound academic rigor, but conclusions drawn in "Explanation" and "Conclusion" sections veer into supersessionist Christian replacement theology. For example, Goldingay makes Gabriel's interpretation in Daniel 8:20–26 a fulcrum pointing to Jesus' comments toward scribes and Pharisees in Matthew 23:32. He goes further and states that Gabriel's words justify 1 Thessalonians 2:16 "in light of [the Jews'] refusal to acknowledge Jesus."[19] Goldingay is not the first Christian reader that uses Daniel to callously pair divine judgment toward the Jewish people, nor will he be the last. Readings like Goldingay's find roots in Protestant

Christian Reformers like Martin Luther and John Calvin, establishing a dangerous and oddly unquestioned precedent.

Goldingay makes Jesus into Daniel's form, focus, and prophetic intent, as he continually cites New Testament books in reference to what Daniel ultimately means. He justifies this through an evangelical Christian theological lens, arguing that the overt Israelite historical import takes a backseat to Daniel's eschatological theological significance: "Jesus's coming implements in the most far-reaching way the reign of God on earth that Dan 7 promises. It brings that unveiling of the mystery of God's plan for the world (Eph 3:1–12) that is spoken of here as the opening of the books (v. 10)." Goldingay's supersessionist approach helps the focus and function of what I am doing with this book, as he cements his position by concluding his work with an extended prayer penned by Calvin that reinterprets Daniel as foretelling "that celestial rest which thou hast prepared for us, through the same Jesus Christ our Lord."[20]

Louis Hartman and Alexander Di Lella's Anchor Bible series entry on Daniel digs deep into ancient traditions and languages echoed throughout the text, but Christian fingerprints show themselves through an insistence on using New Testament scriptural examples to explain Danielic imagery and ideas. Relating Daniel to Revelation is a common scholarly practice (each scholar discussed here does so with remarkable consistency), but Di Lella goes further to include what he calls "parallels" to Daniel's vision in chapter 10 to Paul's conversion in Acts.[21] Such unsolicited connections accentuate how mainstream interpretations cannot help but echo their Christian forbearers. Further, affixing unrelated New Testament scriptures that just happen to contain similar imagery underscores the limitation of standard Christian hermeneutics.

Adela Yarbro Collins penned a lengthy excursus in John Collins' *Daniel* commentary dedicated to addressing "The Influence of Daniel on the New Testament" that details the numerous connections Christian interpreters make between Daniel and the New Testament.[22] Rigorous and academically grounded, Adela Collins' essay illustrates and illuminates deep-seeded reception histories. One can only speculate about possible motives for including her New Testament work in a commentary focusing on a book from the Hebrew Bible, but, within the context of our exercise, it makes sense. She unpacks biased interpretations that make Daniel a New Testament portent because said interpretations are the unquestioned norm. She withholds value judgment about each author's conclusions but underlines conspicuous holes in their hermeneutical logic.

Despite Adela Collins' deft work, in the same commentary John Collins follows an allegorical trajectory like Hartman and Di Lella by using New Testament scripture citations to explain Daniel. He describes Daniel's behavior at Daniel 6:11 as "midway between the two styles of prayer contrasted in the Beatitudes: the 'hypocrites' who 'love to stand and pray in the synagogues and at the street corners, that they may be seen by men,' and Jesus' recommendation, 'go into your room and shut the door and pray to your Father who is in secret' (Matt. 6:6)."[23] Such presumptive readings assume that the reader wants or needs New Testament assistance in understanding how Daniel behaves, as the biblical text itself expresses no such need.

Unlike aforementioned readers, Stephen Miller dispenses all pleasantries or subtleties to make Jesus the central focus of Daniel, claiming that Jesus himself accepts Daniel's authorship and origins.[24] Miller claims Jesus' teachings that resemble events unfolding in Daniel prove Daniel's sixth-century BCE date, making the unprovable claim that Jesus likely believed Daniel existed and authored the book.[25] Such speculation remains highly specious as it confirms how haphazardly Christian readers imprint specific understandings onto a book that says and offers nothing about Christianity or Jesus. Likewise, Tremper Longman makes Jesus the center of what he calls "Biblical Revelation" to claim that Daniel contributes to "how the Old Testament anticipates [Jesus'] coming."[26]

Striking consistencies from these sampled Christians beg the question: Have Christian interpreters always read Daniel this way, or are such interpretations novel and recent? They are neither novel nor recent. Christians reading Christianity into and onto Daniel is as old as Christian biblical interpretation itself. Second-century CE Christian apologist Justin Martyr makes Daniel into a de facto Christian tome, arguing Daniel points to the coming of Jesus Christ as the Messiah with each "Son of Man" reference. Justin also doubles down and reads the stone at Daniel 2:34 as supporting Jesus' divine lineage: "To affirm that he was cut out without hands signifies that he was not a product of human activity, but of the will of God, the Father of all, who brought him forth."[27] Fellow second-century CE Christian thinker Irenaeus takes a similar approach to read Jesus as the Daniel 2:34 stone, which makes sense knowing that Irenaeus read and respected Justin's work.[28] Irenaeus likes Justin's work so much that he quotes Justin in *Against Heresies*, a move that underlines interpretive cross-pollination in early Christianity.

Christian theologian and writer Hippolytus of Rome flourished in the late second and early third century CE. During this period, he produced two works on Daniel: a commentary and *scholia* of exegetical insights. He interprets Daniel as profoundly Christian. The unknown fourth individual walking in Daniel 3's furnace becomes Jesus, and he says Daniel is a "witness of Christ."[29] He meticulously lays out a timeline for Jesus' return using Daniel 8–12 as his guide, further cementing his Christianization despite his preface claim that he wishes "to give an accurate account of the times of the captivity of the children of Israel in Babylon."

The work of these first- and second-century CE Christians becomes paradigmatic as centuries pass but the Christianization of Daniel persists. Fourth-century Catholic theologian Cyril of Jerusalem reads Daniel and dedicates more discussion to Jesus defeating the Antichrist than anything else in his Catechetical Lectures on the text. Cyril uses Daniel as a pawn to support his antichrist claims, saying, "We speak not from apocryphal books, but from Daniel," before detailing his reading as a road map for the coming of both the antichrist and Jesus as the "Son of Man."[30] St. Jerome follows suit in reading Christian dogma and doctrine into Daniel, as does Theodoret of Cyrus.[31]

Such widespread acceptance of Daniel as a Christian text underlines the need to push against mainstream hermeneutical grains. Growth and proliferation of interpretive methods in the 1960s through 1990s, known as the postmodern or poststructuralist era, broadened scholarly approaches to Daniel, thereby introducing ideas that themselves become trends.[32] Of the most recent trends, the dominant interpretive strain attached to Daniel revolves around reading the book as imperial resistance literature. Daniel becomes a theological tool kit of sorts for Christians to follow Daniel's Israelite example, to ultimately "resist" contemporary imperialism. Danna Nolan Fewell articulates this position directly: "The book of Daniel may be the Bible's foremost book of resistance literature against political domination."[33] Anathea Portier-Young concurs with Fewell and contends, "No book of the Hebrew Bible so plainly engages and opposes the project of empire as Daniel."[34]

Yet this "Daniel as imperial resistance" reception trajectory carries tensions that call for further attention, including but not limited to economic class, ethnicity, and gendered identities. An immediate red flag is the reinforcing nature of Daniel's approach to imperialism, an idea we will trace through each chapter of this book. Foregrounding the contradictory essence of reading Daniel as anti-imperial sets the stage for reconsidering Daniel 1, a chapter built around Nebuchadnezzar's insistence on bringing wealthy, handsome, and aristocratic Israelites of royal lineage into his court. Daniel and his friends use their elevated access to better themselves after getting Nebuchadnezzar's conversion to their faith in Daniel 2, where they do not so much oppose empire as much as they reinforce surrounding political systems without systemic change. Daniel 1–6 calls certain kings into question, but the notion of empire consistently stands blameless. Further, Daniel 7–12 rejects human monarchical structures only to favor a divinely installed imperial government. If anything, Daniel resembles a tool of authoritarian placation more than a vessel for imperial defiance.

The point of this opening chapter, and this book in general, then is this: repeating the same handful of interpretations locks Daniel in a cage and severely undercuts what the text and its words might do and say for contemporary audiences. The deconstruction unfolding here is more a reconsideration of interpretive trends than a formal accusation of how people read the Bible. The goal is quite simple: What happens to Daniel, its stories, and possible meanings when pressed beyond traditional Christian thought? Possible answers lie in the text itself.

1

Daniel 1 Reconsidered

1.1 Translation

1 When it was year three of Jehoiakim's kingdom of Jerusalem, Nebuchadnezzar, king of Babylon, came to Jerusalem and laid siege upon it.

2 And Adonai placed Jehoiakim, king of Judah, and vessels of the House of Elohim into his [Nebuchadnezzar] hand. He [Nebuchadnezzar] brought them into the land of Shinar into the house of his god, and he placed the vessels in the treasury house of his god.

3 And the King [Nebuchadnezzar] commanded Ashpenaz, his chief eunuch, to bring sons of Israel, ones whose seeds came from royalty and nobility.

4 Children that are without any blemish and pleasing with appearance; and with understanding of all wisdom and knowing knowledge and understanding learning, with strength in them, to stand in the temple with the king. And they are to be taught literature and language of the Chaldeans.

5 And the king appointed them daily portions from the king's portion and from his wine. They were to be educated for three years, and at the end of that they were to be stationed before the king.

6 And among the sons of Judah were Daniel, Hananiah, Mishael, and Azariah.

7 And the chief eunuch gave them names. He gave Belteshazzar to Daniel; and to Hananiah, Shadrach; and to Mishael, Meshach; and to Azariah, Abednego.

8 And Daniel set it upon his heart that he wouldn't be defiled by the portion of the king or his wine, and Daniel asked the chief eunuch, that he might not defile himself.

[9] And Elohim gave Daniel trust and compassion before the chief of the eunuchs.

[10] And the chief of the eunuchs said to Daniel, "I fear my lord the king that appointed your food and your wine; what if he sees your faces more sullen than the young men your age? You will endanger my head with the king!"

[11] And Daniel spoke to the steward which the chief of the eunuchs had appointed over Daniel, Hananiah, Mishael, and Azariah.

[12] "Test your servant for ten days and give us vegetables and we will eat them, and water and we will drink it.

[13] Then let us, in front of you, compare our appearances with the appearance of the young men eating portions from the king; then do with your servants as you see fit."

[14] And he listened to their speech and tested them for ten days.

[15] And at the end of ten days it was seen that their appearance was better and the skin fatter than each of the young men that had eaten from the portions of the king.

[16] And so the steward took their portions and drinking wine and gave them vegetables.

[17] And these four young men, God gave to them knowledge and understanding of each book and wisdom; and to Daniel understanding of visions and dreams.

[18] And at the end of the days which the king established, the chief eunuch brought them before Nebuchadnezzar.

[19] And the king spoke with them and among them all, no one was found to compare Daniel, Hananiah, Mishael, and Azariah; so they stood before the king.

[20] And each matter of wisdom, understanding that the king placed before them, they were found to be ten times more than each of the magicians and conjurers from throughout the kingdom.

[21] And Daniel was there until the first year of King Cyrus.

1.2 Reading against the Grain

Daniel 1 starts with a bang: Babylonian king Nebuchadnezzar storms Judah, besieges the capital Jerusalem, and takes it by force. According to verse 1, these events unfold during the reign of Jehoiakim to orient the reader to history preceding and surrounding Nebuchadnezzar's siege. Rejecting a nondescript "once upon a time in a faraway land," the verse situates Jerusalem—Judah's political, religious, and economic capital—as the chapter's geopolitical context. What happens in Daniel 1 happens in Jerusalem. After Daniel shows the "where," it gives a "when": the third year of King Jehoiakim's rule. These references to a king and his reign carry historical and cultural weight, but, despite their considerable cultural importance, readers often cast aside Jehoiakim and Judah to focus on Daniel and his three friends. Such an interpretive move is unwise, as it undercuts how Daniel presents Israel as ripe for foreign influence while also showing us the historical-literary context.

Modern interpreters view ancient Israel with an idyllic romanticism that paints the small nation as a utopian commonwealth that tragically collapses without warning. Biblical and historical sources, however, tell a different story. One must question said romanticism surrounding ancient Israel's fall, as the Bible speaks of great instability from the monarchy's inception, starting in 1–2 Samuel, continuing through 1–2 Kings, and into biblical prophetic literature. For example, the prophet Samuel speaks on YHWH's behalf and candidly warns the Israelites in 1 Samuel 8:1–18 about the dangers of monarchical rule. The Israelite people beg Samuel for a king, to which he responds:

> 11 He said, "These will be the ways of the king who will reign over
> you: he will take your sons and appoint them to his chariots and
> to be his horsemen, and to run before his chariots; 12 and he will
> appoint for himself commanders of thousands and commanders of
> fifties, and some to plough his ground and to reap his harvest, and to
> make his implements of war and the equipment of his chariots. 13 He
> will take your daughters to be perfumers and cooks and bakers. 14 He
> will take the best of your fields and vineyards and olive orchards and
> give them to his courtiers. 15 He will take one-tenth of your grain and
> of your vineyards and give it to his officers and his courtiers. 16 He
> will take your male and female slaves, and the best of your cattle and
> donkeys, and put them to his work. 17 He will take one-tenth of your
> flocks, and you shall be his slaves. 18 And in that day you will cry out
> because of your king, whom you have chosen for yourselves; but the
> Lord will not answer you in that day." (NRSV)

Despite Samuel's admonition, the Israelites still crave a king. Samuel (with YHWH's aid) grants their wish, setting in motion events leading to the nation's eventual division and destruction.

Stories of incompetent Israelite leaders driven by lust, greed, and selfishness saturate 1 and 2 Samuel and 1 and 2 Kings. YHWH strips Israel's first king, Saul, of divine favor, causing the troubled monarch to lose his mental and political stability. Saul's fall prompts David's insurrection and successful coup. David then falls prey to his sexual appetites and loses control of himself, his family, and his kingdom. Amnon, David's oldest son, dies at the hands of his half-brother Absalom. Absalom then tries overthrowing his father's government only to die brutally at the end of a short-lived revolt. Then Adonijah, David's fourth son, appoints himself king, only to have David's wife Bathsheba trick the aging David into seating her son Solomon on the throne. According to 1 Kings 11:1–13, Solomon's rule suffers like his father's, after he follows his sexual proclivities and disobeys the Israelite deity by marrying and allowing non-Israelite women to influence him. Solomon's son and successor Rehoboam led poorly and overworked the Israelite people, prompting the ten northern Israelite tribes to secede and form another sovereign kingdom. Biblical sources make clear that the United Monarchy split in two from within, with Northern Israel having its king (Jeroboam) and capital city (Samaria) separate from Southern Judah's Rehoboam and Jerusalem.

Jehoiakim's political rise in Judah also carries historical implications with deep theological ramifications. Second Kings 23:33 tell us Pharaoh Neco II appointed Jehoiakim as a vassal following Egypt's failed campaign to commandeer Haran from the Babylonians. Neco II exploited Jehoiakim as a pawn in Egypt and Babylon's battle for political and military supremacy, stripping away any inkling of Jehoiakim's allegiances to Israel and their deity. Second Kings 24:1 reveals that after the Babylonian ruler Nebuchadnezzar took over Jerusalem, he too made Jehoiakim a vassal for three years until Jehoiakim rebelled and failed, ultimately dooming the nation and its people to exile. Jehoiakim failed his people because, according to 2 Kings 23:37, "[h]e did what was evil in the sight of YHWH, just as all his ancestors had done." These kings failed their god and their people, losing their power and leaving space for non-Israelite leaders (like Neco II and Nebuchadnezzar) to fill the void. Following God yields prosperity, but rejecting the deity leads only to disaster for the king and his kingdom. In short, Israel's kings and their failings show Samuel's prophecy coming true with considerable prejudice.

Beginning Daniel with explicit references to Judah and Jehoiakim brings these monarchical failures roaring to the fore. It recalls palace intrigue that led to the divided Israelite monarchy and the aftermath of poor Israelite leadership. Despite historical uncertainty surrounding Daniel's initial composition, the book carries the considerable burden of reminding readers of how Jehoiakim rules Southern Judah, a nation separated from Northern Israel.

Nonbiblical sources show us Judah's fall to Nebuchadnezzar was anything but swift, nor was it unforeseen. Nebuchadnezzar's Babylon was a known force in the ancient Levant, as the empire's considerable economic and military might yielded palpable historical significance.[1] For example, chronicle 5 of the *Babylonian Chronicle* tablets housed in the British Museum talk at length about Nebuchadnezzar's conquering, with line 12 of the Lacuna reading, "He encamped against the city of Judah and on the second of the month Adar he captured the city (and) seized (its) king."[2] The *Assyrian and Babylonian Chronicles* underline Nebuchadnezzar's power and the reach of his grasp, presenting a tallied list of the lands he conquered, the peoples he subdued, and the kings he overthrew. Therefore, Daniel 1's opening verses should not shock the reader. Nebuchadnezzar sieged Jerusalem and ruled Judah like he did in any other part of his empire, making the Southern Israelite kingdom just another cog in his proverbial imperial wheel. The unremarkable nature of Judah and Jerusalem's fall against the historical backdrop of Nebuchadnezzar's political machinations highlights the Babylonian king's unmovable nature: he took what he wanted, however he wanted, for the benefit of himself and those he kept in close company.

Verse 1's historical insight underlines the theological import of verse 2: the Israelite God *gives* Jehoiakim, Jerusalem, and its inhabitants into Nebuchadnezzar's possession. The deity's role in Nebuchadnezzar's success makes the interpreter regurgitate the "Sovereignty of God" paradigm propagated by John Calvin. These readings claim to build upon themes of hope and divine control amid uncertainty and upheaval, but letting this kind of theology go unquestioned yields problems. For example, claiming Daniel shows "God is in control" devalues suffering and struggle caused by war and political strife. Further, it bolsters theologies that devalue individual human lives, making dead innocent civilians into pawns of divine political games. It also creates space for toxic determinism to rule, echoing the horrors of Manifest Destiny, Hitler's Germany, and any other atrocities committed in the name of someone's "God."

The question becomes why: Why does Daniel say that God gave Israel into foreign control? Why does this position receive no pushback in the text, and for what purpose does Daniel set such an openly colonized stage? The answer may lie in considering the existential fallout from Israel's split and eventual fall: would the Israelites rather believe in a god that controls everything, even if those things happen to be quite terrible? Or would they rather take comfort in the uncertainty of the divine's role in political, economic, and religious upheaval? This, then, underlines a different paradigm for reading Daniel uncovered in these first two verses: perhaps questioning dogma and doctrine is the heart of Daniel's interpretive possibilities. The Daniel character often asks questions and seeks answers, so why should someone reading Daniel take ideas therein at face value? Why not push against traditional notions of divine sovereignty, and why not engage theological diversity by reading Daniel 1:2 as an interpretation of the events after the fact instead of an "as it happened" retelling?

The theological question is now this: Why do Daniel's writers say God is the one that allowed Nebuchadnezzar to take over? Why not blame Jehoiakim? What is at stake with placing the burden on God working with a foreign, non-Israelite invader? Interpreters like Robert Allen Warrior and Renita Weems raise such questions with persistence and well-founded theological frustration about the Bible writ large, yet their positions stay minoritized or, in some cases, overlooked. Warrior rereads Joshua's conquest narratives through an indigenous lens, making the deity's words in Genesis 15 ring with horror: "To your descendants I give this land. The land of the Kenites, Kenizzites, the Kadmonites, the Hittites, the Perizzites, the Rephaim, the Amorites, the Canaanites, and the Jebusites." Warrior speaks to the cold, hard reality of believing in a god that conquers, saying, "As long as people believe in the Yahweh of deliverance, the world will not be safe from Yahweh the conqueror."[3] Weems focuses her approach around the role of gender in prophetic marriage metaphor, in which God is the pious, faithful husband and Israel is the promiscuous, cheating wife. Weems' marriage metaphor shows that this husband-God punishes his wife, Israel, for "her" indiscriminate relationships with other deities, thereby explaining why Israel fell:

> The marriage metaphor, with its intense preoccupation with exclusive devotion and loyalty to one husband, would prove to be a helpful lens through which they and their audiences could view what they might see as the causes of the nation's demise. According to the metaphor, Israel's destruction was the result of the nation's tendency to worship and rely on foreign gods.[4]

Reading verses 1 and 2 through lenses like those of Warrior and Weems changes God's blessing of Nebuchadnezzar drastically, moving it from approving divine sovereignty to destructive divine complicity. People suffering from Nebuchadnezzar's successful coup now ask questions of why and how: Why would their god punish so many for Israelite leadership's failings? Why does the narrative neglect commoners who die, who lost loved ones, and whose worlds get changed forever? How can they be God's people despite falling prey to political power? Did God cede Judah to Nebuchadnezzar, or is that how Daniel reconciles this Babylonian triumph against Israelite aspirations?

Questioning Daniel's presented political theology challenges traditional Christian notions, doctrine, and dogma. Leaders benefiting from Nebuchadnezzar's victory may see the leadership change as a minor inconvenience, while average Israelites may tell a different story. This opens the door to highlight how chapter 1 fails to mention or consider Israelites outside royal and aristocratic classes. Yes, Daniel and his friends are Israelites, but what kind of Israelites are there? Verses 3 and 4 answer this question. At verse 3, Nebuchadnezzar wants Israelites "whose seeds come from royalty and nobility." This means Nebuchadnezzar wants (and gets) rich, aristocratic Israelites. Verse 4 offers further details about what kind of Israelites Nebuchadnezzar wants beyond their affluent lineage: they must be intelligent and good-looking. Prioritizing physical appearance is common throughout the Bible, as 1 Samuel 9:2 describes Saul, the first Israelite king, as "handsome" and "there was no man among the sons of Israel more handsome than he."[5] Saul's fate as Israel's king might prompt hesitation with Nebuchadnezzar's requirements, but Daniel 1–6 shows only success for Daniel and his compatriots. Such prosperity seemingly contradicts biblical sentiment around people like King David and YHWH's instructions to Samuel in choosing and then anointing the new king: "Do not look on his appearance or on the height of his stature, because I have rejected him; for the Lord does not see as mortals see; they look on the outward appearance, but the Lord looks on the heart" (1 Sam 16:7). Invoking such expectations about outward appearance and intellectual capacity also indicates a certain class interplay between the haves and have-nots, as those who are rich are handsome while the impoverished are undesirable.

Nebuchadnezzar also wants male Israelites "with understanding of all wisdom and knowing knowledge and understanding learning" so that they may be educated in Chaldean literature and languages. Literacy in the ancient world was virtually nonexistent, and Daniel's connections to education set him and his friends apart.[6] Faith alone does not single out Daniel and his friends. Nebuchadnezzar pulls them into palace servitude because of their access to economic and academic privilege. Daniel is no ordinary Israelite, nor are his friends "salt of the earth" citizens trying to make their way under foreign leadership. The foursome is handsome, wealthy, educated, and capable of learning. Daniel and his friends do not represent the typical Israelite; they are Israelite aristocratic men, through and through. The text's focus on what kind of Israelite men Daniel and his friends are makes such descriptors integral to the chapter's broader narrative. A pressing question then arises: If Daniel and his friends are rich and powerful nobles handpicked to serve Nebuchadnezzar, who is this chapter for? Despite such textual intentionality, Christian interpretations avoid the consequences of presenting four well-bred and privileged Israelites as representing the larger Israelite collective.

Interpreters downplay Daniel and his friends' economic and educational status with noticeable consistency. John Collins acknowledges a connection to Jewish royalty and nobility but gives this information minimal interpretive weight.[7] Carol Newsom emphasizes their educational capacities, arguing that knowledge and acquiring knowledge persist thematically throughout Daniel. Newsom builds on these themes to emphasize Daniel and his friends' training by highlighting how aristocratic youth, not common laypersons, received educational access and opportunities.[8] And yet, Newsom puts minimal interpretive consequence on their societal background. Seow also stops short of meaningful engagement, marking said access and opportunities as simply "instrumental in the fulfillment of the will of God."[9] Such interpretive defaulting toward seeing the Israelite's situation as divine opportunity undercuts the severity of the situation.

Reference to "the Chaldeans" in verse 4 seems like a throwaway reference, but Chaldeans were an elite educated class in the Babylonian Empire entrusted with astrology and predicting the future.[10] Chaldeans appear throughout the Hebrew Bible as adversarial figures of the Israelites. According to the Bible, destruction follows the Chaldeans everywhere they go. God uses deliverance from the Chaldeans as evidence of Israel's divine favor in Genesis 15 with Abram's covenant. Chaldean armies wreak havoc throughout the books of Kings and Chronicles. Second Kings 25 highlights Chaldean armies as dictatorial forces that destroy Jerusalem's walls to take stolen plunder to Babylon. Ezekiel, Jeremiah, and Isaiah speak at length about Chaldean military might and lament Israel's inability to stop their imperial control.

By instructing Daniel and his friends according to Chaldean literature and language, Nebuchadnezzar makes these four Israelites adversaries to their own people. Assimilation is a standard colonization tactic, as making the captured like the captor allows the captured to become the captor. One would think that Daniel and his friends would oppose such indoctrination at the hands of their Babylonian overlords, but they stay silent on the matter. It seems the four Israelites are content with their lot, especially when we consider how following the king's orders cements them into the upper echelons of Babylonian power.

Mentioning Ashpenaz by name in verse 3 doubles down on the chapter's interest in Babylonian palace intrigue. At this point in the chapter, the only Israelite name mentioned thus far belongs to Jehoiakim, a king that God undermines through military defeat and occupation at the hands of Nebuchadnezzar and the Babylonians. Daniel 1 shares nothing about political and social changes outside Nebuchadnezzar's court, which sets the stage for the rest of the book. Readers hear from only affluent nobility, royalty, and the military infrastructure designed to sustain the status quo. Ashpenaz is no different, as the Hebrew describes this person as Nebuchadnezzar's "chief of his eunuchs."[11] Popular translations like the NRSV and NIV favor words like "official" and "master" to describe Ashpenaz, doing a considerable disservice to persons relying on said translations for an accurate engagement with the text itself. I translate the word סָרִיס as "eunuch" because that is its most common translation throughout the Bible. It can mean a high-ranking military official, but in this context Ashpenaz is a high-ranking military official *because* he is a eunuch.[12]

We have acknowledged these characters' economic background and educational status, but stopping there is insufficient. Making these men God's instruments because they are handsome, wealthy, and intelligent is destructive and limiting. Readers may see themselves falling short of cultural beauty and intelligence standards, thereby ruining their chances to be agents and emissaries for God. Putting undue emphasis on physical and intellectual capacities makes them into quasi-religious superheroes, with lives unattainable for commoners. King Nebuchadnezzar excludes and includes as he chooses, so ascribing his whims to the will of God leads only to theological ruin. Verses 5 through 8 only underline the accentuation of the chapter's narrow socioeconomic scope, but verse 6 adds an interesting wrinkle: it says "among them were Daniel, Hananiah, Mishael, and Azariah," meaning the king selected other Israelites beyond Daniel and his friends. We learn nothing more about these additional Israelites, as they go unrecognized, unheard, and unseen in the narrative.

Daniel 1's silencing does not stop there, as Nebuchadnezzar erases the main four Israelites' indigenous names: Hananiah, Mishael, Azariah, and Daniel are now respectively Shadrach, Meshach, Abednego, and Belteshazzar. One would think interpreters would call out and reject this kind of imperial suppression, but the opposite is true. Traditional Christian readings exclusively use imperial names for Hananiah, Mishael, and Azariah with little to no reference given toward this drastic Israelite cultural erasure. Children's Bibles, church curricula, and preached sermons tell tales of Shadrach, Meshach, and Abednego, but Daniel 1 explicitly states these "names" are Babylonian labels and not the characters' Israelite names.[13] One could argue that the ongoing use of Shadrach, Meshach, and Abednego in interpretations aligns with the text's use of these names, but such an argument fails to consider why Daniel 1 (and eventually Daniel 3) uses their colonized names instead of given birth names. This radically reorients their names and their role in the larger Daniel narrative, as their Israelite heritage becomes of little consequence compared to what Nebuchadnezzar wants of them. The names Shadrach, Meshach, and Abednego remind us of unchecked imperial power and control, making it more even confounding as to why the text uses Daniel's Israelite name and not the Babylonian Belteshazzar. What makes him worthy over and against his peers?

Complexity around the characters' names underlines the narrative and interpretive baggage Daniel carries both within and beyond the Bible. Evidence points to the biblical Daniel character as part of a much larger Daniel literary corpus extending outside the Bible.[14] Outside the Bible, Daniel is more of a cultural hero than a particularly religious one. Knowing this can help us understand why Daniel rejects the king's food and wine. Daniel's actions in verse 8 appear more personal than cultic, as he chooses not to defile himself according to his will and his choices. What, then, is the point and purpose of Daniel's decision to reject the initial food offering? Daniel 1:8 says Daniel did not want to "defile" himself, but this justification offers little in terms of Daniel's rationale. "Defile" here is the Hebrew גָּאַל, and its biblical use paints a broad understanding of defilement; it suggests nothing specifically having to do with Israelite purity requirements. Further, God does not instruct Daniel to abstain from consuming the king's portions or wine, nor does the text say Daniel's decision receives divine favor. Yet this absence of God does not stop readers and interpreters from placing a form of opaque divine intervention onto Daniel's choice.[15]

Scholars agonize over why Daniel rejects the first offerings only to accept water and vegetables from the king in verse 12. Some readers argue the rations defile Daniel because it comes from Nebuchadnezzar's supply, while others present accepted resolutions from other scholars without comment.[16] Other Christians claim Daniel's choices show resistant class solidarity among fellow exiles, but such a claim ignores how and why Nebuchadnezzar selects Daniel and his friends because they come from wealthy Israelite nobility. Daniel is no "man of the people" here, as the text tells us Daniel rejected one form of Nebuchadnezzar's foodstuffs for something else from the king's fare. Israelite purity laws about food shed no light on Daniel's decision as well, since "portion of the king" is a generic phrase for foodstuffs, and "wine" is the common word יַיִן in Hebrew.[17] Nothing about these descriptions denotes cultic impurity, nor does the text lend particular significance to Daniel rejecting something the king offers. Far from an act of resistance, Daniel's dietary choices then become an act of quid pro quo. Kings gain power by exerting their will, so Daniel tests Nebuchadnezzar's diligence in making people accountable to his commands.

Daniel tries to work the system for his benefit, and his conversation with Ashpenaz in verses 9–13 highlights his borderline reckless self-confidence. Ashpenaz' expressed anxiety also underlines what is at stake for Ashpenaz, as he fears for his own life at the expense of Daniel's curious request. Daniel 1:9 does say that God gives Daniel trust and compassion before Ashpenaz, but this raises a perplexing theological issue: Did God know what Daniel was going to do before Daniel did it? If so, why does the text withhold this information from the reader? Because as it stands at verse 9, it is as if God plays "catch up" to align Daniel's choice with God's ability to assist. Interpreters argue that God's actions toward Ashpenaz on Daniel's behalf reflect Daniel executing God's will.[18] However, one could just as easily contend that God gives Daniel trust and compassion before Ashpenaz because Daniel made a mistake and God protects him despite the error. It is quite paradoxical that God grants Daniel the tools necessary to survive after giving Jerusalem over to Nebuchadnezzar. What exactly *is* God's plan in this story, if such a thing even exists?

Readings underlining God's alleged sovereignty in Daniel 1 indirectly highlight the expendable nature of humans throughout the story. God hands Jerusalem to a foreign king despite the massive communal trauma such an event brings. Ashpenaz expresses anxiety and fear about Daniel's choice, meaning that God's actions in granting Daniel trust and compassion before Ashpenaz force the chief eunuch to act against his will. Ashpenaz becomes nothing more than a pawn in Daniel's game. Chapter 1 lays out no threats toward Daniel and his friends, and, even in learning

Daniel's plans, Ashpenaz knows that *his* head, not the heads of these four Israelites, is at stake. God and Daniel stand ready to sacrifice this otherwise innocent person to accomplish an unforeseen and unarticulated purpose. This highlights an ongoing theme in chapter 1: God accommodates plans of a select few while standing silent and inactive toward anyone else.

Thus far we have heard more from the Babylonians (Nebuchadnezzar and the chief eunuch) than the deity and Daniel. Daniel first speaks in Daniel 1:11–13, and his ambiguity underlines his dubious mission. Daniel speaks to an appointed steward and not Ashpenaz to accommodate his dietary request, meaning Daniel sidesteps Ashpenaz' hesitation. It is a bizarre example of breaking the chain of command because, according to verse 9, God grants Daniel favor before the chief eunuch, not subordinates. Daniel does not get the answer he wants from Ashpenaz and removes him from the equation. Daniel 1:16 confirms that the steward switches the prescribed rations for vegetables, allowing plausible deniability for a high-ranking official but creating space for an unnamed steward to suffer possible consequences. The question then becomes this: Why include Ashpenaz in the first place, if Daniel takes another route? The answer reiterates an earlier theme: in Daniel, the nameless matter little beyond narrative expendability.

Lucky for our nameless steward, things work in Daniel's favor. Daniel and his friends look healthier and fuller than other (again nameless) men that took the king's initial portions. God finally weighs in on the situation in verse 17, granting the foursome knowledge and wisdom alongside Daniel's ability to understand visions and dreams. The plan works in that it grants these selected Israelites a preeminent spot in Nebuchadnezzar's court, but to call it a "plan" is a questionable approach. Mainline interpretive threads highlight Daniel's success as evidence of divine sovereignty, but such a practice is rife with theological problems. Daniel cajoles his way to the top without ever questioning the systems that allow him, a man of considerable wealth and knowledge, to gain more status and more connections. Further, divine favoritism toward the powerful conflicts with anti-imperialism biblical narratives like Exodus and 1 Samuel 8. What do these inconsistencies mean, and how might contemporary readers resolve them?

Mindful of Daniel's tactics, chapter 1 ends with Daniel and his friends safe, but at what cost? We hear nothing about the other candidates beyond a passing "among them all" in verse 19, meaning they exit the story as quickly as they arrived. God acts sporadically and haphazardly throughout Daniel's ploys. God favors Nebuchadnezzar to begin the chapter, then positions the chief eunuch Ashpenaz to act favorably toward our heroes, only to have Daniel circumvent Ashpenaz to accomplish his goals. Finally, God gives the foursome the knowledge and skills to succeed; according to verse 20, this makes them exemplary. Nebuchadnezzar himself does not remark on their appearance, as verse 15 offers the passive verbal construction "it was seen" regarding how they look. Thus, nothing Daniel does regarding food affects the outcome, creating space to argue that Daniel's actions do nothing to bolster his success. Verses 20–21 show Daniel does his job well, ten times better than his peer magicians and conjurers. Only by God's decision do these men gain knowledge and understanding to succeed, making Daniel's food machinations null. Despite that, Daniel now has his position of power in the court of the man responsible for destroying the temple and the nation of Israel.

1.3 So What?

Now comes the tricky but worthwhile part: What do we, as contemporary Christian readers, do with this text? How can we reassemble the pieces set before us? We do not live in biblical Israel during Babylonian occupation, and it is highly unlikely that someone of Israelite royal lineage will read this. And yet, the tensions uncovered in Daniel 1 reflect difficulties people face in striving to do the work of God. Readers employ texts like Daniel for instruction, guidance, or affirmation, turning biblical texts into a guide or "life coach" of sorts for uncovering "the will of God." But these scriptures can be so much more than keystones of positivity and affirmation. They can (and do) challenge the reader to reconsider and reflect on what side we take regarding power, control, and placation.

"Reflect" is a keyword for engaging Daniel, or any biblical text for that matter. Considering Daniel 1 as a mirror reflecting the reader changes the discussion. Do we see what we *want* to see in this story of political maneuvering, or do we have the courage to consider how Daniel 1 reflects reality? What is the difference between these two questions, and how might our answer reflect our religious communities and us? We frequently insert ourselves as the more righteous and victorious characters, thereby making the narratives into stories unapologetically paralleling our successes, failures, wants, and needs. But what if identifying with characters in the story is off base? What if Daniel 1 is devoid of righteous or pious exemplars? Instead, what if the text is a mirror designed to make us candidly consider, "What am I actually in this story?"

A surface reading sees Daniel as someone standing up for what he believes and using that determination to subvert imperial expectations for personal success. However, reading deeper and pressing harder highlights just how little Daniel changes with his actions, as he uses systems of power for his gain based on no other motivation than his own. Further, God is the sole reason for the Israelite situation, and God remains the primary actor in Daniel's success. Daniel 1's presentation of God repeatedly sides with the powerful without ever considering the role of an average Israelite. What is one supposed to do with this God? How must we respond to a God that hands over innocent people to maniacal rulers? Further, what is the reader to do about imperial systems that take people from their homelands, change their names, indoctrinate them, and make them regime puppets? A daring solution lies in seeing the narrative resolution as an ongoing question: is the world a series of divinely ordained and unchangeable norms, or does Daniel 1 uncover and reflect the absurdity of *not* asking questions and defaulting to passive indifference?

Daniel's theological rationalization of war carries an inherent interpretative flexibility, as God did not give Jehoiakim and Judah into Nebuchadnezzar's hand. Historical sources confirm that the Babylonian king took the Israelite people and their homeland by force. This was not divine intervention; it was the continued rolling of one man's attempt to rule the known world. Covering Nebuchadnezzar's actions and Daniel's choices with an umbrella of divine sovereignty leaves average Israelites (and the soldiers fighting the battles) to fend for themselves. Contemporary history shows just how destructive such an approach to divine sovereignty can be, as religious leaders and politicians ascribe horrendous violence as divinely certified with apologetic religious fervor. Destroyed people and places become unwilling martyrs meant to "save" a selected, chosen few. For American Christians like Billy Graham, the bombs exploding over Hiroshima and Nagasaki brought peace and certainty of God's divine plan, prompting the evangelical leader to let out a celebratory "Hallelujah" after their successful detonation.[19] Charles Swindoll takes things a step further and says God's role in Daniel 1 points to one "truth":

> International terrorism, rogue nations with nuclear capabilities, predictions of environmental catastrophe, and government and business corruption seem to point toward the fact that our civilization is on a pathway of destruction. How are we to make sense of such a world? For Christians, our tendency is to focus on the particulars of

> prophecy, but the best place to start is by looking at the big picture of God's plan.[20]

Evangelical justification of suffering through divine sovereignty defines Daniel 1's place in contemporary Christian contexts.[21] But reading Daniel 1 in this way is shallow, limiting, and dangerous. The text begs us for deeper considerations of divine sovereignty.

Dominant theological positions make divine sovereignty synonymous with fate or absolute divine control. This means that nothing happens outside of God's purview and control, all but eliminating free will and human choice. Claiming that Daniel 1's sovereignty indicates universal predetermined circumstances and consequences is theologically reductionist and dangerously indifferent, especially mindful of widespread suffering. Daniel 1 underlines the considerable difference between inflexible notions of divine sovereignty and the thing Christians call "the will of God." God is far from "in control" in this chapter. Like the finite freedom of humanity, Daniel faced limited choices. All he could do was ask and hope things would work in his favor. Nothing was certain or sovereign. Daniel did what Daniel had to do to survive. Such limitations reflect the true nature of empire, as death becomes increasingly certain as empires spread. God intervenes to protect Israel and Daniel from themselves, as acts of full rebellion against considerably more powerful forces often lead to total annihilation. But reading the surrender of Israel to Nebuchadnezzar as God blessing such military aggression seems to be the opposite of what chapter 1 can say.

It is with the precarious balance between God's mediation and Daniel's choices that chapter 1 lives into its reflective capacity. Daniel 1 puts the mirror back onto the reader and entreats us to consider: What and who does this story reflect? Does it reflect the inscrutable will of God in control of and over all things? Or does it show that such understandings of God's work borders on self-righteous idolatry? Does Daniel reflect complicity, or do Daniel's unknown motives and opaque decisions spur us to consider the work and will of God differently? Defaulting to making ourselves feel better and reassured presents a prideful and narrow understanding of God. Would readers still praise God's wisdom and control if Daniel failed? How often do we relish in successes, then refuse to seek God amid failure?

So it is with this first chapter that Daniel lays its cards on the table as it pushes the boundaries of what the Bible can be and do, making us reconsider what this thing we call "the Bible" actually is. Daniel's initial theological issues only increase compared to what the Daniel character says and does. Further, asking what the story is trying to tell us becomes far too limiting, as the proper question may be, "What might Daniel 1 be saying about us?" Do we make decisions and hope God steps in to support our choices? Or do our lives leave out the perennially unnamed but perpetually harmed? Christians frequently use texts like Daniel 1 to justify our decisions and positions, but what makes Daniel's success admirable? Asking these questions may yield no answers, but that just might be the most daring and powerful message Daniel 1 can offer.

2

Daniel 2 Reconsidered

2.1 Translation

1 In the second year of Nebuchadnezzar's reign, Nebuchadnezzar dreamed dreams, such that his spirit disturbed him and his sleep came upon him.

2 And the king said to summon the enchanters, the sorcerers, and the Chaldeans to tell the king his dreams, and they came and they stood before the king.

3 And the king said to them, "I dreamed a dream and it troubled my spirit to understand this dream."

4 And the Chaldeans spoke to the king (Aramaic): "O King, live forever! Tell the dream to your servants and we will declare the interpretation."

5 The king answered the Chaldeans, saying, "This is a public decree: if you do not make known the dream and its interpretation, your limbs will be torn and your houses be made into a dunghill.

6 But if you declare the dream and its interpretation you will receive gifts, a portion, and great honor from me—only tell me the dream and its interpretation."

7 They answered a second time, saying, "Let the king tell his servants the dream and we can make its interpretation known."

8 And the king answered, saying, "I know with certainty that you are stalling for time because you see that I have a public decree:

9 that if you do not tell me the dream, there is one verdict for you. You have conspired among yourselves to speak lying and corrupt words before me until the time changes. Only tell me the dream and I will know you can declare its interpretation."

10 The Chaldeans answered before the king, saying: "There is no man on the earth who can make known what the king demands! For no great king or ruler has asked such a thing from any magician or sorcerer or Chaldean.

11 The thing that the king asks is difficult, and there is no man who can make it known to the king except the gods, whose dwelling is not among flesh."

12 Because of this the king became exceedingly angry and very furious, and commanded that all the wise men of Babylon be destroyed.

13 And the decree was put out, and all the wise men were to be killed; they sought Daniel and his friends, to execute them.

14 Then Daniel replied with prudence and discretion to Arioch, the king's chief of the executioners, who had gone out to execute the wise men of Babylon.

15 And he asked, saying to Arioch, the king's chief official, "Why is the decree from before the king so urgent?" Arioch then made the matter known to Daniel.

16 So Daniel went in and requested from the king that he give him time and that he tell the interpretation to the king.

17 Then Daniel went to his house and made known his matter with his friends, Hananiah, Mishael, and Azariah.

18 And he asked them to seek mercy from God of the heavens concerning this mystery, in order that Daniel and his friends might not perish with the rest of the wise men of Babylon.

19 Then the mystery was revealed to Daniel with a vision of the night, and Daniel blessed the God of the heavens.

20 Daniel responded and said, "May the name of God be blessed, forever and ever, for wisdom and power are his.

21 For he changes the times and the seasons, removes kings and raises up kings, gives wisdom to wise men and knowledge to those knowing understanding.

22 He reveals deep and hidden things, knows what is in the darkness, and the light dwells with him.

23 To you, God of my ancestors, I give thanks and praise for you have given me wisdom and power and have now made known to me what we asked of you, making known the matter of the king."

24 Therefore Daniel went to Arioch, whom the king had appointed to destroy the wise men of Babylon. And he spoke to him thusly: "Do

not destroy the wise men of Babylon! Bring me in before the king and I will tell the king the interpretation."

25 Then Arioch brought Daniel before the king with haste and spoke to him thusly: "I have found one from the sons of the exiles of Judah who can make known the king's interpretation."

26 The king answered and spoke to Daniel, whose name was Belteshazzar: "Are you able to tell me the dream that I have seen, and its interpretation?"

27 Daniel answered before the king and said: "The mystery of which the king asks, no wise men, conjurers, magicians, or diviners are able to make it known to the king.

28 But there is a God in heaven who reveals mysteries, and he has made known to Nebuchadnezzar what will occur in the latter days. This is your dream and visions of your head upon your bed:

29 To you, O King, your thoughts that came up as you were upon your bed concern what will be hereafter, and the revealer of mysteries made known to you what is to be.

30 And as for me, this mystery was not revealed to me because of wisdom that I have compared to other living beings, but in order that the interpretation be made known to the king and so that you may know the thoughts of your heart.

31 You, O King, were looking, and lo! There was a great statue! This statue was mighty and its countenance was extraordinary. It was standing before you and its appearance was frightening.

32 The statue's head was of fine gold, its chest and arms of silver, its belly and thighs of bronze,

33 its legs of iron, its feet partially of iron and partially of clay.

34 As you looked a stone was cut, one not with hands, and it struck the statue upon its feet of iron and clay, and it crushed them.

35 Then the iron, the clay, the bronze, the silver, and the gold were crushed and became as the chaff of the summer threshing, and the wind carried them away so that no trace of them could be found. And the stone that struck the statue became a great mountain and it filled all the earth.

36 This was the dream; now we will tell the king its interpretation.

37 You O King, the king of kings, to whom God of the heavens gave the kingdom, the power, and the strength, and the glory,

38 into your hand he gave all humans, wherever they dwell, the
beasts of the field, and the birds of the heavens, whom he made ruler
over them all, you are the head of gold.
39 And after you shall rise another kingdom, inferior to yours, then
a third bronze kingdom, which shall rule all the earth.
40 And there shall be a fourth kingdom, strong like iron; just as
iron crushes and shatters everything, this iron will crush and shatter
all these.
41 And as you saw the feet and toes made partially from the potter's
clay and partially from iron, it shall be a divided kingdom, but some
of the iron's strength will be in it, just as you saw the iron mixed with
the soft clay.
42 And the toes of the feet, which were partially of clay and partially
of iron, so shall the kingdom be partially strong and partially brittle.
43 And as you saw the iron mixed with the soft clay, so shall they
mix with one another in marriage, but this will not hold together
with that, just as iron does not mix with clay.
44 And in the days of those kings the God of the heavens will establish a kingdom that will never be destroyed, and it shall not be left to
another people; it will crush and bring to an end all these kingdoms
and it will stand eternally.
45 Just as you saw the stone cut from the mountain not by hands,
and that it crushed the iron, the bronze, the clay, the silver, and the
gold, the great God has made known to the king what will be hereafter. For the dream is certain and its interpretation is trustworthy."
46 Then King Nebuchadnezzar fell upon his face and worshipped
Daniel and commanded an offering and soothing incense be poured
out for him.
47 The king responded to Daniel and said: "Truly your god is god of
gods and ruler of kings and revealer of mysteries, for you have been
able to reveal this mystery!"
48 Then the king promoted Daniel and gave him many gifts and
made him ruler over the entire province of Babylon and chief prefect
over all Babylon's wise men.
49 And Daniel made a request of the king, and he appointed
Shadrach, Meshach, and Abednego over the work of the province of
Babylon, but Daniel remained in the court of the king.

2.2 Reading against the Grain

Just like Daniel 1, chapter 2 begins with an emphasis on Nebuchadnezzar. But Daniel 2 also does something peculiar with its language: it switches from Hebrew to Aramaic at verse 4 for no apparent reason. The only other place Aramaic appears in the Bible is the book of Ezra, making Daniel's language change stand out even more. What is most peculiar about the shift is the text does not tell us why. Further, at verse 4 it changes from Hebrew to Aramaic by literally saying, "And the Chaldeans spoke to the king (Aramaic)" in Hebrew, then "O King, live forever!" in Aramaic. English translations insert the preposition "in" to make the text say, "in Aramaic," but I use parentheses around the word to reflect the text's more raw approach. The text returns to Hebrew at Daniel 8:1, meaning Daniel 2:4a through 7:28 is in Aramaic, and scholars do not know why. Aramaic was a lingua franca, or common language, during the Persian period in which Daniel is set.[1] So it makes sense that the people in Daniel 2 speak Aramaic, but moving from Hebrew to Aramaic without rationale is puzzling. There is no solution as to why the change happens, with scholars doing what I do here: noting the change and acknowledging the absent resolution.

Verse 1 sets the narrative table by dating itself to the second year of Nebuchadnezzar's reign. If one constructs a makeshift timeline starting with Daniel 1, Daniel 2 takes place a year or two after Daniel and his friends and the food gambit. Daniel himself appears late in the chapter at verse 14, a literary move that lets the reader see the foreign king and associates' thoughts and wants. Scholars point out that the second-year notation is odd considering that three years is the prescribed length of education put upon Daniel and his friends in chapter 1. For example, Seow notes that year two demarcates Daniel's growing interpretive prowess, and Newsom digs deep into text-critical discussions around a variant rendering "two" as "twelve."[2] Such is the dominant interpretive narrative around the timestamp: Did chapter 2 unfold during Daniel's training? Is it a misprint? Or is the author's timeline wrong?

Yet such questions neglect the ramifications of another chapter opening with Nebuchadnezzar, a foreign king, as its primary focus. Chapter 2 makes no mention of Daniel and his friends until verse 13, making the alleged protagonist a minor player in the unfolding narrative. The more one reads Daniel 2, the more one realizes this chapter is just as much Nebuchadnezzar's story as it is Daniel's. Daniel plays a considerable role in interpreting Nebuchadnezzar's dream, but one cannot deny the innate curiosity arising from considering why Nebuchadnezzar gets so much narrative attention.

Nebuchadnezzar's behavior toward trusted advisors in verse 2 sheds possible light on the situation. The king summons "enchanters, sorcerers, and the Chaldeans" to help understand his most recent dreams. Notably missing from this list is Daniel, the man in the previous chapter that wowed Nebuchadnezzar so much that the king appointed him to the royal court. Why the disconnect? Why not consult and utilize the considerable resources at Nebuchadnezzar's disposal instead of limiting his options? One could argue that here again the theme of incompetent kings appears, as Nebuchadnezzar forgets the very people he appointed. Nebuchadnezzar's incompetence could prove Daniel's larger anti-imperial sentiment as the king goes from promoting Daniel and his friends to seemingly forgetting their existence. Further, Nebuchadnezzar requests the impossible of his experts by seeking both the dream and its meaning without his divulging the dream's contents. Nebuchadnezzar then threatens his officials with dismemberment for failure but counters his menace by offering whoever meets the demands gifts and great honor. Nebuchadnezzar knows what he wants, but how he wants it done reflects considerable instability.

Nebuchadnezzar's radical either-or behavior makes the king a caricature of himself, issuing decrees that threaten to reshape entire governing structures if these enchanters, sorcerers, and Chaldeans cannot fulfill the impossible task of reading the king's mind. Interpreters read the king's decisions and build up to Daniel's arrival as setting the stage for Daniel's protagonist entrance. However, Nebuchadnezzar receives the dream, not Daniel. The dream's message is for Nebuchadnezzar, not Daniel. Further, if one believes the dream comes from God, that means God speaks directly to Nebuchadnezzar. This makes Nebuchadnezzar, not Daniel, the chapter's central character. Daniel is merely a vehicle to interpret the dream and share its message with Nebuchadnezzar.

And yet just as chapter 2 is about Nebuchadnezzar, it is simultaneously *not* about the troubled contentious king. Nothing about the king's words or actions makes him more remarkable than other kings spread throughout Daniel. His behavior is erratic with raw and immature emotions. Inexperience permeates Nebuchadnezzar's narrative persona, making Daniel's Nebuchadnezzar a pale imitation of historical Nebuchadnezzar's ruthless and focused approach to domination. Who then is this king? How might he function in the larger Daniel narrative? Nebuchadnezzar's Chaldean cadre carry our collective confusion as they call out his bizarre behavior in 2:10, exclaiming, "There is no man on the earth who can make known what the king demands!" The advisors do what Nebuchadnezzar asks in advising a next move, but he finds their input lacking since they cannot tell him the dream. He petulantly orders all Babylonian wise men to face execution. The king's laughably outrageous behavior brings chapter 2 firmly into the satirical arena, as the king listens to no one and runs his kingdom by making up and changing rules to an unwinnable game with no discernable point.

And it is in this bizarre panorama that Daniel finally makes his way into the narrative. Like Daniel 1, Daniel 2 masterfully makes the reader think Daniel is the solution to all narrative problems up to this point, as the threat to his life in verse 13 feels quite empty considering Daniel's previous success. Like Daniel 1, Daniel resolves threats against him and his friends by cajoling a top official to save Daniel's neck. Daniel does not fight for the lives of average Israelites, because the king does not target run-of-the-mill citizens. Daniel once again acts for his own benefit according to his own need, and, just like chapter 1, God is markedly absent. Daniel's behavior in 2:17 reflects this divine absence as he asks his friends (using their Israelite names) to seek God's insight and assistance in accomplishing the king's request. This means Daniel approaches Nebuchadnezzar in verse 16 with uncertainty about the outcome. Readers may describe Daniel's actions here as reflecting his faith in God, but closer inspection highlights Daniel's palpable uncertainty.

The first sign Daniel is in over his head is his request for more time. Nebuchadnezzar grants the Israelite dream interpreter more time, giving Daniel something he withheld from his inner circle. Nebuchadnezzar gives no reason or rationale, and the text tells the reader nothing about how or why the king arrives at this decision. This makes Nebuchadnezzar and Daniel a match made in bureaucratic heaven, as the king acts according to his feelings at any given moment and Daniel acts according to his self-interest. Selflessness is not these characters' strong suit.

Daniel's request of his friends at verse 18 reflects desperation, as the man known in Christian circles for interpretive prowess and direct connection to God seeks outside help. Daniel is, in effect, using his friends to (hopefully) prevent the extermination of Daniel, his friends, and Babylonian wise men. Interpretive strands paint Daniel as a heroic figure set apart to broadcast and celebrate God's sovereignty over events as they unfold. Such readings neglect evidence pointing toward the opposite narrative reality. Daniel relies on luck and irrational self-confidence alongside the hope that God will bail him (and the Babylonian wise men) out of their predicament. Luckily for Daniel, he gets the answers he seeks in a night vision in verse 19, but here, again, God stays silent. God does not swoop and cut away the chaff of confusion and looming death. Instead, God answers their prayers with a night vision, giving Daniel tools necessary to face the king.

Before praising God and regaling Daniel's piety, we must consider the people Daniel tries to save and from what Daniel saves them. Nebuchadnezzar wants to execute all Babylonian wise men, not average Israelites or other common folks. This means Daniel's actions ensure the safety of an elite group of politically and socially connected Babylonians, a move countering any sense of anti-imperial sentiment. Daniel's actions reflect a pro-empire orientation that comforts the king and ensures that Israelite adversaries will continue to survive and thrive. Daniel and his friends face death not because of their Israelite heritage; they face death thanks to their Babylonian royalty connections. This makes for radically different interpretive possibilities, as Daniel's actions reflect a distinct Babylonian loyalty.

Daniel's response at verses 20–23 follows Daniel's choices and Daniel's choices alone, as he continues buttressing the Babylonian status quo. Daniel's beautifully written words praise God for answering prayers as he showers adulation upon the deity, going as far as to describe God as "God of my ancestors." Here Daniel has not given up on his god despite the horrors wrought upon Israel and its people, calling to his ancestors in praising the God of Abraham, Moses, and Noah. Despite efforts toward highlighting his Israelite bona fides, Daniel's words feel hollow given how Daniel uses this newfound knowledge. Instead of using his divine connection to overthrow his oppressors, Daniel uses it to comfort Nebuchadnezzar. This reduces God to something that Daniel picks and chooses from according to his wants. God is now a tool for Daniel to exploit, setting dangerous theological precedence. Is God just "there" when someone needs God and is otherwise absent? Does it take more than one person beseeching the divine to get the deity's attention? And does God fight only for the politically connected and affluent?

Daniel insists on telling Nebuchadnezzar himself, once again using divine wisdom for face-to-face time with a foreign ruler that took Israel's land by force. Arioch brings Daniel before Nebuchadnezzar, and Nebuchadnezzar strangely talks with Daniel like the two never met. Verse 26 also lets the reader know that Daniel is Belteshazzar, something made abundantly clear in chapter 1. Narrative inconsistencies between Daniel 1 and

Daniel 2 prompt scholars to claim these chapters existed independently until later in the canonization process.[3] This means the Nebuchadnezzar of Daniel 2 neglects Daniel because this king is not the Nebuchadnezzar of Daniel 1. Such an approach makes sense given the stand-alone nature of each chapter in Daniel 1–6. It makes even more sense when comparing the tone, content, and apocalyptic focus of Daniel 7–12 with the straightforward narratives in chapters 1–6. This speaks to the possibility of Daniel being more of a "glue" character in a larger literary corpus than a central protagonist, making Daniel and his friends the common denominator in otherwise disparate stories.

Each chapter then stands independent as an artifact with unique points and purposes, making these chapters partners in conversation rather than one story beginning in chapter 1 and ending in chapter 6. Reimagining chapter 2 as one seat at the interpretive table creates space for diverse, ongoing, and dynamic readings that make us consider adventurous questions, like, "How does the God of Daniel 1 differ from the God of Daniel 2, and what might that say about the communities that held these stories as sacred?" Or "Nebuchadnezzar and all the other kings in 1–6 never seem to learn any lesson despite all they see and hear from their Israelite captives; what does that say about their capacity to lead and learn?" The list can go on and on, making what happens in these chapters more than just a narrative journey from Point A to Point B. Despite such rich possibilities, mainline interpretations favor safer and simpler readings that reduce Daniel, his friends, and these kings to pawns in the grander narrative of God's sovereignty. Through that lens, God's alleged power and might mean so little to Nebuchadnezzar that the obstinate king cannot remember Daniel well enough to contact him to interpret this dream.

Daniel lays out the dream for the king and the reading audience, offering considerable detail because no one (including the reader) knows anything about the dream at this point except the king. Daniel certainly takes advantage of his moment before the king: he speaks for nineteen verses and fills the page with grandiose adulation toward the king, going as far as to call Nebuchadnezzar "the king of kings" at verse 37. One could argue that Daniel speaks hyperbolically here, perhaps indirectly mocking Nebuchadnezzar. Daniel's next words in verse 38 defy such an approach, however, as he appears quite genuine in praising Nebuchadnezzar. He attributes Nebuchadnezzar's success to divine providence, corroborating Daniel 1:1–2. Indeed, there is a sense of theological consistency across these opening two chapters, and it does align with accepted Christian notions of divine sovereignty. Mindful of that, it is most peculiar that this sovereignty extends to Nebuchadnezzar and his rule as king. Daniel 2 portrays Nebuchadnezzar as a divinely appointed ruler, cementing the king's place in the larger cosmological structure.

Daniel 2:37–37 expands the political theological statement from Daniel 1:2, saying all humans, wherever they dwell, along with the beasts of the field and the birds of the heavens, fall under the king's dominion. Daniel simultaneously interprets the dream and adulates the monarch, as praise toward Nebuchadnezzar echoes Daniel's words about God in Daniel 2:20–23. There Daniel praises God's power and wisdom, situating the deity in control over time, kingdoms, and knowledge. God "reveals deep and hidden things, knows what is in the darkness, and the light dwells with him." Similarly, Nebuchadnezzar is "the king of kings" and the one to whom God bestows power, strength, glory, and the very kingdom of Israel. All humans fall under Nebuchadnezzar's rule wherever they dwell, meaning that Daniel believes this foreign king's authority defies limits. Daniel moves beyond humans, claiming Nebuchadnezzar reigns over every animal of the field and bird of the sky. It seems the only entity more powerful than Nebuchadnezzar is Daniel's God, and one could even debate that, as the only other being that knows the contents of Nebuchadnezzar's dream is God. God and Nebuchadnezzar's knowledge about the dream is identical, thereby giving the foreign king deity-like knowledge.

The one thing Nebuchadnezzar lacks is confirmation about what the dream means. Daniel and his interpretive skills come into play here, but the question remains: Would God have given Daniel, or anyone else for that matter, the dream's interpretation without someone asking for it? God chooses Nebuchadnezzar to receive the dream and carry its contents without Nebuchadnezzar's request. The dream confuses Nebuchadnezzar, meaning God pours out this divine message upon an incapable non-Israelite receptacle. Why not give the dream to Daniel and eliminate the monarchical go-between? On top of this odd choice of dream receiver, giving Nebuchadnezzar the dream is callous because, as Daniel's interpretation shows, the known world hinges upon the dream's meaning. In theory, if Daniel's friends neglect Daniel's request, the world loses the dream and its interpretation, people die, and God's giving Nebuchadnezzar the dream becomes a mistake. Detractors to this type of reading may use divine sovereignty as their retort, but understanding sovereignty this way makes humans nothing more than thoughtless automatons. Even worse, defaulting to a "God will make things right in God's time" sovereignty invalidates anyone who perished from Nebuchadnezzar's forces.

Verses 28–30 confirm Nebuchadnezzar's place as one of the chapter's protagonists when Daniel describes God as a mystery revealer. This mystery falls upon Nebuchadnezzar. God shows Nebuchadnezzar the future as the king sleeps, a move that makes the king God's information channel to the human realm. God blesses Nebuchadnezzar's rule with this dream, but that is paltry compared to Israel's God giving the Babylonian monarch celestial secrets with cosmological significance. Does God now favor Nebuchadnezzar because the king took Israel by force? Or has God always favored Nebuchadnezzar, making Israel's rise and eventual fall a conduit for getting to Nebuchadnezzar's reign? Daniel's words in verse 30 highlight how God gives Nebuchadnezzar the dream and intends its interpretation for the king and only the king. Daniel believes that God cares for Nebuchadnezzar's heart, suggesting an intimate relationship between the deity and the king. The book may bear Daniel's name, but through two chapters the book's affection belongs to Nebuchadnezzar.

We have yet to discuss the contents of the dream and its interpretation, and that is on purpose. Christians put considerable interpretive stock in Daniel 2's statue and the variety of metals, practically ignoring the rest of what happens in chapter 2. The statue is an important part of the chapter, but it is just that: one part of a larger piece. These Christian readings take the statue and the metals comprising it as metaphors representing weakened proceeding kingdoms (i.e., a lesser metal equals a lesser kingdom). Such metaphors are apt in understanding the obvious in chapter 2, but acknowledging these metaphors and stopping there leaves much to interpret. For example, Daniel inflates Nebuchadnezzar's ego in presenting Babylon as the gold kingdom and thereby the pinnacle of the current historical trajectory. Making Nebuchadnezzar "the head of gold" also removes Nebuchadnezzar's culpability, suggesting that what unfolds lies beyond the control, and in turn accountability, of the current Babylonian king. One could argue Daniel's statue interpretation makes Nebuchadnezzar the first failure, meaning Daniel tells the foreign ruler that his fruitless reign culminates in destruction. However, that is not what Daniel says. Daniel does not suggest the king should fear the interpretation, nor does he present Nebuchadnezzar at the mercy of a sovereign God. Rather, Daniel's words alleviate the king's anxiety and make Nebuchadnezzar feel so elated that he worships Daniel, has him anointed, praises Daniel's god, and promotes Daniel to province ruler and chief prefect of Babylonian wise men. Divine wisdom now pacifies a foreign oppressive ruler's anxiety, which Daniel then wields to buttress his and his compatriot's career aspirations. Daniel helps only himself, his friends, and Nebuchadnezzar.

Just as Daniel uses the golden head to appease Nebuchadnezzar, so too do Christian interpreters use the statue and its metals to assuage and commend each other. Countless readers, both living and long dead, project themselves upon said statue, reducing Daniel 2 to nothing more than a political or personal apocalyptic totem. Contemporary street preachers distribute flyers proclaiming the end of the current age and use Daniel 2 as one foundational apocalyptic text to build their argument. Timeworn (and still accepted) readings from European Christian church fathers follow similar paths and present Daniel as the keystone to unlocking and understanding history. Yet returning to the text shows that, except for Babylon and Nebuchadnezzar as the golden head at verse 38, the metals and kingdoms remain distinctly nondescript. All we know about these symbolic kingdoms is just what the text says: they represent kingdoms. Further information about these empires and their identities is unavailable.

And yet, deficient evidence does not stop interpreters from projecting themselves and their circumstances onto Daniel 2. Christian readers take considerable effort in reconstructing history according to how they read the statue, culminating in their respective current geopolitical landscapes. For example, Christian thinker and theologian Jerome's fourth-century CE commentary is a definitive Christian paradigm through which Christian interpretations still flow. Jerome says the silver is "the empire of the Medes and Persians" because as silver is lesser than gold, so too is the Mede and Persian empire compared to Nebuchadnezzar's Babylon.[4] Jerome continues and bends biblical narrative history toward his own by making the third empire of bronze into "the Alexandrian empire, and that of the Macedonians, and of Alexander's successors." This means Jerome squeezes three separate imperial entities with Alexandria, Macedonia, and Alexander's successors into one of Daniel 2's kingdoms. He reads three empires as one to claim the iron empire "clearly refers to the Romans."[5] Jerome lived and worked in fourth- and fifth-century Rome, meaning he quite literally makes his time the apex of Daniel's statuesque history.

Jerome's presumptuousness is contagious, as alleged "unbiased" and "historical" readings continue for over one thousand years, leading up to, within, and beyond the Protestant Reformation. Martin Luther reads the fourth kingdom as the Roman Empire with considerable self-assurance, with Giovanni Diodati, John Calvin, and other Protestant Reformers following the same trend.[6] Protestant interpretation of Rome as the fourth kingdom is a not-so-subtle way of pinning anti-Catholic sentiment upon Daniel 2, a move further highlighting the pattern of placing one's own adversaries onto Daniel's unknown and unnamed antagonists. It is also worth noting that the era's Catholic interpretation is equally anti-Protestant and pro-Jesus, showing a remarkable interpretive consistency between these two adversarial Christian factions.[7]

Like the fourth kingdom and the statue, ancient and modern Christian readers make chapter 2 about Jesus via the stone in verses 34, 35, and 45. Daniel sees the rock in question in verse 34, saying "a stone was cut, not one with hands." Verse 35 calls it "the stone," and verse 45 adds to the description in verse 34: "the stone cut from the mountain not by hands." The text offers this and only this about the stone—nothing more, nothing less; anything interpreters add comes from their minds. Just like the discussion around the metals and their meaning, contemporary Christian readings of Jesus as the stone build upon a dominant strain of interpretation. As early as the second century CE, Justin Martyr writes extensively about Daniel and the Old Testament in *Dialogue with Trypho* to prove Jesus is the fulfillment of all scriptures, including and especially Daniel.[8] Jerome uses the stone to pivot his reception toward Jesus and the virgin birth, saying, "However, at the final period of all these empires of gold and silver and bronze and iron, a rock (namely, the Lord and Savior) was cut off without hands, that is, without copulation or human seed and by birth from a virgin's womb."[9] Similarly, fifth-century CE Christian Theodoret of Cyrus uses Daniel 2 to support the virgin birth: "So we learn from Old and New Testament that our Lord Jesus Christ was called stone: it was cut from a mountain without hands being used, being born of a virgin independently of marital intercourse."[10] Augustine of Hippo also falls prey to Christian projection, saying, "We know that the stone cut from the mountain without hands is Christ, who came from the kingdom of the Jews without a human father."[11]

Contemporary readers etch this "Jesus as the stone" into the modern era, creating an unquestioned norm based on specific men's antiquated opinions. Yet modern Christian voices present this interpretation as brand new or something their own, cementing the reading into doctrine-level entrenchment.[12] These interpretations focus on the stone's origins, specifically it being cut not by human hands, thus continuing the cascade of baseless conclusions revolving around Daniel confirming Jesus' heavenly origins and virgin birth. Making this stone solely about Jesus is limiting, dangerous, and anti-Semitic. It reinforces Christian supersessionist approaches to Daniel and eliminates more daring considerations of what the text might be doing. For example, readers rarely, if ever, consider exactly who and what it is that the stone will destroy. We Christians read ourselves as the ones the stone is thrown on behalf of, meaning we survive and claim victory. We read ourselves as the ones benefiting from fallen empires and earthly destruction. In doing this, we fail to consider that we might be the ones facing destruction.

Verses 35 and 45 make it clear that this stone destroys *all* empires. Despite unilateral destruction, Nebuchadnezzar finds peace in Daniel's words in verses 46–59. One would think the news about his empire's final destruction would chill Nebuchadnezzar's spine; instead, he celebrates. Why does he celebrate? And why does he promote Daniel for sharing that the kingdom will fall into utter ruin, lost to history? The dream reflects Nebuchadnezzar's anxieties about his role and power: what he has can swiftly fall, and he stands powerless to stop it. The stone destroys all empires, not just one or a select few. All. Only the eternal kingdom that the stone becomes will survive. Why, then, would anyone consider themselves victors among the chaos? We Christian readers speak warmly about this eternal kingdom because we far too often read ourselves as the people inhabiting this future principality. For example, second-century CE Christian thinker Irenaeus interprets the eternal kingdom as filled by just and righteous Christians. Augustine reads it simply as the extant Christian church. Modern interpreters project positive readings onto the stone as well, making it a vehicle for God breaking into human existence to institute one final and decisive rule. Just like Nebuchadnezzar, Christian readers celebrate the stone's arrival as a culmination and vindication. According to these interpreters (and despite the profound lack of textual support), powerful Christian foes fall, and Christians take their rightful place under God's rule.

The king's praise befuddles commentators to the point of claiming that Daniel 2 reflects editorial redactions, meaning Nebuchadnezzar's response to his empire's destruction excludes the fifth stone kingdom.[13] Yet such readings dodge the pressing issue of Nebuchadnezzar's extant response. Claiming the king celebrates without full knowledge of what we, the readers, know is disingenuous to contemporary religious communities. Nebuchadnezzar is, in effect, celebrating his own demise. Or perhaps he understands he will be long dead before the stone makes its appearance, excusing him from blame for those the stone will crush. Nebuchadnezzar celebrates because he knows his fate differs from proceeding leaders, which is why he promotes Daniel. This good news also yields success for Daniel and his friends, as their fates now match the king's: something bad will happen to someone else during a time far removed from their generation. Everyone gets what they want and then some, leaving us readers to ponder: What is the point of all this?

2.3 So What?

Christian scholars often read parables in the Old and New Testaments as open to interpretation, encouraging readers to insert themselves according to their life's journey. This reflects interpretive flexibility inherent to parables. A similar approach could yield considerable interpretive fruit for texts like Daniel 2. Christian readers frequently align themselves with Daniel. We make his moves and motives match our own, reading ourselves as downtrodden Israelites thriving among foreign powers. Yet one could argue that Daniel's role in this second chapter amounts to little more than an extended cameo. Nebuchadnezzar, not Daniel, is just as much the main character as anyone else in chapter 2. Nebuchadnezzar's feelings, thoughts, and emotions take center stage, with Daniel playing a minor part against a larger narrative background.

All of Daniel's decisions revolve around Nebuchadnezzar. Daniel appears in verse 13 only after Nebuchadnezzar's execution decree. God grants Daniel's friends the wisdom and insight necessary to satisfy Nebuchadnezzar's request, but only after Daniel requests it through his friends. Daniel himself declares that God has shown Nebuchadnezzar God's ultimate plans for the coming future. In verse 30, Daniel says God showed Daniel the dream and its interpretation "in order that the interpretation be made known to the king and so that you may know the thoughts of your heart." Daniel even embodies Nebuchadnezzar in retelling the dream, describing what the king saw in verses 31, 41, 43, and 45. Further, Daniel compares everything to Nebuchadnezzar's kingdom, a move that makes the foreign king the centerpiece upon which this dream and history hinges. All this unfolds because Nebuchadnezzar is the primary protagonist in Daniel 2. His wants, thoughts, and needs drive the narrative forward, and the chapter quite literally revolves around him.

Yet such an approach defies Christian receptions, as interpreters downplay Nebuchadnezzar's role and make him a pawn in God's larger plan. Such receptions stretch back to the earliest known Christian interpretations and continue among contemporary readers. For example, Jerome argues the king receives the dream "in order that he might give glory to god."[14] Third-century CE Christian writer Hippolytus takes a similar stance, claiming that "the vision was concealed from the king" in order that Daniel "might be shown to be a prophet."[15] Sixteenth-century German Christian Reformer and theologian Johann Wigand expands on this interpretive stream and, in so doing, highlights a pressing issue surrounding how Christians read Daniel 2:

> The purpose of the chapter also has three points. First, God wanted to confound the skill of the world's so-called bright lights. He permitted them to destroy themselves since they were not able to understand the secret mysteries of God. Second, God wanted to reveal hidden and future things that the true God might be acknowledged and glorified. Third, God wanted to bestow on his church a witness of his presence and truth to lighten their affliction in exile.[16]

Wigand inserts God and the Christian church into the chapter, despite neither making an appearance. Even Wigand's work echoes other readings when he claims God "wanted to confound" and "permitted" things to happen in Daniel 2. Justin Martyr laid down such a reading as early as the second century CE with his *Dialogue with Trypho*, followed by Jerome in the fourth century CE and Theodoret of Cyrus in the fifth century. These early Christian interpreters and their contemporaries insert God wherever they like, setting a dangerous precedent that exposes the limits of unchecked fatalism. Approaches like this limit what contemporary readers can do, as this type of reading goes unquestioned to the point of becoming paradigmatic.

Reading against this fatalistic interpretive grain creates avenues for bold reconsiderations. According to verse 1, Nebuchadnezzar simply "dreamed dreams" as he slept. The text ascribes no divine origin or purpose to the dream and its contents. Thus, what unfolds reflects Nebuchadnezzar's genuine uncertainty and exposes the capricious nature of people wielding considerable power. Something as random as a dream sparks Nebuchadnezzar to make outlandish requests that could result in multiple pointless deaths. As noted earlier, Daniel intervenes only because he and his friends are possible victims. Further, God pays attention to the situation only after Daniel's friends beseech the deity, meaning that according to this text God sits idle as events unfold. Is God absent or otherwise too busy to step in? Or could this story offer space for reflecting on how Daniel, his friends, and Nebuchadnezzar treat the deity? Is God a vending machine that waits on the cries of a select few before risking any kind of intervention? Or could Daniel 2 be a critique of this kind of "pray and God will answer" religiosity?

Understanding the divine in this manner reflects a dangerous trend among Christians in the United States. We make prayer a tool if it is advantageous to us. We thank God when things go well, like when we receive a promotion or our child does well in school. But our theological worlds change when life's realities slap us back into the present. We wonder where the God that blesses and gives has gone when cancer ravages our bodies or violence shatters our communities. We treat God like God is only for us, until God is not, crafting a troubling cycle of theological uncertainty. Sermons teaching God's sovereignty as laid out in Daniel 2 only reinforce these theological missteps, prompting us to assuage our anxieties and sadness under the guise of "part of God's plan." We wait in expectant hope for the stone of Daniel 2 to crush our enemies and place us in our rightful spot atop God's new and perfect kingdom.

But what if instead of saving us, the stone comes to destroy us? What if our behavior and our actions are the very things God wants to eliminate in favor of God's wants as opposed to our narrow and self-imposed understandings of Christianity? Because whether we like to admit it, American Christianity has become an imperial religion. More American politicians are Christian than any other religion combined (and it is not even close). Christians make up the majority of the U.S. Supreme Court, making laws and institutions reflect Christian biases. Despite such power, Christians read our misbegotten sense of persecution into Daniel 2. In failing to recognize this reality, we reject our own complicity (and, in some cases, outright partnership) in American oppression. We default to naïve fantasies about idealized places in the cosmic order and, in so doing, allow imperial evil to reign unchecked. We American Christians become so engrossed with our ideas of ourselves that we fail to see that we, Christians in America, are more like Nebuchadnezzar than we are not.

One need only consider the history and origins of the United States to see the side we stand on: Christians colonized the land that became the United States, then made it into a global economic power through centuries of enslavement. Primary sources and historians back up this claim with overwhelming consensus.[17] Christopher Columbus, a devout Christian, set sail in 1492 dreaming of spreading his faith alongside European economic interests. Sixteenth-century conquistador Pedro Cieza de León speaks of the Spanish impact on indigenous peoples and lands:

> We, Christians, have destroyed so many kingdoms. For wherever the Spaniards have passed, conquering and discovering, it is as though a fire had gone, destroying everything in its path.[18]

On September 6, 1620, male pilgrims aboard the Mayflower signed an agreement that makes clear the point and purpose of their efforts:

> Having undertaken for the Glory of God, and Advancement of the Christian Faith, and the Honour of our King and Country, a Voyage to plant the first colony in the northern Parts of Virginia; [we] do by these presents, solemnly and mutually in the Presence of God and one another, covenant and combine ourselves together into a civil Body Politick, for our better Ordering and Preservation, and Furtherance of the Ends aforesaid.[19]

In 1656 a Dutch traveler writing from New Netherland recalls:

> The Indians . . . affirm that before the arrival of the Christians, and before the smallpox broke out amongst them, they were ten times as numerous as they now are, and that their population had been melted down by this disease, whereof nine-tenths of them have died.[20]

Christian settlers, like Nebuchadnezzar, create cultures of fear and intimidation that leads to dependence on the oppressor from the subjugated. European Christian colonizers forced indigenous peoples to convert to Christianity or face death. Conversions, however, did not mean permanent protection. For example, in March 1782, British armies forced the native Delaware peoples from their homes with false accusations of theft and abetting murderers. Roxanne Dunbar-Ortiz describes what happens next:

> Condemned to death, the Delawares spent the night praying and singing hymns. In the morning, Williamson's men marched over ninety people in pairs into two houses and methodically slaughtered them. One killer bragged that he personally had bludgeoned fourteen victims with a cooper's mallet, which he had then handed to an accomplice.[21]

Examples like this go on and on. Christianity may not have begun as the empire's religion, but in colonizing hands it became one.

Christian conquering continues from there. "Manifest Destiny" drove us Americans to move west across the continent because we believed God destined us to do so. Countless people died, and entire civilizations perished. What is worse now is how divided we Americans remain about our imperial status. Discussions around banning historically accurate books fill our computer screens and news cycles, as people fear what might come from increased public awareness surrounding the actual history of the United States. Christians believed God gave this land into our hands, rationalizing lives we took with claims of everything being in God's all-knowing control. We American Christians put God on whatever side we take with total disregard for the suffering of others.

Historical cycles of war and violence roll on, presented as inevitabilities to endure rather than realities to change. For example, Russia invaded Ukraine in 2022 among considerable public outcry. American news stations displayed pictures of the dead along the streets of Kyiv and spoke with political pundits about the how and why of Russia's latest foray into global war. Evangelical periodicals like *Christianity Today* filled their pages with news and views from evangelicals for evangelicals, as refugees fled for the lives of their children and themselves. Ukrainian evangelical leaders shared prayers and insights with *Christianity Today*, allowing an "on the ground" glimpse into war-torn Christian thought. Pastors and leaders sought wisdom, strength, and focus. Others, like Yuriy Kulakevych, took the opportunity to bash Orthodox Christians:

> I am praying for supernatural restoration during short nights of sleep! Everyone is doing their best—physically, mentally, and spiritually—but some, and especially the youth, need delivery from posttraumatic stress. Yet amid the darkness of war, I am praying for the evangelization of the nations in the Russian Federation, with the gospel hidden by the black robes of the Orthodox priests.[22]

Missionary Vadym Kulynchenko sees the invasion as proof for Eurasia and the Middle East as "the epicenter of God's end times prophecies," and Sergey Rakhuba sees the war as a faith test: "It is easy to trust God when nothing is happening . . . but as the love of Jesus shines through tragedy, we can still find hope and joy."[23]

American evangelicals took similar yet altogether distinct positions. Pat Robertson claimed Russian president Vladimir Putin is "being compelled by God. He went into Ukraine, but that wasn't his goal. His goal was to move against Israel, ultimately."[24] Franklin Graham tweeted support for the Russian dictator: "Pray for President Putin today. This may sound like a strange request, but we need to pray that God would work in his heart so that war could be avoided at all cost."[25] Graham and Robertson's respective

Putin support sounds eerily like Christian receptions painting Nebuchadnezzar as a troubled but ultimately divinely chosen leader, a move that reinforces ideological positions leading to more war and more death.

Ardent focus on Russia's invasion highlights deep-seated American Christian imperialism. The United States and its allies wrought war and destabilization around the globe, reducing governments across South America and the African continent to nothing more than pawns for our economic gain. For that reason, it is well within the parameters of Daniel's rhetoric to read our current empire as the one facing destruction. For us, the message of Daniel 2 seems clear: the coming of God's judgment will destroy all earthly empires, including and especially ours. Should we wait for the placation? Or should we act with liberation from these prisons of our own making?

3

Daniel 3 Reconsidered

3.1 Translation

1 And King Nebuchadnezzar made an image of gold, and its height was sixty cubits and its width was six cubits. He (the king) set it up in the plain of Dura in the province of Babylon.

2 The king sent to gather the satraps, the prefects, and the governors, the counselors, the treasurers, the justices, the magistrates, and all the officials to come to dedicate the image which King Nebuchadnezzar set up.

3 The satraps, the prefects, and the governors, the counselors, the treasurers, the justices, the magistrates, and all the officials of the provinces gathered for the dedication of the image which King Nebuchadnezzar had erected. As they stood before the image which Nebuchadnezzar had erected,

4 the herald proclaimed aloud to everyone: "You, the people and nations, to all languages, are commanded

5 at the time when you hear the sound of the horn, pipe, lyre, trigon, harp, drum, and music of every kind, fall and give worship to the golden image that Nebuchadnezzar the king erected.

6 And whoever does not fall and worship, he will immediately be cast into the midst of the fiery furnace to burn."

7 Thus, when all the peoples heard the sound of the horn, pipe, lyre, trigon, harp, drum, and music of all kinds, all the people, nations, and languages worshipped the golden image which Nebuchadnezzar the king erected.

8 When this happened, certain Chaldeans came forward and brought accusative charges against the Jews.

[9] They declared and said to Nebuchadnezzar the king: "O King, live forever!

[10] You, the king, made a decree that each man that hears the sound of the horn, pipe, lyre, trigon, harp, drum, and music of every kind, shall fall and worship the golden image.

[11] And whoever does not fall down and worship, he will be cast into the midst of the fiery furnace to burn.

[12] There are certain Jews that you appointed over the work of the affairs of the province of Babylon: Shadrach, Meshach, and Abednego. They do not serve you, O King; they do not serve your gods, and they do not worship the golden image that you erected."

[13] Then Nebuchadnezzar was enraged and furious. He said, "Bring me Shadrach, Meshach, and Abednego." Then these men were brought before the king.

[14] Then the king answered and said to them, "Is this true, Shadrach, Meshach, and Abednego? You do not serve my gods or worship the golden image which I erected?

[15] Now, if you are ready, any time you hear the sound of the horn, pipe, lyre, trigon, harp, drum, and music of every kind, to fall down and worship the image that I made . . . but if you don't worship, immediately you shall be cast in the midst of the burning fiery furnace. Who, then, is a god that shall deliver you from my hands?"

[16] Shadrach, Meshach, and Abednego answered, saying, "O King Nebuchadnezzar, we don't need to answer you regarding this matter.

[17] If the god whom we serve is able to deliver us from the burning fiery furnace and from your hand, O King, may he deliver us.

[18] But if not, may be it known to you, O King, that we do not serve your gods or worship the golden image which you set up."

[19] Then Nebuchadnezzar filled with rage and the expression of his face changed toward Shadrach, Meshach, and Abednego. He answered, saying to heat the furnace seven times hotter than normal.

[20] And he told his strongest warrior men of his army to bind Shadrach, Meshach, and Abednego to cast them into the fiery burning furnace.

[21] Then the men bound their tunics, trousers, hats, and clothes and cast them into the midst of the fiery burning furnace.

[22] Because this order from the king was so urgent and the furnace was heated to excess, the men that brought up Shadrach, Meshach, and Abednego were slain by flames of the furnace.

23 And these three men, Shadrach, Meshach, and Abednego, fell bound into the midst of the flaming, fiery furnace.

24 Then Nebuchadnezzar the king was astonished and stood alarmed. He answered and said to his counselors, "Were these three men not cast bound into the midst of the fire?" They answered and said to the king, "True, O King."

25 He responded and said, "Lo! I see four men unbound and walking in the midst of the fire, and there is no harm upon them! And the appearance of the fourth is one like a son of gods."

26 Then Nebuchadnezzar approached the door of the fiery burning furnace. He answered and said, "Shadrach, Meshach, and Abednego, servants of the Most High God: come out and come here." Then Shadrach, Meshach, and Abednego came out from the midst of the fire.

27 And the satraps, prefects, governors, and counselors of the king gathered to see these men whose bodies did not burn, and the hair of their heads was not singed, and their tunics were not harmed, and the smell of fire did not pass between them.

28 Nebuchadnezzar answered and said, "Blessed be the god of Shadrach, Meshach, and Abednego, who sent a messenger to deliver his servants that trusted in him. They set aside the king's command and yielded their bodies instead of serving and worshipping any god except their god.

29 Therefore, I set out a decree that all people, nations, and languages that speak negligence against the god of Shadrach, Meshach, and Abednego, their limbs shall be torn and their houses shall become a dunghill; for there is no other god that is able to deliver in this way."

30 Then the king promoted Shadrach, Meshach, and Abednego in the province of Babylon.

31 Nebuchadnezzar, the king of all peoples, nations, and languages that dwell throughout the earth: "May peace grow in abundance!

32 I declare that the signs and wonders that the Most High God has done good before me.

33 How great are his signs! How strong are his wonders! His kingdom is an eternal kingdom, and dominion is from generation to generation."

3.2 Reading against the Grain

A surface reading of Daniel 3 yields predictable results: Shadrach, Meshach, and Abednego stand for their faith against difficult odds. Through supernatural intervention, they find prosperity among Babylonian elites and bring praise, glory, and honor to their deity. And yet, Daniel 3 holds considerable theological and political complexities that make us reconsider unchecked power, blind allegiance, political corruption, and the human cost of political maneuverings. But a most important avenue for interpretation arises alongside theological tensions raised in Daniel 1 and 2: Why is God still so markedly absent?

Like the first two chapters, Daniel 3 mentions Nebuchadnezzar first. The Babylonian king is just as constant as Daniel and his friends in these three chapters, so much so that one could again argue he is another protagonist in this monarchy-centric narrative. Reading chapters 2 and 3 in succession highlights an oddity in Nebuchadnezzar's behavior: How does he respond to the dream of a weakened, then ultimately destroyed, metal and stone statue, with gold symbolizing his Babylonian kingdom? By building a golden image for his kingdom to valorize. Nebuchadnezzar is either naïve, foolish, incompetent, or a combination of the three, as building a golden edifice after dreaming of a fallen statue that symbolizes the eventual end of all human empires is shockingly on the nose. It is as if Nebuchadnezzar mocks himself.

Verse 1 says Nebuchadnezzar "made an image," but Nebuchadnezzar did not build this himself. Political leaders, both ancient and modern, lay claim to things they never touch as their own, as if to say they "made" the very thing they discuss. Though leaders may provide the funding and supply the workers for such a project, their hands only lift hammers and shovels at ceremonial groundbreaking ceremonies. Such is the likelihood here, with Nebuchadnezzar placing this golden image in Dura, a Babylonian providence. Notice that my Daniel 3 translation lacks "statue" for the word describing the structure. The Aramaic word here is צְלֵם. It appears throughout the chapter referring to this thing made of gold, commonly read as a "statue." Translations vary with this word, as versions fluctuate between "statue" and "image."[1] There is no historical evidence supporting the existence of such a statue or image. Fifth-century BCE Greek historian Herodotus writes about two golden statues made in the image of Zeus and Cyrus the Great, saying nothing about one built for or by Nebuchadnezzar.[2] Further, insufficient evidence leaves scholars divided as to the particulars of this place known as Dura. It is a common Babylonian location name, but specifics beyond that rely purely on conjecture.[3] This means Daniel 3 begins with two historical impossibilities, as no evidence exists of either Dura or the image's existence. One could argue this is a rhetorical move telling the reader up front that Daniel 3 is fiction set within the parameters of the known world. The fantastical nature of Daniel 3 only supports such a claim. For example, according to Daniel 3:2–5, Nebuchadnezzar calls everyone together to make them bow before this image whenever they hear "music of every kind." Such a decree is outlandish, impractical, and unenforceable. Reading the king alongside the fictional Dura and image makes Nebuchadnezzar a clear caricature, propped up to create an impossible, no-win scenario for Shadrach, Meshach, and Abednego.

Verse 7 continues this satirical vein by saying that all people, nations, and languages worshipped Nebuchadnezzar's image. One must wonder how exactly the king and his compatriots expected this worship to unfold. The Babylonian kingdom stretched for hundreds of miles. Did dutiful Babylonians drop everything anytime music filled the air to migrate to the statue? Did they turn and simply face in the image's direction, or is the situation so absurd that it carries its hyperbolic improbability with pride?

Verse 8 supports reading Daniel 3 as borderline satirical, as "certain Chaldeans" accuse observant Jews of disobeying the empty decree. These Chaldeans' actions display no subtlety, as their accusations in verses 9–12 show that this ludicrous decree is nothing more than a poorly veiled attempt to entrap Shadrach, Meshach, and Abednego. Reading Daniel's connective narrative tissue helps us understand what motivates the Chaldeans: jealousy. They resent the Israelites because in Daniel 1:20 the king praises the Israelites' efforts as "ten times more than each of the magicians and conjurers from throughout the kingdom." In short, the Chaldeans feel threatened and hatch an elaborate, vain scheme to eliminate their adversaries.

The Chaldeans lavish praise upon Nebuchadnezzar at verse 9 but commit a critical misstep at verse 10 in claiming the king made the decree concerning the statue. According to verses 2–6, the king orders the statue's dedication; this otherwise unknown "herald" in verse 4 makes the command to worship the golden image. The king says nothing about worshipping the statue until verse 13 after he orders Shadrach, Meshach, and Abednego before him. One could argue that Nebuchadnezzar never made the decree and that the first he hears of it is in verses 10–12. Why else would the Chaldeans describe the king's own decree and, in essence, tell him about a binding directive done in his name without his knowledge?

Further, why does Nebuchadnezzar seem confused by the Israelite trifecta's actions, given that the first two chapters end with the king heaping praise upon the foursome and their deity? Nebuchadnezzar appears profoundly and comedically out of the loop, leaving one to consider who runs this kingdom: the appointed monarch, his loyal and paranoid delegates, or no one, leaving the kingdom to function according to the wants and whims of someone different depending on the moment and circumstances. The Chaldeans also appear disconnected from the king's comings and goings, as in verse 12 they criticize the Israelite trio because "they do not serve your gods, and they do not worship the golden image that you erected." Daniel 1 and 2 end with Nebuchadnezzar taking the Israelite god as his own, so these three men *do* worship one of Nebuchadnezzar's gods. And verse 12 becomes more peculiar after Nebuchadnezzar affirms the Chaldean at verse 14, asking the trio, "Is this true . . . you do not serve my gods or worship the golden image which I erected?" The king's words then echo Daniel 1:2 as he rebukes the Israelites and mockingly asks, "Who, then, is a god that shall deliver you from my hands?" Irony saturates this moment. Nebuchadnezzar asks if the Israelite deity can save them from his hands despite the second verse of Daniel's first chapter explicitly saying that God gave Jehoiakim into Nebuchadnezzar's hand. Nebuchadnezzar misunderstands that the God he mocks put him in power, begging the question: What does this say about Nebuchadnezzar's ability to grasp what unfolds around him? Further, does Nebuchadnezzar know God is using him? And if so, does that make Nebuchadnezzar yet another pawn in this divine game? One would think Shadrach, Meshach, and Abednego would remind the king of his change of heart toward their deity from chapters 1 and 2, but they stay silent. What really happens here, and why do so many characters seem so oblivious?

Such profound narrative amnesia highlights the surreal level of caricaturing in Daniel 3, as only the reader knows about the preceding chapters and the events therein. Shadrach, Meshach, and Abednego answer with confident disdain in verses 16–18 and say nothing about Nebuchadnezzar's previous declarations two chapters prior. Everyone in Daniel 3 works outside the purview of chapters 1 and 2. Narratively, this makes sense: if the three Israelites remembered and reminded Nebuchadnezzar of his past religious declarations, then we have no story. Further, if Nebuchadnezzar remembers chapter 2's dream, he builds no statue and makes no decree. That is not what happens here, prompting a return to a guiding question: What exactly is happening in Daniel? How does Daniel 3 contribute to the larger narrative complexities laid out thus far, and what messages might it carry for contemporary readers?

One crucial element in considering what this story is doing and for whom is to consider how Daniel 3 uses the trio's Babylonian aliases and not their given Israelite names. Perpetuating Shadrach, Meshach, and Abednego as their names highlights a persistent and unquestioned issue. No trace of the Israelites known as Hananiah, Mishael, and Azariah remains; only Shadrach, Meshach, and Abednego endure. Children's Bibles ignore how the popular names associated with the trio are not their actual names. Christian interpreters make inconsequential annotations about these Babylonian titles and fail to press the issue. Daniel retains his Israelite name as his primary title, with his "Belteshazzar" title appearing sporadically in chapters 1, 2, 4, 5, and 10. Such a literary move creates an identity hierarchy of sorts, as the biblical narrator deems only Daniel worthy of going by his Israelite name.

One could therefore argue that calling these Israelites Shadrach, Meshach, and Abednego is yet another literary signpost pointing toward chapter 3's layered literary complexity. The Chaldeans speak to the trio's Jewish ancestry at verses 8 and 12, making this the only place where something beyond their Babylon names marks their identities. It would be one thing for only Nebuchadnezzar to use their Babylonian monikers, but here the opposite is true. Such reinforcement of Babylonian oppression and identity destruction makes one wonder on whose side the biblical narrator stands. Claiming that these names reflect their ability to work and thrive under oppressive foreign systems loses merit following Nebuchadnezzar's anger and vitriol upon learning of their disobedience. It is as if Nebuchadnezzar completely forgets what these men did for him in chapter 2 and what they did for themselves in chapter 1. They are merely cogs in this king's wheel or, worse, pawns in Daniel 3's narrative, moved to bring Nebuchadnezzar and God closer.

Because make no mistake: Nebuchadnezzar changing from his gods to the Israelite deity is Daniel 3's traditional accepted point and purpose. Christian interpreters read Daniel 3 as a triumph over ungodly heathen Babylonians, as readings lavish praise upon the Israelite trio's faith and trust in their deity. However, said readings disregard the cost of any decisions the king or Israelites make. Nebuchadnezzar turns to God at the story's end, so according to Christians everything getting to that point is worth it. Christians across centuries default to making Daniel 3 a story of divine favor, but, like all decisions, making God favor one group over others carries dangerous consequences.

Said consequences appear in the aftermath of the three Israelites' response. Rage fills Nebuchadnezzar's body so much that according to verse 19 his face changes, making his anger physically obvious. Mirroring his own rage, Nebuchadnezzar orders the furnace so hot that flames engulf and kill the men bringing Shadrach, Meshach, and Abednego. We know nothing about these slain men beyond their physical strength and their dying for the sake of Nebuchadnezzar's brashness. And yet, Christian commentators use the attendants' deaths as proof of God's power and might, as the three Israelites survive something so deadly that it causes the accidental death of unnamed and unknown temple servants. Christian readers back in the second century played up these men dying as an act of judgment, with Hippolytus claiming the soldiers died because the fire "recognized and punished the guilty" and "did not touch the servants of God."[4] Ninth-century Christian thinker Isho'dad of Merv goes further and claims "divine intervention" killed the guards "in order that the king and the Babylonians might not think that because of hallucination or illusion those youths made the fire harmless."[5] So it seems insufficient to say these men died, as in the hands of Christian interpreters their deaths function as an "I told you so" to Nebuchadnezzar on behalf of Shadrach, Meshach, and Abednego's god. Such readings are destructive and dangerous, as they reflect spite-filled theologically triumphalist approaches rooted in revenge upon one's enemies.

Triumphant readings also undercut the moment's severity for Shadrach, Meshach, and Abednego. Christians read Daniel 3 knowing that divine intervention ensures the three Israelites' collective survival. Experienced readers know how the story ends. The men in peril do not. Their words in verse 17 support the moment's vulnerability and their risk when they say, "If the god whom we serve is able to deliver us . . ." Either they lie to Nebuchadnezzar, or their fates stand unknown. Or they failed to think through their decision, resulting in the deaths of at least three unknown unnamed men. One could argue the trio's faith is naïve and selfish, returning to the "God as divine vending machine" theme set up in chapters 1 and 2. God also keeps a flair for the dramatic, swooping in at the final minute and saving our heroes. Why does God wait, wasting so much time and costing the guards their lives? Why not step in earlier and prevent anything from happening in the first place? A story without drama is unremarkable. Thus, Daniel 3 adorns its narrative with men who risk and a God that waits without explanation.

Nebuchadnezzar's response at verse 24 feels cartoonish but consistent with how preceding chapters depict the king. In Daniel 1, Nebuchadnezzar is unaware of what happens in his kingdom among his servants, making space for Daniel, Shadrach, Meshach, and Abednego to manipulate Nebuchadnezzar's political system for their benefit. In Daniel 2, Nebuchadnezzar asks the impossible from his closest advisors and orders their execution because they are unable to complete said impossible task. Now, in chapter 3, Nebuchadnezzar's emotions run wild because three Israelite men do what everyone, including the reader, expects them to do in remaining loyal to God. One could argue the Chaldeans knew the trio would reject such a decree, meaning that they knew the kingdom and people in it better than the king himself. Nebuchadnezzar's anger reflects this surprise and, when paired with the impossible decree, reflects the king's inability to fulfill basic leadership functions. He is much more of an oafish baron than a fearsome king.

The king's men throw Shadrach, Meshach, and Abednego clothed into the flames, only for those men (and their clothes) to emerge unharmed. Christian readings argue that the men enter the scorching-hot flames clothed and that God's power keeps their garments from burning. Such readings fly in the face of previous justifications for why the king's soldiers died tossing Shadrach, Meshach, and Abednego into the fire. Propositions of the fire's ability to judge between the righteous and unrighteous prompt one to ask what the clothing did to justify being spared, as clothes cannot choose righteousness since they are inanimate objects.

Mainstream readings ignore such questions and instead focus on the mysterious fourth figure. This fourth figure sends shockwaves throughout the narrative itself and the Christian interpretations surrounding it. Verse 24 again lets readers see Nebuchadnezzar's feelings as he stands with astonished alarm, saying at verse 25, "Lo! I see four men unbound and walking in the midst of the fire, and there is no harm upon them! And the appearance of the fourth is one like a son of gods." The Aramaic phrase דָּמֵה לְבַר־אֱלָהִין, translated here as "like a son of gods," sends Christian readers into a Christological fervor. Irenaeus reads this figure as Jesus, saying he is God's "Word, as he willed it for the benefit of those who saw."[6] He then pivots (unprompted) to claim that this fourth figure is the stone from Daniel 7, thereby shoehorning Jesus into yet another of Daniel's metaphoric images. Hippolytus takes the opportunity to make this scene about Nebuchadnezzar, proclaiming this figure is Jesus, "the Son of God," and claims the figure fulfills scriptural prophecies foretelling "that the Gentiles would recognize him incarnate."[7] In an amusing turn, Nebuchadnezzar's response shocks Jerome: "I do not know how an ungodly king could have merited a vision of the Son of God."[8] This consternation makes Jerome claim the figure is an angel that "foreshadows our Lord Jesus Christ." Even though the fourth is not Jesus, Jerome cannot help himself in tying the unnamed figure to the Christian Messiah.

I could list more timeworn readings alongside recent Christian receptions that use this fourth figure to point toward Jesus. This would be redundant and fruitless, as that interpretive trajectory is shockingly consistent. Modern scholars like James Montgomery, C.L. Seow, John Collins, Sibley Towner, and Carol Newsom acknowledge this interpretive stream but neglect critical consideration for how such interpretations affect Daniel 3. The simple fact is Daniel 3 leaves the fourth figure's identity a mystery. Shadrach, Meshach, and Abednego never mention or acknowledge the entity. The only person that makes any guess about the figure's identity is Nebuchadnezzar with this "son of gods" moment. Nebuchadnezzar's guess finds support throughout the Bible and other literature of the ancient Levant.[9] For example, in Exodus 4:22, God instructs Moses to tell Pharaoh, "Israel is my firstborn son," meaning Israel is the collective metaphoric representation of God's offspring. Genesis 6:4–6 mentions beings known as "sons of God" (בְּנֵי הָאֱלֹהִים). Similarly, Job 1:6 and 2:1 describe beings that come before God as בְּנֵי הָאֱלֹהִים, literally "sons of God." God tells Nathan in 2 Samuel 7:14 that King David's offspring (aka King Solomon) will be God's son and God will be his father. Just because Nebuchadnezzar says he sees some sort of divine son does not mean that person is Jesus. Far richer and varied possibilities exist.

Who or what exactly is this fourth person, unbound walking among the fire? The only information we know about this entity comes from Nebuchadnezzar. No one else in the text mentions the fourth, nor does anyone corroborate Nebuchadnezzar's claim. Such sparse evidence leaves the metaphor wide open. It could be an angelic figure, sent to protect Shadrach, Meshach, and Abednego. It could be Nebuchadnezzar's anxieties about the moment manifested by seeing a specter. Or, staying in line with previous Old Testament iterations of Israel as God's child, it could be a metaphoric representation of Israel standing in and among the flames, staring back at its oppressor. Or it could be a symbol of God's enduring presence among such tumult.

What if this mysterious, unknown, and unnamed figure is all the above and more? Nebuchadnezzar's seeing the fourth among the flames prompts him to call out Shadrach, Meshach, and Abednego from the flames. This prompts the king's cadre to gather around and pay witness to unsinged hairs and unharmed clothes. The fire left no smell on the men, as if they never drew close to the flames, much less walked around in them. Nebuchadnezzar's excitement now prompts him to make a decree, unlike someone making a decree for him earlier. He blesses their God, praises them for disobeying his commands, and promotes them (it would not be the end of a Daniel story in chapters 1 through 6 without political expediency and promotion). Yet the king fails to learn from previous mistakes, as, at Daniel 3:28, Nebuchadnezzar orders

> that all people, nations, and languages that speak negligence against the god of Shadrach, Meshach, and Abednego, their limbs shall be torn and their houses shall become a dunghill; for there is no other god that is able to deliver in this way.

Nebuchadnezzar learns nothing about the practicality of ruling a kingdom as we get yet another decree dictating how citizens can worship. Like the earlier decree, this one is equally unenforceable. What should be a hopeful turn toward worshipping and praising the Israelite god simply falls flat, as Nebuchadnezzar makes similar claims and remarks in Daniel 1 and 2, only to abandon them without remorse in Daniel 3.

Indeed, Shadrach, Meshach, and Abednego stand by their faith and keep their lives, but chapter 3 leaves little impression beyond that according to Christian interpretations. One could argue that God uses the situation to prove divine power over Nebuchadnezzar and, in turn, coerce the king into changing laws regarding the statue. Yet knowing what we know about Nebuchadnezzar, we know it is just a matter of time before he forgets Shadrach, Meshach, Abednego, and their god, creating space for this cycle to repeat itself.

3.3 So What?

So, what then is the point of this story? How might modern interpreters expect to use Daniel 3 in ecclesial, communal, and personal settings? What relevance does this chapter hold for contemporary readers? Avenues for understanding this story could begin in a traditionally unexpected but relevant place: What if Daniel 3 is continuing the satirical trend begun in Daniel 1 and 2? What if, instead of presenting these characters and their choices as a series of yes-no or right-wrong binaries, we read them filled with satirical versatility? Few genres are as misunderstood (and misused) as satire. Initial responses to satire often boil it down to simple but shockingly oblivious parts that defang what satire can be, making it a shadow of itself. Readers may think satire makes fun of something simply for the sake of making fun. But the function of satire differs from such hasty understandings. It creates space for bold and creative interpretations that mock and deride to critique, and even heal, Christianity's self-inflicted theological and ecclesial wounds.

Terry Lindvall's dissection of ancient and contemporary satire incorporates biblical and apocalyptic imagery from Revelation, calling satire "a two-edged sword" that "wounds to heal" as it "mocks to remake and reconcile."[10] Through Lindvall's lens, satire can create literary "traps" that ensnare the reader into laughing at their own mockery and critique. Satire, then, parodies to condemn and challenge readers to reconsider their place in the narrative and respective contexts. Lindvall's approach dovetails our reconsideration of Daniel quite nicely, as he reads Hebrew prophets as satirical experts applying rhetorical skill with religious and historical wisdom to craft razor-sharp critiques designed to compel and inspire change. Applying this lens to Daniel 3 unlocks the chapter's vast interpretive and theological possibilities, as such a move boldly makes us consider who and what the story critiques.

What, then, might Daniel 3 be satirizing, and who might be the "butt" of such jokes? As shown thus far (and as preceding chapters will show), Christian scholars consistently bring one character to the front of Daniel's interpretive conversations: God. Countless Christian readers make Daniel 3 yet another example of divine sovereignty and end the discussion there. Such readings celebrate God's control over Daniel's dire situation and make the faith of Shadrach, Meshach, and Abednego the model for readers. And yet, upon rereading Daniel 3, God's conspicuous absence paired with the divine's selective behavior highlights an intriguing possibility: What if Daniel 3 critiques the very notion of divine sovereignty? Further, what if Daniel 3 satirizes God's apparent passive indifference, thereby highlighting the need to reconsider this very thing that people call "God"? Christian readers rarely consider the problems of waiting for "God's timing" and use stories like chapter 3 to support their claims. We celebrate the "good" in life by praising God. We cite faithful behavior and belief as cornerstones of our religious convictions. Yet as this "good" gives way to the dreaded "bad," our language for God takes a dramatic shift. We wonder where God went, lamenting and yearning for bygone days when God's presence covered us so wonderfully that we could almost see a divine figure walking among and alongside us.

The shallowness of understanding God this way is its own theological critique, which Daniel 3 highlights with extreme prejudice. Defaulting to reading Daniel 3's God as unquestionable in timing and perfect in outcome undervalues bolder theological claims at play. It reduces God to something we seek when realities of human existence, like sickness from unexpected illness or sadness from sudden death, knock at our door. Or worse when our choices bring struggles or sufferings upon ourselves and others. Shadrach, Meshach, and Abednego had innumerable opportunities to seek divine guidance. Instead, they stand idle as events unfold, forcing God to intervene. Such blatant passivity with this "wait and see" approach to God neglects the active steps that their deity makes throughout the Bible. This is the same God that, according to Genesis, saw the chaotic mess existing before creation and made it into the living, breathing, and vibrant world that we call home. Exodus presents God as restless and angry on behalf of his peoples' mistreatment at the hands of a tyrant, prompting God to step in and use Moses to chart a path to freedom.

But God's intervention can also yield questionable and downright immoral outcomes. The same God that freed the Israelites from a tyrant in Exodus becomes tyrannical toward Canaanites in Joshua and drowns the very world created in Genesis 1 and 2 with the great flood in Genesis 6–9. Daniel 3's divine inconsistency then becomes reflective of theological duplicity spread throughout the Bible, prompting us to consider a courageous theological proposition: perhaps Daniel 3's God mirrors the very duplicity of how people see God. We want divine control and sovereignty, but we never consider who suffers from what we think God "should" do. We reject these struggles in favor of "everything happens for a reason," neglecting the far-reaching consequences this position has for the world at large. We limit God to favor what we selfishly think is best. We celebrate walking among the flames and forget the people that lost their lives so that we might prosper. We, like this chapter's three Israelites, turn to God for necessity or convenience.

And this fails to reconsider the fourth figure in the flames. The ongoing Christianization of Daniel 3 and this fourth figure generates remarkably destructive consequences. For example, inspired by the New International Version, *Read with Me Bible*—a book of selected biblical stories with illustrations intended for children of early elementary school age—makes a distinct stylistic choice. The illustration going with a synopsis of Daniel 3:25 features a wide-eyed and shocked Nebuchadnezzar. His vision falls upon Shadrach, Meshach, Abednego, and a fourth unnamed figure standing unharmed in the fiery furnace. What makes this illustration remarkable is that the fourth figure looks like Jesus as depicted in the New

Testament section of this children's Bible. He wears a white robe with a colored sash across his chest. His face bears a brown, well-trimmed beard, and his brown hair stops just above his shoulders. Even more peculiar is how the accompanying synopsis reads, "And the fourth looks like an angel," a translation differing from NIV's more literal, "and the fourth looks like a son of the gods."[11] The illustration plus this translation plants in the minds of young readers the idea of either Jesus or an angel saving Israelite men. At the least, the text holds zero evidence supporting Jesus or an angel in the flames. At worst, this interpretive move normalizes painful supersessionist replacement theology by inserting Jesus into this Israelite story, thereby undercutting non-Christian interpretive possibilities.

So, who or what is this fourth figure? What might he mean or represent through our reconsidered lens? As noted above, Nebuchadnezzar is the only character in the chapter that ventures a guess. The text offers no information beyond that. But maybe this is the point. Sparse textual support paired with how interpreters understand the fourth figure unveils more about us than Daniel 3. Christian readers stand ready to name characters that the text leaves unnamed and unknown, continuing the trend from Daniel 2 as Christians label the metals and statue according to their enemies, meaning we make those destroyed kingdoms into whomever and whatever we want to destroy. Similarly, Christian readers hijack Daniel 7 and the fourth beast with readings that border on becoming conspiracy theories. We make these things into what we want them to be and what they need to be to justify whatever theological, political, and social narratives we construct. By projecting ourselves and only ourselves onto this fourth being, we limit the text.

Where, then, are we to pull meaning from this confounding chapter? By turning the interpretive lens on ourselves, points of clarity appear. Do we see God as a divine parachute, waiting to bail us out at the last minute? Or do we see the flaws in that theology, and seek more? Are we trampling over the silenced few, like the king's soldiers dying in "fulfillment of God's will"? Or do we open our eyes to who and what surrounds us, daring to consider how we might fit into their story as opposed to how they fit into ours? Are we the ones thrown into the flames, or are we the ones doing the throwing? Is Nebuchadnezzar a king worth mocking or an example to consider, making us ask if we are the ones being critiqued as opposed to the ones doing the critiquing?

4
Daniel 4 Reconsidered

4.1 Translation

1 I, Nebuchadnezzar, was at ease in my house and prospering in
my palace.

2 I saw a dream that frightened me; upon my bed visions of my
head alarmed me.

3 So I made a decree, to bring before me all the wise men of Babylon, to make the interpretation of the dream known to me.

4 Then the magicians, the enchanters, the Chaldeans, and the
astrologers came in, and I spoke my dream before them, but they
could not make its interpretation known to me.

5 At last, Daniel, whose name was Belteshazzar after a name of my
god, came in before me; a spirit of holy gods was in him, and I spoke
my dream before him:

6 "Belteshazzar, chief of the magicians, whom I know has a spirit of
holy gods within you, and of every mystery, none is too difficult for
you. The dream that I saw, tell me its interpretation.

7 I saw, seeing with my head upon my bed, and lo! A tree at the
center of the earth and its height was great.

8 And the tree was great and strong, and its top reached the heavens, and it was visible to the end of the entire earth.

9 Its leaves were beautiful, and its fruit was plentiful, and food for all
within it; under it, animals of the field were shaded. Birds of the heavens nested in its branches, and from it all the living things were fed.

10 And looking, I saw visions of my head upon my bed and lo! A
lookout, a holy being, descending from the heavens.[1]

11 He cried aloud and spoke thusly: 'Cut down the tree and chop off its branches; strip its foliage and scatter its fruit. May the animals flee from beneath it and the birds from its branches.

12 But as for its stump and roots in the ground, leave them with a band of iron and bronze in the new grass of the field. May he be bathed in the dew of the heavens, and may his share be with the animals of the field in the grass of the earth.

13 May his heart be changed from that of a human, and let the heart of an animal be given to him. And may seven times pass over him.

14 This sentence is by decree of the lookouts and the decision by order of the holy ones, in order that the living may know that the Most High rules over the kingdom of mortals, and he can give it to anyone he wills and sets it over the lowest of men.'

15 This is the dream that I, Nebuchadnezzar the king, saw. And you, Belteshazzar, tell the interpretation because all the wise men of my kingdom were unable to make it known to me. But you are able, for a spirit of holy gods is in you."

16 Then Daniel, whose name was Belteshazzar, was distressed for one moment. And his thoughts terrified him. The king answered and said, "Belteshazzar, do not let the dream and the interpretation alarm you." Belteshazzar answered and said, "My lord, may the dream be for people that hate you and its interpretation for your enemies.

17 The tree that you saw, which was great and strong, and its top reached to the heavens and was visible to all the earth,

18 with lovely foliage and bountiful fruit and food for all, under which animals of the field lived, and in whose branches birds of the heavens dwelled.

19 You are it, O King, which has become great and strong. Your greatness has grown and reached to the heavens and your dominion to the end of the earth.

20 And the king, who saw a lookout, a holy being, descending from the heavens and saying, 'Cut down the tree and destroy it but leave its stump and roots in the ground, with a band of iron and bronze in the new grass of the field; and may he be bathed in the dew of heaven and may his share be with the animals of the field until seven times pass over him.

21 This is the interpretation, O King, and it is a decree of the Most High that has come upon my lord, the king.

22 And you shall be driven from humanity, and your dwelling will be with the animals of the field. You shall feed on grass like oxen, and you shall be drenched in the dew of the heavens. And seven times will pass over you until you know that the Most High rules over the human kingdom and that he can give it to anyone he wishes.

23 And as it was commanded to leave the stump and roots of the tree, your kingdom shall be confirmed to you when you know who rules the heavens.

24 Therefore, O King may my counsel be good for you. Break away from your wrongdoings in righteousness and iniquities with mercy for the oppressed; that way, your prosperity may be prolonged."

25 All this came upon Nebuchadnezzar, the king.

26 At the end of twelve months, he was walking about the palace of the kingdom of Babylon.

27 The king answered and said, "Is this not the great Babylon, which I have built as a royal house by my mighty power and for my honorable majesty?"

28 While the words were in the king's mouth, a voice fell from the heavens: "To you, O King Nebuchadnezzar, it is declared.

29 You shall be driven from society, and your dwelling shall be with the animals of the field; you shall eat grass as the oxen, and seven times shall pass over you until you know that the Most High rules over the human kingdom and gives it to whomever he pleases."

30 Then the sentence was immediately fulfilled against Nebuchadnezzar. He was driven from human society, and he ate grass like oxen, and his body was drenched by the dew of the heavens until his hair grew as long as eagles' feathers and his nails like a bird's claws.

31 And when those days ended, I, Nebuchadnezzar, lifted my eyes to the heavens, and my knowledge returned to me. And I blessed the Most High, and I praised and honored the one who lives forever, for his dominion is an everlasting dominion and his kingdom is from generation to generation.

32 All dwelling on the earth are accounted as nothing, and he does what he wills with the hosts of heaven. And those dwelling on the earth, there are none that can stay his hand and say to him, "What are you doing?"

33 At that time my reason returned to me, and my majesty and countenance were restored to me for the glory of my kingdom. My

counselors and nobles looked for me. I was reestablished over my kingdom, and still more greatness was added to me.

[34] Now I, Nebuchadnezzar, praise and extol and honor the king of the heavens, for all his works are truth and his ways are just, and whoever walks in pride he is able to bring low.

4.2 Reading against the Grain

Daniel 4's opening is confusing. Most English translations begin with Nebuchadnezzar wishing prosperity to all peoples, nations, and languages, followed by praising the signs and wonders of "the Most High God." What makes this confusing is Daniel 4:1–3 in English translations is Daniel 3:31–33 in Aramaic versions. English translations use verse and chapter numbers based on a collection of sources known as the Old Greek version (OG) of Daniel and not the Aramaic. Verse and chapter numbering differs between the Aramaic and OG, creating an interpretive quagmire as Aramaic Daniel 4:1 is OG Daniel 4:4.[2] Thus, what English translations present as Daniel 4:4 is actually Aramaic Daniel 4:1. Choices made in English translations of this chapter and numbering system are also inconsistent: English translations begin chapter 4 according to the OG chapter and numbering, but said translations rely on the Aramaic as the primary translation source. In short, interpreters organize according to one source (OG), then translate another (Aramaic).

As someone who spends my professional life studying Daniel, I am just as confused by this choice as you may be. To make matters worse, scholars dodge the issue. For example, Collins and Newsom address the discrepancy but neglect *why* such discrepancy exists, making us hard-pressed to find answers to why the Aramaic versions take priority over the OG.[3] It remains a complex issue with abundant possible (though highly uncertain) resolutions. At its center lies a distinct choice that translators made and continue to make. That choice builds on what mainstream interpreters have always followed, and modern interpreters do not want to "break the mold." We allow ourselves to be bound by choices built around previous interpretations that drive modern readings.

Mindful of this Aramaic-OG discrepancy, we turn to chapter 4, which opens with yet another dream from Nebuchadnezzar. Once again Nebuchadnezzar remains the central protagonist. Such repetition highlights Daniel's ongoing narrative cycles, as Daniel 1–6 echo each other to become episodic, sharing stand-alone stories united by shared characters in similar situations, driven by similar outcomes. For example, Daniel's persistence in Daniel 1 yields considerable success, setting the pattern he and his friends follow throughout the first six chapters. In Daniel 2, Nebuchadnezzar dreams of a giant statue, then Daniel 3 makes a giant statue a key plot device. Shadrach, Meshach, and Abednego face certain death in the flames of chapter 3, only to find salvation from an unknown figure. Similarly, Daniel faces certain death in chapter 6 in the lions' den, only to emerge unharmed.

Like the repetitive and episodic nature of Daniel 1–6, Christian interpretations of Daniel 4 get stuck on repeat regarding divine sovereignty. For example, Theodoret starts his reading in earnest by addressing what he considers to be the chapter's central theme:

> [Nebuchadnezzar] treated his subjects very harshly and had reached such a state of arrogance as to think that he was greater and more powerful than not only the so-called gods but even the true God. . . . Nothing of what was done by him would have happened without God's permitting it and wanting to call to account for impiety those who had suffered this from him.[4]

Theodoret makes the dream a lesson designed for Nebuchadnezzar to learn God's unquestioning and unwavering sovereignty. Jerome takes a similar approach and expands his lens, making Nebuchadnezzar into a metaphoric stand-in for Satan by connecting the king's downfall to Jesus' words in Luke 10:18: "I watched Satan fall from heaven like a flash of lightning." Jerome turns this chapter into a conduit for highlighting Jesus' strength over and against Satan (despite neither Jesus nor Satan making an appearance).

Such understandings of divine sovereignty continue through the Reformation. Calvin makes it apologetic, saying that the dream "was a kind of entrance and preparation for repentance" so that Nebuchadnezzar would know that God is God and Nebuchadnezzar is only human.[5] Johannes Oecolampadius and Philip Melanchthon claim that the dream and subsequent transformation is God punishing Nebuchadnezzar's arrogance, making the chapter into a well-intentioned learning opportunity for the king. These samples show how easily Christian readers wed the narrative with their theology, but the callous nature of their interpretations is quite shocking. One can almost hear these venerated church leaders say, "What else could this chapter be about, beyond affirming and confirming God's triumphant power?"

Recent Christian interpretations use divine sovereignty to make Daniel 4 into a quasi-motivational self-help story, using Nebuchadnezzar as a model for Christian repentance.[6] Despite incorrectly making Daniel a book about Christian piety, such readings may be onto something: Daniel 4 takes considerable interest in Nebuchadnezzar's innermost thoughts and feelings. It is Nebuchadnezzar's chapter down to its very structure. For example, unlike Daniel 2's third-person narration, Daniel 4 uses a first-person narrator. This offers an intimate look into the king's psyche as he responds to another dream at verse 2. The king orders all Babylonian wise men before him as he did in Daniel 2, but Nebuchadnezzar again does not contact Daniel when calling the wise men, suggesting the king's memory is faulty or that Daniel 4 is indeed a self-contained story. Daniel arrives at verse 5, but Nebuchadnezzar continues using the first-person pronoun "I," meaning Daniel is there for Nebuchadnezzar's sake.

The king greets Daniel by his Babylonian name, Belteshazzar, then explains the name's meaning. Nebuchadnezzar claims that the name means "a name of my god" because Daniel "has a spirit of holy gods." Narratively speaking, this is strange because thanks to chapter 1 we already know Daniel's Babylonian name is Belteshazzar. The name's accompanying explanation also raises questions. J. Collins points out how the king's "implied etymology" in verses 5 and 6 is "mistaken" as the name "Belteshazzar" means something different.[7] Seow and Newsom take similar stances in opposing claims about "a spirit of holy gods," referencing Nebuchadnezzar's polytheistic background. Such language parallels Hebrew phrasing that describes YHWH in Joshua and Joseph in Genesis.[8] Nothing Nebuchadnezzar says about the name makes sense, highlighting the messiness of this introduction.

Nebuchadnezzar hails Daniel, aka Belteshazzar, as "chief of the magicians" at verse 6. Acknowledging Daniel's position makes it even more peculiar that Nebuchadnezzar did not just summon Daniel and Daniel alone. Why trifle with subordinate interpreters instead of Daniel, the so-called chief magician? Nebuchadnezzar gawks over Daniel because "of every mystery, none is too difficult for you," then lays narrative melodrama on thick with, "The dream that I saw, tell me its interpretation." The Babylonian king then lays out the dream in theatrical detail, complete with the hokey interjection "lo!" and repeated use of adjectives like "great," "strong," and "plentiful." Nothing Nebuchadnezzar says here is subtle.

The dream opens with a healthy and vibrant tree at the earth's center, whose top stretches into the heavens with branches visible "to the end of the entire earth." On the surface, this image is positive and comforting. All creation surrounds and benefits from it. Its power and might extend across the land with profound beauty. The tree's branches hold abundant fruit; their shade comforts land animals and provides space for birds to nest. All living things feed from the tree's plentiful offerings. Verse 13 announces the arrival of a figure, described as "a lookout, a holy being." This lookout orders the destruction of the tree, its branches, its foliage, and its fruit, causing all its beneficiaries to flee. There is much to unpack with this dream, but, before we consider interpretations, we must wrangle with this heavenly being in verses 10, 14, and 20.

Pinning down who or what exactly this "lookout" is opens a floodgate of interpretive possibilities. English translations traditionally render the Aramaic phrase עִיר וְקַדִּישׁ as "holy watcher." Daniel 4 is the only time in the entire Hebrew Bible that עִיר is a heavenly being, hence why my translation aligns with the simpler and more descriptive "lookout." My translation follows Goldingay's rendering of "lookout" because histories of interpretation place considerable weight upon the word "watcher."[9] First Enoch, a book considered noncanonical in every Christian denomination except for the Orthodox Tewahedo Church, uses "watcher" to describe corrupted fallen angels. Scholars call 1 Enoch 1–36 the "Book of the Watchers" for its detailed descriptions of these "watchers" wreaking havoc across creation and causing the flood in Genesis 6–9. The character in Daniel 4 is not a corrupted or fallen angel. He is clearly in good standing with the deity, as his word carries the weight of God, described here with the title "the Most High." The lookout is simply a divine emissary, sent on God's behalf like Daniel 2's stone cut not by human hands.

This lookout's arrival begins the cosmic tree's destruction. Trees have practical and allegorical purposes throughout the Bible and ancient Levant, symbolizing life, growth, and sustenance. Trees also represent protection, power, and strength. They carry considerable narrative utility, as their meager seedling origins lead to generational beauty, provisions, and support. The tree of life and the tree of the knowledge of good and evil in Genesis 2 are the most known biblical trees, and both play a considerable role in the Adam and Eve story. The tree of life appears throughout the Bible and receives pointed divine protection after Eve and Adam eat from the tree of the knowledge of good and evil.[10] Tree symbolism extends beyond the Bible, with literary and iconographic examples found throughout ancient Egypt, Sumer, Assyria, and Nebuchadnezzar's Babylon.[11] Gods and goddesses find rest and strength in trees. Deities fight over who gets to claim them as their own. They can also represent the very gods and goddesses themselves. Nebuchadnezzar's dream tree echoes that rich imagery and symbolism, as it connects the earth to the celestial realm and provides food, shelter, and comfort.

Knowing the literary fullness of trees and what they embody makes the narrative weight of Daniel's interpretation fall flat. He tells Nebuchadnezzar what everyone reading the chapter already knows: this tree represents Nebuchadnezzar. So just like the felled statue in chapter 2, this fallen tree is a metaphor for the king. Daniel also retells the dream's content (something Daniel, the king, and the reader already know). Daniel's interpretation here feels beat-for-beat like the interpretation in chapter 2, but, unlike chapter 2, the dream's meaning scares Daniel. Thus far kings, not Daniel, experience fear, distress, and terror, leaving space for Daniel's confidence to shine and mock each so-called king's might and strength. These roles switch in verse 16 as the dream distresses and terrifies Daniel. Now Nebuchadnezzar is the comforter as he assuages Daniel, saying, "[D]o not let the dream and the interpretation alarm you." Daniel's response to the king is odd and borderline sycophantic: "My lord, may the dream be for those that hate you and its interpretation for your enemies." If Daniel is indeed a stand-in for pro-Israelite anti-imperialism, why feel distressed about a dream foretelling Nebuchadnezzar's downfall?[12] Further, why does Daniel brownnose the king and wish the distressing interpretation upon Nebuchadnezzar's enemies (which, according to the Bible and history, include the Israelites)?

Reading how Christians sidestep Daniel's obvious affection toward Nebuchadnezzar entertains as much as it disheartens. We tie ourselves in interpretive knots trying to justify Daniel's clear admiration and affinity. Ephrem says Daniel operates out of "respect for the king," which implies Daniel respects the man responsible for Jerusalem's destruction and leaves space to consider Daniel as a pro-Babylonian "sell-out."[13] Jerome sees Daniel feeling "sorry for the man who had conferred on him the greatest honor" to avoid charging the king "with sinful pride."[14] Despite their clear allegiance to Nebuchadnezzar and the power structures he controls, these readings are not misguided or unfounded—quite the opposite. Readings like Ephrem and Jerome's highlight how Daniel's emotions align with decisions he made earlier. Daniel knows that if Nebuchadnezzar is happy, Daniel gets a promotion. If the king is unhappy, Daniel will die. Daniel is pragmatic as he looks to save his own skin. Yet Christian readers give Daniel's potential pragmatism next to no pushback. His pious goals never veer in their eyes. Interpreters consider Daniel's motivation and then neglect what his appeasement means: Daniel's concern lies with Nebuchadnezzar's feelings over and against the foreign king's overdue comeuppance. Historical evidence highlights Nebuchadnezzar's ruthless brutality, and anything suggesting otherwise is naïve at best and propaganda at worst. Nebuchadnezzar is thoroughly unworthy of Daniel's sympathy, yet Daniel gives it to him.

On top of this, Daniel's dream interpretation overlooks those suffering from the king's reign and those that will suffer during and following his downfall. The dream itself romanticizes Nebuchadnezzar's rule by depicting the tyrant as a robust and magnanimous tree that feeds all and turns away none. One could argue the dream reflects Nebuchadnezzar's fantasies about his rule, meaning that God builds up Nebuchadnezzar's pride only to tear it down (quite literally). If this is the case, why give the reader Nebuchadnezzar's perspective alongside Daniel's sympathies?

Another side to this argument exists, one that Christian interpreters overlook: If the dream represents Nebuchadnezzar, does that make his rule effective and successful? Think about it: this tree gives food and shelter throughout the earth. It takes root in the earth's very heart and reaches far into the heavens. Based solely on the dream itself, the life the tree allows seems quite stable. Why destroy the tree? If it does so much good for so many, why wield divine might to undo it?

And is the tree even destroyed? Verse 12 describes a stump left over from the tree, wrapped with iron and bronze. Most Christian receptions largely ignore the stump and focus on the destruction of the tree itself.[15] Yet others weigh how stumps can grow back. For example, Collins and Duguid cite Isaiah and Job to draw parallels to biblical allegories that present Israel as a stump awaiting regrowth.[16] These scriptural references add a twist to Daniel's stump imagery: reading Daniel's stump through other biblical uses makes Nebuchadnezzar's stump into a symbol of expectant hope. Isaiah 6 and 11 use stump and root imagery to convey hope for Israelite renewal and regrowth after the exile. Job 14 employs a similar "stump = hope" symbolism, which makes sense within the context of Job's postexilic Israelite ambitions for rejuvenation. If Nebuchadnezzar is meant to be a "bad guy," such imagery makes no sense. Is Daniel implying that Nebuchadnezzar can also find renewal? If so, is this hope for Israel or Nebuchadnezzar?

Claims for Daniel 4 being pro-Israel fall flat as evidence suggests that Daniel 4 is a story about Nebuchadnezzar's renewal and redemption. We hear this chapter from his perspective, and his portrayal is overly sympathetic. Daniel speaks very highly of the king and experiences fear on the king's behalf. Nebuchadnezzar comforts Daniel, and Daniel is receptive. The tree symbolizing Nebuchadnezzar supplies food and shelter for anyone and everyone. Further, verses 23–24 confirm the dream's intent: to prolong Nebuchadnezzar's kingdom and personal prosperity. According to Daniel 4, God gave Nebuchadnezzar a dream designed to make the king "know who rules the heavens" and "break away from your wrongdoings in righteousness and iniquities with mercy for the oppressed." Chapter 4 is not about Daniel or the Israelites. It is a story about how Nebuchadnezzar is a "good king" in God's eyes.

The rest of the narrative underlines and cements the chapter's pro-Nebuchadnezzar slant, as the long-awaited "punishment" gets one verse. Verse 30 describes what happens to the king, and verse 31 ends it as quickly as it began. What happens in verse 30 demoralizes the king, but saying it equals cutting a tree down to its stump is a dramatic overstatement. Nebuchadnezzar knowing why he must experience this defangs the experience. Any sense of actual discipline toward the king disappears, and what he will eventually get is little more than a slap on the wrist.

Chapter 4 heads toward its end at verse 31 with more of Nebuchadnezzar's first-person narration. Christian readers claim the king learns his lesson. Humility replaces arrogance as Nebuchadnezzar's existential journey gives him a nihilistic approach to existence as he learns his place in the created order. But that is all Nebuchadnezzar does: he acknowledges his place in the world order without permanent consequences. Nebuchadnezzar praises "the Most High" and exclaims: "[F]or all his works are truth and his ways are just, and whoever walks in pride he is able to bring low." Everything else after the king's exile suggests nothing has changed. Nebuchadnezzar gets back his reason, majesty, and monarchical glory. As verse 33 says, "I was reestablished over my kingdom, and still more greatness was added to me." Nebuchadnezzar listens to God, and the chapter ends like it began: with Nebuchadnezzar in charge. Paired with chapter 1, this closing address bookends Nebuchadnezzar's reign with a shocking sense of divine approval. According to Daniel 1, God gave Israel into Nebuchadnezzar's hand. God reminds Nebuchadnezzar of the divine hierarchy after the king loses his way in chapter 4. But Nebuchadnezzar still rules Babylon.

Since nothing about Nebuchadnezzar's position changes, we must reconsider Nebuchadnezzar's so-called "lesson." Early Christian readers do little more than regurgitate the story itself and Nebuchadnezzar's thoughts therein. Theodoret (oddly) acknowledges Nebuchadnezzar remembering his divine placement "as the person who had previously administered the mighty kingdom."[17] Ephrem takes a similar pro-Babylonian stance and makes Nebuchadnezzar the example par excellence for people following God:

> Through that punishment, which God inflicted on [Nebuchadnezzar], [God] shows that he gives back to each one his properties with justice and impartiality and humiliates those who walk in arrogance; and he mortified [Nebuchadnezzar] who was too full of [himself] and behaved arrogantly, so he will break the audacity of people similar to [Nebuchadnezzar] with similar consideration.[18]

Ephrem makes chapter 4 into a reminder of sorts, essentially saying, "Like this king, God will humble us when we're arrogant, too!" Ephrem is like other fourth- and fifth-century Christians in that they seem far too comfortable accepting Nebuchadnezzar's punishment as just and sufficient. The trend unsurprisingly continues into the Reformation, so much so that Calvin chalks up chapter 4 as proof of "how this world is administered by God's secret providence and that nothing happens but what he has commanded and decreed."[19] Interpreters stand content to accept the outcome as divine and apt but such contentedness prevents them from considering the fallout of Nebuchadnezzar's continued reign.

Because this reign indeed goes unquestioned in the text. Daniel 4 doubles down on both the king and the monarchy-style government. At verse 32, Nebuchadnezzar says:

> All dwelling on the earth are accounted as nothing, and he does what he wills with the hosts of heaven. And those dwelling on the earth, there are none that can stay his hand and say to him, "What are you doing?"

Note that Nebuchadnezzar says "all" dwelling on the earth—not just him. Nebuchadnezzar feigns empathy here, claiming everyone is subject to the same rules. He says that all people, including him, "are accounted as nothing." This theological statement aligns with unchecked fatalism in Ecclesiastes, but that does not make this sentiment about the human condition any less troubling. Do we readers take this lesson to heart as well? Do we account for nothing, as the king says? Is this something Nebuchadnezzar takes to heart? Or could it serve other purposes? Verse 33 suggests the king may have ulterior motives: "I was reestablished over my kingdom, and still more greatness was added to me." Nebuchadnezzar skillfully builds upon the reasoning of verse 32 to claim that his position of power is what God wants. Just as Nebuchadnezzar is subject to God, Daniel 4 reiterates humans as subject to divinely appointed rulers. One could say Daniel 4 presents a world in which everything accounts for nothing under God's ultimate power. Despite this, Nebuchadnezzar remains eager to justify his power. Daniel 4 accomplishes that by reinforcing Babylonian power structures as part of God's divine cosmology. This reinforcement carves an intriguing possibility for modern interpretations: Daniel 4 contains all the pieces necessary to be pro-Babylonian propaganda. I know this claim may receive considerable pushback, but a basic understanding of propaganda applied to Daniel 4 highlights too many consistencies to ignore.

One could argue that the difference between propaganda and genuine narrative is a matter of interpretive choice. I agree with this argument. It supports my position. Expertly crafted propaganda hides in plain sight, making readers forget why any writing wants to persuade. Because, in the simplest times, propaganda aims to persuade. Propaganda, as I understand it, has four characteristics: it (1) holds a persuasive function, (2) is for a sizeable target audience, (3) represents a specific group's agenda, and (4) uses faulty reasoning and/or emotional appeals.[20] Veracity and sincerity with any form of propaganda are irrelevant.[21] What matters is that Daniel 4 wants to persuade its readers into thinking the Babylonian Empire is natural and just. It does so by co-opting the Israelite Daniel figure and using Israelite religious language to make Nebuchadnezzar into the idealized Israelite repentant king.

One could push back against claims of reading Daniel 4, an ancient text, through the lens of modern propaganda. And yet, scholars studying ancient Egypt speak openly about pharaohs and other leaders wielding propaganda.[22] Evidence shows that as far back as the fourth millennium BCE, Egyptian royal powers used propaganda to "communicate their emerging dominance with images that conveyed a narrative of their growing supremacy."[23] They chiseled artistic depictions on walls, wore elaborate headgear, and built massive statues (some of which still exist) to persuade onlookers with awe, aura, and mystique. Such examples exist throughout the book of Daniel: Why else would Nebuchadnezzar erect a giant statue for everyone to bow down to and worship? It did not come from the goodness of his heart, nor did he make it a public works project. Daniel 3 makes it clear the king wanted people to know that he controls the kingdom.

Daniel 4 follows a similar path; only this time the thing to admire is Nebuchadnezzar's shallow humility under the guise of divine order.

For contemporary readers to say that Daniel 4 cannot be propaganda is to be naïve. Too often we let biases about what people tell us the Bible "is" cloud our judgment. This is one point and purpose of deconstruction: to make us aware of our biases and how they affect what we do with the Bible—because Daniel 4 quite clearly wants to persuade us. It leads us to believe that Nebuchadnezzar is a good, divinely appointed king that just needs a chance at correction. Unlike Pharaoh in Exodus, Nebuchadnezzar's fate lies not at the bottom of a sea but in the seat of a throne. It wants us to believe that Nebuchadnezzar learned his lesson, then gained divine favor, resulting in a prosperous and just reign. Nebuchadnezzar talks about knowing his place in the divine order, and the chapter concludes with the Babylonian king still in power. We know better. History knows better. We have considerable evidence for Nebuchadnezzar's ruthlessness. We know of his brutality and of the brutality of others like him that claim their power comes from God. We know his armies looted, pillaged, and destroyed in the name of king and kingdom. We also know Nebuchadnezzar does not break the mold, because his brutality was normal and accepted among monarchs. Indeed, one could argue that Daniel 4 is all about divine sovereignty and that Nebuchadnezzar's place in the chapter makes us consider who exactly that sovereignty is for.

4.3 So What?

What do we do with Daniel 4 as it lays out Nebuchadnezzar's journey in considerable detail, giving us a firsthand look at what he thinks, feels, and wants? How can we preach and teach it? What can something this sycophantic be for us? It is indeed Nebuchadnezzar's chapter, through and through. Acknowledging this raises more questions than it answers. If the chapter fits the parameters of imperial propaganda, what can it mean for modern-day Christians? How do we as contemporary interpreters push against dominant streams of interpretation? Responding to these questions falls back to the reality of choice.[24] What choices do we have with Daniel 4? And what do those choices mean for what we do with the Bible in general? Katheryn Pfisterer Darr's work with Ezekiel offers considerable assistance for our questions. Darr engages Ezekiel's violent sexual imagery and destructive theology by challenging us readers to accept responsibility for our choices. This is the nature of religious growth, Darr argues, because such growth "entails assuming responsibility for the decision we make in interpreting the Bible."[25]

So, what then do we do? How do we respond to a text that so clearly supports something as corrupt and vile as imperial colonization? Darr asks a similar question about God's villainous behavior in Ezekiel, to recommend something elegant, bold, and profound in its simplicity: say no. Respond to Daniel 4 with a firm and expectant "no." Darr refuses to accept Ezekiel's message of destruction, death, and exile as "the punishment of a just God."[26] Ezekiel, like the rest of the Bible, is a product of its time and place. Wisdom and experience fill its pages and entreat us to listen as a conversation partner about this thing that we call "God." Like all conversations, sometimes disagreements arise. What is to stop us from protecting ourselves by simply saying no to Daniel 4?

We Christians, evangelicals specifically, learn early in our lives that the Bible is "always right." If we claim the Bible is incorrect, so-called experts call us unlearned or too inexperienced to understand the text's deep and mysterious purpose. We learn to always say "yes" to the Bible, even when we know the Bible is wrong. We know it is wrong to justify enslavement, war, famine, and other atrocities as justified punishment under the guise of "God's plan." The "always yes" approach is so entrenched that this "no" response receives considerable criticism. Disgruntled readers may question my Christian faith and argue this reading is too agenda-driven, but the reality is every scholar has an agenda. No one approaches biblical interpretation neutrally (despite claims otherwise). Blindly saying "yes" to everything the Bible contains leads only to destruction.

Tracing dominant Christian readings only supports this claim. Christians say "yes" to Daniel 4 without considering what that "yes" means in practice. These "yes" responses perpetuate oppression to the point of carelessness. Evidence supporting my argument is plentiful and shocking. Jerome, Ephrem, Theodoret, Augustine, and other early Christian readers build their entire readings off this "yes" approach with divine sovereignty. The trend continues into and after the Reformation as Calvin, Luther, Diodati, and Oecolampadius never consider why Daniel presents a corrupted king as an idealized redemptive figure. Modern readers only carry this thread through and effectively double down on it. For example, Seow concludes his interpretation of Daniel 4 thusly: "The human ruler is finally to be an agent of divine will, a vehicle through which the greatness and sovereignty of God are universally made known."[27] John Owens takes this idea further and is somehow more forthright in the chapter's message: "Such a historicized account could be used during the threat or dominance of any tyrannical ruler to be encouragement and direction to a downtrodden defeated people."[28] Smith-Christopher makes the chapter's lesson one of "wait for God": "To say that God truly reigns is to make human authority tentative, temporary, and always liable to being disregarded in favor of the higher authority."[29] These examples span nearly two thousand years, and each reflects the overwhelmingly passive and banal approach Christians take with Daniel 4.

In saying no, do we reject Daniel 4's place in the Bible? Do we cut it out or look only at passages that say what we want them to say and do what we want them to do? No. We do the opposite. We face difficult texts with courage and strength. We, like Darr with Ezekiel, say, "I cannot follow you on this one, Daniel." Then we ask ourselves why we cannot follow. We consider how to live like people of God. We reject Christian passivity that suggests God will simply fix corruption and evil via divine lessons. Do we also have the courage necessary to again ask which side are we on: the side of Nebuchadnezzar or the side of God? Daniel says over and over that Nebuchadnezzar's reign is divinely ordained. Does this reflect reality as it is, or does it reflect a skewed sense of the world built into imperial domination? Daniel 4 wants to persuade us that earthly rulers, no matter how vile, can be redeemed without actual redemption. Such messages make us reconsider our relationship to the powerful: Should we question them? Or is everything they do part of God's ultimate plan? History shows that simply defaulting to "God's plan" leads only to death and destruction. We are right to suspect and question those in power, especially when they (or others on their behalf) claim God gave them their position.

Idealistic notions of God's plan and divine sovereignty permeate the modern American political landscape. President Donald Trump, an American evangelical Christian darling, in 2022 said that "God made the decision" following the U.S. Supreme Court's overturning of the *Roe v. Wade* decision.[30] Following the 2020 United States presidential election, Dr. Robert Jeffress, a prominent evangelical pastor from Dallas, Texas, defended then president-elect Joe Biden to concerned Christians. Writing an opinion piece for *Fox News*, Jeffress assures Christians despondent over Trump's defeat:

> Human governments and rulers change at God's direction and design. Our faith and our salvation lie not in any human ruler, but in the ruler of rulers, the King of kings. We have to remember that even

> though the occupant of the White House is changing, the One who occupies the throne of Heaven hasn't changed.[31]

Jeffress wrote to a wide and eager audience, as one-third of Americans believed God influenced Trump's election.[32] Jeffress claimed President Obama fell under that same umbrella as well, as did Trump's energy secretary Rick Perry. Perry, an open evangelical Christian, claims, "You know, Barack Obama doesn't get to be the President of the United States without being ordained by God. Neither did Donald Trump."[33] Southern Baptist Convention leader Dave Miller continued the trend and even cites Daniel 4 to justify President Obama's second term: "God chose that Barack Obama would be the president of the United States."[34]

Divine-sovereignty rhetoric around Biden, Trump, and Obama pale compared to George W. Bush's thoughts about himself. Said Bush on why he decided to run for president: "I've heard the call. I believe God wants me to run for president."[35] Pressed about this statement, Bush doubled down:

> I feel like God wants me to run for president. I can't explain it, but I sense my country is going to need me. Something is going to happen, and, at that time, my country is going to need me. I know it won't be easy, on me or my family, but God wants me to do it. In fact, I really don't want to run. My father was president. My whole family has been affected by it. I know the price. I know what it will mean. I would be perfectly happy to have people point at me someday when I'm buying my fishing lures at Wal-Mart and say, "That was our governor." That's all I want. And if I run for president, that kind of life will be over. My life will never be the same. But I feel God wants me to do this, and I must do it.[36]

I could go on for pages more about governors, senators, mayors, and other elected officials that either claim a divine mantel or have it put upon them. The fact remains that each president listed above has blood-soaked hands. Each is responsible for the deaths of thousands and the suffering of millions. Progressive Christians point to presidents like Biden and Obama as "lesser evils" in election years, but the sheer number of deaths allowed (and often ordered) by each of these men defies imagination. According to one study by Brown University, the twenty-year war on terror killed nine hundred thousand people.[37] Herein lies the essential problem with claiming a leader, any leader, carries divine appointment: that theological logic means God appointed those presidents, meaning God is responsible in this instance for the deaths of nearly one million people.

It is in pushing against such notions of divine sovereignty that we find a renewed sense of purpose for Daniel 4. Through this reading, Daniel 4 becomes a warning to all that may read it. The voices of the Israelites that suffered and died under Nebuchadnezzar's hand hold it up to us as a mirror, entreating us to ask where we stand. People like Nebuchadnezzar show us just how far unchecked power can reach and how dangerous it can become. It can infiltrate the things we care about and love the most, all while claiming to be part of "God's plan." We cannot allow Nebuchadnezzar's word to be the final say on his rule, nor can we let cries about "divine sovereignty" become excuses for death and dismay. We must channel the voice and hope of readers like Darr as we seek the workings of the living God: "Sometimes, we embrace painful texts not because we agree with their answers, but because they force us to wrestle with crucial questions."[38]

5

Daniel 5 Reconsidered

5.1 Translation

1 Belshazzar, the king, made a great feast for one thousand of his nobles and in the presence of the thousand he was drinking wine.

2 Belshazzar spoke, under the wine's influence, to bring the vessels of gold and silver which his father Nebuchadnezzar had taken from the temple in Jerusalem so that the king and his nobles, his wives and his concubines, might drink from them.

3 So they brought the vessels of gold that were taken from the temple, the house of God in Jerusalem, and they drank from them, the king and his nobles, his wives, and his concubines.

4 They drank the wine and praised the gods of gold and silver, bronze, iron, wood, and stone.

5 Then immediately, there appeared the fingers of a man, and they wrote next to the candlestick upon the plaster of the wall of the temple of the king; and the king saw the palm of the hand which was writing.

6 Then the king's countenance changed and his thoughts alarmed him. And the joints of his hips loosened, and his knees knocked together.

7 The king called loudly to bring in the conjurers, Chaldeans, and astrologers. The king declared and spoke to the wise men of Babylon: "Of each man, the one who reads this writing and shows me its interpretation shall be clothed in purple and have a gold chain placed upon his neck, and he shall rule a third of the kingdom."

8 Then they came in, all the king's wise men, and they could not read the writing or tell the king its interpretation.

9 Then the king, Belshazzar, was greatly alarmed, and the color of his countenance changed, and his nobles were perplexed.

10 The queen, on account of the words of the king and his nobles in the banquet house, entered. The queen declared and said, "O King! Live forever! Do not allow your thoughts to alarm you and do not let your countenance change.

11 There is a man in your kingdom with a spirit of holy gods in him. And in the days of your father he was found to have insight, understanding, and wisdom of the gods in him, and the king, Nebuchadnezzar, your father, made him the highest of the magicians, conjurers, Chaldeans, and astrologers for your father the king.

12 All this because an excellent spirit, knowledge, and understanding to interpret dreams, explain riddles, and solve problems were found in this one, Daniel, whom the king named Belteshazzar. Now let Daniel be called and he will give the interpretation."

13 Then Daniel was brought before the king. The king answered and said to Daniel, "So you are him. Daniel. One from the sons of the exile of Judah.

14 I have heard about you, that a spirit of holy gods is in you, and that illumination, insight, and excellent wisdom are found in you.

15 And now the wise men, the conjurers, have been brought in before me to read this writing aloud and make its interpretation known to me. And they were not able to give the interpretation of the matter.

16 And I have heard that you are able to give interpretations and solve problems. Now if you are able to read the writing aloud and make its interpretation known to me, you shall be clothed in purple and have a gold chain upon your neck and shall rule one-third of the kingdom."

17 Then Daniel answered and said before the king: "May your gifts be for yourself and give your rewards to another. But the writing I will read aloud to the king, and make the interpretation known to him.

18 You, the king, God the Most High gave kingship and greatness and glory and majesty to Nebuchadnezzar, your father.

19 And from the greatness which he gave him, all peoples, nations, and languages were trembling and fearful before him. He killed those he wanted to kill, and those he wished to keep alive, he kept alive. He honored who he wanted and humbled whoever he wished.

20 And when his heart was lifted up and his spirit grew strong so that was proud, he was brought down from the throne of his kingdom, and his glory was taken from him.

21 He was driven from the sons of men, and his heart was made like that of an animal, and his dwelling was with wild asses. He was fed grasses of oxen, and his body was bathed with the dew of the heavens until he knew that God the Most High was ruler over the kingdom of men and appoints whomever he wishes over it.

22 And you, his son, Belshazzar, have not humbled your heart even though you know all this!

23 You have lifted yourself up against the Lord of the Heavens. The vessels of his house have been brought before you, and you and your nobles, your wives, and your concubines have been drinking wine with them. And you have praised the gods of silver and gold, bronze, wood, and iron, which do not see and do not hear and do not know, and the God in whose hand is your breath and all to him are all your ways, you have not honored him.

24 So from before him was the hand sent, and this writing was inscribed.

25 And this is the writing which was inscribed: Mene Mene Tekel and Parsin.

26 This is the interpretation of the matter: Mene, God has appointed your kingdom and completed it.

27 Tekel, you have been weighed on the scales, and you have been found wanting.

28 Peres, divided is your kingdom, and it shall be given to the Medes and Persians."

29 Then Belshazzar spoke, and Daniel was clothed in a purple robe and a chain of gold upon his neck, and a proclamation was made that he shall become ruler of one-third of the kingdom.

30 That night, Belshazzar the Chaldean king was slain.[1]

5.2 Reading against the Grain

Daniel 5 opens with an abrupt shift: Nebuchadnezzar is gone. Now Belshazzar is king. Verse 2 claims Belshazzar is Nebuchadnezzar's son, but, according to historical evidence, this is untrue. Further, according to this same evidence, Belshazzar did not become king after Nebuchadnezzar. Nabonidus, the final Babylonian king ruling in the fifth century BCE, is Belshazzar's father. Cuneiform inscriptions on a clay cylinder called the *Nabonidus Cylinder* and tablets labeled the *Nabonidus Chronicle* repeatedly state Belshazzar was Nabonidus' crowned prince and eventual regent. Belshazzar never had the title "king of Babylon."[2] Early Christian readers, including Jerome, Theodoret, Melanchthon, and Calvin, address the leadership change alongside apparent gaffes with dexterous dodging or outright denial. Jerome first argues that "father" is a common term for ancestors, thereby making use of "father" in verse 2 appropriate and accurate.[3] Calvin takes a similar position: "The Prophet calls Nebuchadnezzar the father of Belshazzar, since it is usual in all languages to speak of ancestors as fathers."[4] Calvin plays fast and loose with his argument, especially the claim that "all languages" use "father" in this manner. In contrast to Calvin's brazen assumptions, Theodoret and Melanchthon simply claim Belshazzar was Nebuchadnezzar's son.[5]

Scholars wrestle to resolve this historical tension, as such an incongruence between history and text seems unmovable. Current interpreters dig deeper into chapter 5's erroneous genealogy with considerable detail, crafting historical timelines around Nebuchadnezzar's posterity to prove their point.[6] Belshazzar was not Nebuchadnezzar's son, nor did he rule after Nebuchadnezzar. Yet a viable resolution for "King Belshazzar" is shockingly simple: calling this man "king" is a literary signpost guiding the reader toward interpretive possibilities. Such signposts highlight Daniel's historically ahistorical nature as it once again takes historical figures and uses them to tell ahistorical stories. The question then becomes this: What might Daniel 5 be doing beyond historical reconstruction and recollection?

In verses 1 and 2, Belshazzar feasts and consumes wine until intoxication. On top of that, the king effectively flaunts his behavior before "one thousand of his nobles." This means Belshazzar makes reckless drunken decrees and acts erratically, erroneously, and irresponsibly. Why share his drunken state with the reader?[7] Is the text trying to apologize for the king's behavior and justify his request for Jerusalem's religious vessels? Or is it doing something else? Belshazzar's arrogance is undeniable. However, citing drunkenness alongside social grandstanding creates space for more explanation and justification than we might like, especially considering that once again the book of Daniel tells of a foreign king exploiting Israelite religious traditions for personal gain.

Verses 3 and 4 expand the scope of the chapter's characters. The king and his nobles, wives, and concubines drink from the vessels and then praise "gold and silver, bronze, iron, wood, and stone." Traditional interpretations ascribe malice to the king's drunken revelry, but the text withholds Belshazzar's motivations. He could drink from these vessels to spite the Israelites and their god, or he could do it simply because he can. The text does not tell us, so scholars and readers fill this narrative gap with their assumptions. Such an approach sets the tone for what people do with

Daniel 5: brandish opinion as fact to create interpretations that tie off into tidy theological proverbs.

Speaking of theology, God is absent in chapter 5, and that absence is quite conspicuous. As with chapters 1–4, discussion about divine sovereignty saturates interpretations, inserting "God" where the deity is a no-show. Daniel 5 is no exception. Characters talk about God, but the chapter shows no overt direct divine action. One particularly presumptuous example is the hand at verse 5. My translation reads, "there appeared the fingers of a man," from the Aramaic אֶצְבְּעָן דִּי יַד־אֱנָשׁ.[8] Verse 5 doubles down on the hand's human provenance: "the king saw the palm of the hand which was writing." Based solely on the text, all we know is that the hand is human, surprises the king in its appearance, and writes on the wall. Additional attributes on the hand are just that: something added. English translations follow this more literal approach and reflect the Aramaic, yet most Christian readers assume the hand has divine origins.

This lack of evidence does not stop Christian readers from making this human hand into a divine instrument. Attributing divine origin to Daniel 5's human hand goes back as far as Jerome and Theodoret, and it continues among contemporary Christians. For example, Iain Duguid titles a section in his commentary on Daniel 5 "A Hand from Heaven" and describes the event as "a revelation from God" without question or hesitation.[9] It appears in children's Bibles as well, with the *Read with Me Bible* saying, "the fingers of a human hand," placed beside a drawing of a spectral hand coming from outside the image frame.[10] Other children's Bibles describe the hand as "ghostly" and appearing "from nowhere . . . floating there, all on its own."[11] Again, nothing in Daniel 5 supports this interpretation. But this kind of interpretation highlights Christians continuing to put God where God is not. Making God every narrative's point and purpose is not only poor hermeneutics but also highly reductive theology. Saying the hand belongs to God severely limits how Christians read Daniel 5, reducing the story to another example of a disobedient king receiving "just" punishment. Yet Daniel 5 is more complex than such hasty theologizing allows, and the king's reaction in verses 6–8 helps us understand why.

The king's immediate fearful reaction in verse 6 corresponds with how other kings reacted to dreams and events in Daniel: his "countenance changed and his thoughts alarmed him." Verse 6 goes further in describing Belshazzar's reaction and includes details that border on cartoonish. The king's hips loosen, and his knees knock together, suggesting an over-the-top "Looney Tunes" style response. Christian interpreters say the fear of

God or some variation of divine reverence prompts Belshazzar's response, but, once again, the text does not say that. The reality is Belshazzar may be afraid because he simply cannot read what the hand writes: in verse 7 he asks the wise men of Babylon to read and interpret the writing. If the king could read it, he would need only the interpretation.

Verse 8 complicates things as the king's supposed experts cannot read or interpret it either, prompting further fear and anxiety. Verse 25 shows us the shocking simplicity of the writing so we cannot eliminate the possibility that the king and experts are either illiterate or too wine-drunk to read. The story goes out of its way to highlight the king's inebriation in verse 2, and, considering the limited literacy rates in the ancient world, it is possible neither the king nor his experts could read. Or to be more precise, perhaps the king and his experts were illiterate. Only a select few could read and write in the ancient world, hence the need for a scribal class.[12] And even then, said scribes faced limitations of working with different languages. However, scribal language limitations are irrelevant because the king never asks for a scribe; he asks for "conjurers, Chaldeans, and astrologers." This further highlights the incompetency of kings in Daniel: Why not request people whose very jobs are reading and writing? Why consult diviners and magicians when a royal clerk might suffice? Either the wine affects the king's judgment more than we like to imagine, or the king is unable to call upon the right people for the job.

The queen interjects at verses 10–11, paving the way for Daniel to offer his reading and interpretation. This means once again the book of Daniel introduces a king, gives the king quite a fright, then finds reason and rationale to bring Daniel on stage later in the story. One could ask why the king fails to summon Daniel sooner, but calling Daniel prematurely would relieve Daniel 5's narrative dramatic tension. The story is subpar if Daniel stands beside the king in verse 1, ready to serve. Mindful of this embellishment for the sake of narrative, the queen's extended introduction of Daniel is peculiar. We, the readers, know what Daniel can do, so why does the queen regale the king (and therefore the audience) with Daniel's exploits? Why not simply say "the queen told Belshazzar of Daniel's exploits and successes"? Her description could highlight the extent of Belshazzar's incompetence, as the queen recalls how Nebuchadnezzar (here again erroneously labeled as "your father") made Daniel "the highest of the magicians, conjurers, Chaldeans, and astrologers." Does this mean Belshazzar does not know who works under him, or does he disregard how previous kings ruled before he took the throne?

Verses 13–16 amplify the chapter's theatricality and give Belshazzar an extended monologue explaining everything that happens to this point in the story. Belshazzar's need to rehash his experience feels unnecessary, but it makes sense within dramatic storytelling. Daniel 5 unfolds without the benefit of universal knowledge among the characters, hence the need for continued exposition. We, the readers, know what comes before Daniel's arrival, and we know the information the king shares with Daniel. On top of this written description, the king barely knows Daniel, much less what he can do. Despite this, he gives the Judean exile considerable (if, within the context of Daniel 5, unearned) trust. Think about it: Belshazzar meets Daniel, then immediately promises him purple robes, a gold chain, and considerable political power. For all the king knows, the writing is inconsequential, and his shaken reaction is nothing more than paranoia accompanying excessive drinking. Further, since neither he nor his experts can read the writing, the king has no way of fact-checking Daniel's reading and interpretation. Daniel could deliver whatever interpretation he wants, regardless of what the words may say. Once again, to Daniel's benefit, we have an incompetent and irrational monarch running the show.

Daniel gets his dramatic sequence in verses 17–29, and he begins by retelling Nebuchadnezzar's Daniel 4 experience. Nothing Daniel says about Nebuchadnezzar's experience in Daniel 4 is new to the reader, so this information is solely for Belshazzar. Daniel's recounting scares and humbles Belshazzar, meaning he employs Nebuchadnezzar's time in the wilderness as an intimidation tactic. It is most telling that despite Nebuchadnezzar's absence, Daniel praises the former king and reiterates that "God the Most High gave kingship and greatness and glory and majesty to Nebuchadnezzar." It seems even after his rule has ended that Nebuchadnezzar can do no wrong in Daniel's eyes. This raises the question of how (and why) Belshazzar became king in the first place: If God is indeed in control of everything in Daniel, how can someone become king without God's blessing?

Standard Christian approaches to Belshazzar's punishment, that he defiled and disrespected Daniel's god by drinking from the sacred vessels, pales in comparison to what Daniel recalls about Nebuchadnezzar. Daniel reminds us in verse 19 that Nebuchadnezzar ruled with fear and killed at will. Yet God gave Nebuchadnezzar the chance to humble himself and turn from evil. This juxtaposes Nebuchadnezzar's bloody history with Belshazzar's drinking wine from the temple vessel, an odd comparison to say the least. Nebuchadnezzar retains his power and stature in Daniel 4, but Belshazzar dies for his actions. Does that mean God cares more about Belshazzar's improper ritual protocols than Nebuchadnezzar's blood-soaked rule? At verse 22, Daniel indicts Belshazzar's failing to humble his heart "even though you know all this," with "this" being Daniel 4 and Nebuchadnezzar's story therein. Preceding verses show Belshazzar did not know Daniel and his exploits, so Daniel is, in effect, blaming Belshazzar for something he does not know. It seems ignorance is an inadequate justification.

Verse 24 returns to the infamous hand as Daniel lays out the king's judgment and punishment. He describes the hand, saying, "from before him was the hand sent," with "him" here implying the deity described in verse 23. Christian readers have long used verses 23–24 to justify the hand's divine lineage, arguing the hand belongs to God or God has given the hand a divine blessing. Daniel's language here is deceptively simple, as his rhetoric creates considerable interpretative space. The Aramaic is מִן־קֳדָמ֫וֹהִי, meaning "from before him." English translations play fast and loose with this Aramaic phrasing, evidenced by the NRSV and ESV's "from his presence" or the New Living Translation's "So God has sent this hand to write this message."

John Collins claims this phrase gives the hand the "state of a divine emissary, like the spirits of 1 Kgs 22:20–22."[13] Collins at least attempts to support this traditional argument with textual evidence, but others simply operate off assumption. For example, Towner paints the handwriting as God "decreed and announced," and Goldingay simply cites Collins.[14] Relating Daniel 5 to a 1 Kings passage in which a spirit talks directly with God is incongruous, as Daniel's hand has no voice and offers no form of consent. Unlike 1 Kings, God is silent in Daniel 5. Daniel speaks for God, and Seow wisely notes this discrepancy: "Daniel interprets the hand as something that has been sent from the presence of God."[15]

Seow's notation points toward a compelling interpretive possibility: How does Daniel's presence in chapter 5 change knowing that Daniel interprets what he sees, instead of merely assuming the hand is divine? Discussion around the hand would be radically different if Daniel 5 referenced God's behavior or spoken words. Instead, we get a sparse description that creates questions about to whom the hand belongs. Is it someone random, fed up with the king's behavior? Or is it God acting in stealth mode? Perhaps Daniel is the culprit, frustrated that a new king cut him out of the royal loop despite his best efforts to please Nebuchadnezzar. The text does not say.

What the hand writes further complicates matters, but remembering illiteracy in the ancient world offers clarity. Daniel presents "Mene, Mene,

Tekel, Parsin" as deep, profound, and mysterious. The reality is much simpler: these words are Aramaic nouns referring to various weights. If the king could read Aramaic, he would know that. He (and his appointed experts) cannot because Daniel's recitation is the first time the reader learns the actual inscription. There are considerable scholarly discussions around textual criticism of these words and their "original" form.[16] Text-critical arguments are inconsequential for us, however, as the version used in churches, personal study, and classroom settings is consistent: the handwriting says, "Mene, Mene, Tekel, Parsin." The dominant narrative argument about these words focuses on their meaning and the riddle-like way the text presents them.[17] One major reason for this lies in the words translating directly to "a large weight, a large weight, one-sixteenth of a mene, half-shekel." Despite their noun forms, Daniel's interpretation focuses on their related verbal forms, meaning "to count/number, to count/number, to weigh, to divide." We do not know if what Daniels says is true; we have his thoughts on the words and nothing else. If Daniel is the only one that can read the text, and the first time we learn what the hand writes is through Daniel, is Daniel making things up as he goes along?

This question grows more compelling after considering Daniel's almost clichéd explanation. Read against the backdrop of Daniel 1–4, Daniel's interpretation is predictable: God is disappointed in another king and will bring about that kingdom's destruction. What makes Daniel 5 unique is Daniel's particularity in claiming the Medes and Persians will soon rule Belshazzar's kingdom. Historically, Christian-focused scholars dig deep into Daniel's Medes and Persians reference, with some claiming the king's lavish banquet happens as the Medes and Persians wait outside the gates.[18] Again, the text does not support such claims. Others, like Towner, read mentioning "Medes and Persians" for what it is: "the stuff of brilliant, colorful storytelling."[19] One can add another layer to Towner's argument, as the written inscription makes no mention of Medes or Persians, making this information one more of Daniel's expositional embellishments.

The story ends with Belshazzar's death. Such a conclusion matches the chapter's opening abruptness, as the king we meet in verse 1 is now dead. Christian interpreters immediately claim the king's death is an apt punishment for his crimes against God, as, unlike previous chapters, Daniel 5 lacks an overt invitation for the king's repentance.[20] Why is Belshazzar denied the chance to change his ways like the preceding king? Further, does the king deserve such punishment for drinking from Israelite vessels? Historically we know Nebuchadnezzar ruled through violence and fear. Daniel's recollection of Nebuchadnezzar offers the king multiple chances to change his ways. What is it about Belshazzar's behavior that warrants such swift and abrupt repercussions? Daniel 5 presents Belshazzar as an illiterate drunk surrounded by incompetence, making him an overt monarchy caricature that elevates Nebuchadnezzar's standing in the larger narrative. Belshazzar contrasts Nebuchadnezzar, the king that Daniel 1 proclaims God installed into power, as a ruler who happens to show up in this story. Daniel uses him to tell a non-Israelite king of his failings, leading to yet another promotion for the Israelite protagonist. Only this time, someone murders the king following Daniel's promotion.

Christian readers take Belshazzar's death as the story's proverbial "icing on the cake," designed to show unrepentant leaders what awaits their arrogance.[21] How do we know if it is divine punishment and not happenstance? Nothing about his death suggests the divine plays a role. The Aramaic verb at verse 30 is קְטִּ֫יל, a passive verbal construction meaning "to kill" or "to slay." This means Daniel 5:30 says, "Belshazzar the Chaldean king was slain." Daniel 5 offers no further details about this slaying, nor does the text name the responsible party. Yet readers still overlay historical assumptions and theological explanations onto how Belshazzar died. For example, Jerome argues the Medes and Persians killed Belshazzar upon taking the city, and Greek historian Xenophon says soldiers stormed the palace and killed the king.[22] Neither of these readings have textual support. Belshazzar came and went as just an avenue for Daniel's gain, with God remaining shockingly absent and unsettlingly quiet.

5.3 So What?

So, what, then, are we to do with this story of a drunken, failed king and his courtesan Daniel? Perhaps more important for the lived realities of contemporary Christian communities is this: How do we approach Christian readings that bog Daniel 5 in theological clichés? The Christian theological orientation laid upon Daniel is in dire need of reconsideration. The issue in question is two-pronged. First, we must radically amend the concept of divine justice. Second, we need to expand past divine justice into a larger understanding of how Christians read Daniel 5 as a manifesto of sorts for God's sovereign control of history. No major Christian reading dares to question the king's fate in Daniel 5. Believing Belshazzar's death as just and warranted connects disparate Christian readings, with each highlighting how Belshazzar got what he deserved to follow a standard "divine sovereignty" tact. Evangelicals like Charles Swindoll address this existential dread and read Daniel 5 to support trite theological truisms: "We don't need to wonder whether God will do something about the evil that goes on in the world. Long ago, He saw its beginning and determined its end. His patience and mercy don't negate His judgment."[23] Towner cites André LaCocque's claim that "history is the bearer of God's judgment. History is both theophany and verdict."[24] Or Seow claims that "the narrator's point, subtly made, is that God's will is being worked out in history after all."[25] Going back further in time, Martin Luther believes the chapter's design is meant to warn other tyrannical rulers: by failing to repent, Belshazzar "loses body and soul, his land and his people with one strike. Indeed this is written to frighten all such tyrants."[26] Gerhard's position complements Luther's: "Just like King Belshazzar . . . when the building of this world and all its kingdoms are soon to be destroyed, it will also happen that people will act secure and will busy themselves with getting drunk."[27] A most disturbing read on Belshazzar's death comes from Theodoret:

> The just judge was therefore within his rights in confining punishment of the former to a specified time, whereas he granted the latter no pardon. In particular, God foresees all future events and thus knows them clearly as if already in the past; so he knew ahead of time the repentance of the former and arranged for his fate accordingly, whereas he knew ahead of time the latter's incorrigible impiety and put a stop to the increase in impiety with death.[28]

According to this approach, God will punish those that follow Belshazzar's arrogance. To Christians, this looks and feels good, right, and appropriate. Lived reality tells a far different story.

People commit acts of considerable evil with impunity. No day passes without headlines of yet another shooting, yet another murder, and yet another act of mindless violence. Politicians openly steal money from supporters to craft golden parachutes. Presidents lie with little to no recourse. Racism, sexism, and other forms of discrimination are so widespread that they seem part of the natural order. Sometimes people committing evil face the cold, hard light of justice. But not all the time. People slip through the justice system's cracks and walk free, while other people living honest, fair lives face cancer, sickness, or poverty despite having done nothing to warrant such fates. Through the Daniel 5 Christian lens of "just punishment and divine sovereignty," everything in history unfolds according to God's will. Is this true? Is it accurate? Did God make colonizers steal millions of people from the African continent, enslaving them to give a select few sugar, cotton, and tobacco? Was it God's will when shooters walked into elementary school buildings, killing children no older than five or six years old? Where was God when indigenous people around the world faced slaughter from people claiming to fight for "freedom?" Is it God's will when a child starves to death on one side of the city when another throws food out because they "didn't like it"?

These are questions we must ask of ourselves, our Bibles, and our interpreters. If we default to believing that God controls all of history, we severely undercut the pain and suffering millions experience daily. This is not to say that God is absent from history, a la Deism. Quite the opposite. The Bible presents God as an active and vibrant force, but what the Bible can call "justice" we call genocide and murder. We know better. Such apparent randomness in judgment and punishment permeates the biblical text.[29] This shows contemporary readers that people long ago faced similar theological anxieties: If God is just, why does so much injustice go unpunished now? Questions like this are essential to Christian thought and practice, and far too often we shy away from asking. Instead, we stay comfortable believing that "everything happens for a reason."

Nothing in Daniel 5 suggests anything that unfolds in its pages accords with God's will. One could argue that Daniel 5 creates space for the opposite, warning us to be suspicious of those claiming to speak for God and to know God's will. God is indeed absent and silent in the chapter, with Daniel and Daniel alone speaking for God. Far too many Christians follow this path and present themselves as unquestioned authorities, but such theological authoritarianism rivals any wickedness the Bible offers. The Roman Catholic Church covered up the abuse of thousands, possibly millions, of children. The abusers often received promotions and relocation as "punishment." The Southern Baptist Convention's report on abuse at every level of its organization shocked the world, with more and more people coming forward as survivors.[30] In these examples and others, faithful, diligent Christians were manipulated by people they trusted, with some told that crimes committed against them were acceptable because the perpetrator is "a man of God."[31] So-called "church leaders" said each survivor "engaged in fornication and needs to be called to repent."[32]

Herein lies the difficulty in reading texts like Daniel 5 as it becomes a case study on why we read the Bible. It contains the pieces necessary to paint a pleasant, borderline cathartic approach to the unjust receiving the punishment they deserve. Holding the text and its interpretations beside hard realities of injustice and suffering tears that painting to pieces, forcing us to rearrange said pieces to reflect how life is and not how we wish it was. I do not claim to be unbiased. The wrongdoings I list reject the kind of divine sovereignty associated with Daniel 5 and show my theological orientation. Daniel 5 has space for such rejection and acceptance, for tension and dissent. Anyone saying otherwise treats the Bible like Belshazzar drunkenly treats the temple vessels, taking something set aside for sacred contemplation and using it as they see fit.

6
Daniel 6 Reconsidered

6.1 Translation

1 And Darius the Mede received the kingdom. He was sixty-two years old.[1]

2 Darius was pleased, and he sat 120 provincial governors who were over the entire kingdom,

3 and over them three superintendents, of which Daniel was one. These provincial governors gave the account so that the king would not take a loss.

4 Then Daniel distinguished himself over the superintendents and provincial governors because a remarkable spirit was in him, and the king planned to appoint him over the entire kingdom.

5 Then the superintendents and provincial governors looked to find charges against Daniel concerning the kingdom. And they were unable to find a charge or a fault because he was trustworthy, and no negligence and fault could be found in him.

6 Then these men were saying, "We will not find a charge against Daniel unless we find it in the law of his god."

7 Then these superintendents and provincial governors crowded[2] over the king and said to him, "King Darius, live forever!

8 We are in agreement: each of the kingdom's superintendents, prefects, and provincial governors, counselors, and governors, to establish an ordinance of the king, and to enforce an injunction, that all who request a petition from anyone, divine or human, for thirty days, except from you, the king, shall be cast into a den of lions.

9 Now, king, establish the injunction and sign the document which cannot be changed in accordance with the laws of the Medes and Persians which cannot be changed."

10 Therefore, King Darius signed the document and injunction.

11 And Daniel, who knew about the signed document, went into his house and had the windows of his roof chamber opened toward Jerusalem, and three times a day he knelt on his knees and he prayed and gave thanks before his god just as he had done previously.

12 Then these men crowded and found Daniel seeking and showing favor before his god.

13 Then they approached and spoke before the king about the injunction, "King, did you not sign an injunction that all who request a petition from anyone, divine or human, with thirty days except from you, the king, shall be cast into the lions' den?" The king answered and said, "The thing stands fast, according to the law of Medes and Persians, which cannot be revoked."

14 Then they answered and spoke before the king that "Daniel, who is from the sons of the exile of Judah, sets nothing upon you, King, or upon the injunction that you signed, and three times daily he requests petition."

15 When the king heard the charge, much distress came over him, and he set his mind upon Daniel to deliver him, and until the sun went down he labored to rescue him.

16 Then these men thronged to overthrow the king and said to the king, "Know, King, that it is a law of the Medes and Persians that any edict and ordinance that the king establishes cannot be changed."

17 Then the king commanded and Daniel was brought and thrown into the lions' den. The king answered and said to Daniel, "May your god, whom you serve continually, deliver you."

18 And one stone was brought and set over the mouth of the den, and the king sealed it with his signet ring and the rings of his nobles, so that nothing could be changed against Daniel.

19 Then the king went into his palace and spent the night fasting; no food was brought to him, and sleep fled from him.

20 Then the king at dawn arose in the daylight and in haste went to the den of lions.

21 And as he came to the den, he cried to Daniel in an anguished voice. The king called to Daniel and said, "Daniel, servant of the living god, has your god whom you continually serve been able to deliver you from the lions?"

22 Then Daniel spoke to the king, "King, live forever!

23 My god sent his angel and shut the lions' mouths, and they did not destroy me, for I have been found blameless before him, and also before you, king, I have done no crime."

24 Then the king was exceedingly glad about it and Daniel, and he said to lift him from the den. So, Daniel was lifted from the den, and no kind of harm was found upon him because he trusted in his god.

25 And the king spoke, and those men that charged accusations against Daniel were brought and thrown into the lions' den, they, their sons, and their wives, and they did not reach the den's bottom before the lions overpowered them and crushed their bones to pieces.

26 Then King Darius wrote to all peoples, nations, and languages dwelling across the entire earth, "May you have abundant peace!

27 I make a decree that across the dominion of my kingdom to tremble and fear before Daniel's god, for he is a living god, enduring forever, and his kingdom shall never be destroyed and his dominion will be until the end.

28 He delivers and rescues, and he does signs and wonders in the heavens and the earth, for he saved Daniel from the lions' hand."

29 And this Daniel prospered in Darius' reign and the reign of Cyrus the Persian.

6.2 Reading against the Grain

Towner opens his Daniel 6 reading with a formulaic Christian interpretation: "It requires no very elaborate reading to discern the subject of Daniel 6."[3] He continues, "God wins in the struggle by stopping the mouths of the lions, to whom Daniel had been thrown as food for them and punishment for him, and so vindicates both himself, his law, and his servant."[4] Towner is not alone in this "God always wins" approach, as it goes back as far as Theodoret, who claims, "Nothing, to be sure, can dull true religion: it spreads its rays everywhere, be it in slave or in captive; far from anything being capable of obscuring its splendor, it spreads its characteristic gleam."[5] Despite the confidence of interpreters, a cursory reading shows us the opposite. Theological complexity and duress at the hands of colonization saturate the chapter. An unknown king makes foolish, shortsighted edicts under pressure from monarchical "yes men." Daniel behaves recklessly and sets dangerous precedent for those who might follow his lead, and an absentee deity gets credit for something that might as well be dumb luck. On top of this, the king praises Daniel's god by subjecting innocent people, including children, to horrific deaths in the hungry lions' mouths. Daniel 6 is anything but straightforward or gleaming in splendor.

Let us start with the obvious: Darius the Mede never existed.[6] There was a King Darius, but he was Persian, not Median. Scholars note this historical discrepancy but neglect what it may mean for interpretation. Perhaps the author makes a mistake and gets the historical information wrong, and the misstep simply stuck. Or somehow Daniel's writers mixed up their information and mislabeled the king, but such a glaring error would have been corrected long before Daniel 6 reached us. It seems this "Darius the Mede" is doing something else in Daniel's larger narrative. I argue that making this nonexistent man the chapter's monarch is yet another literary signpost, guiding readers to remove any association of historical veracity that the chapter might carry.

Making Darius, a nonexistent king, the chapter's appointed ruler is heavy-handed but effective, along the same lines as "once a upon a time" or "a long time ago in a galaxy far, far away." For this reason, the chapter's fantastical nature should be unsurprising, especially given what unfolds. Despite such obvious fictional markers like lions that avoid Daniel but suddenly get an appetite, an unnamed horde of critics whose behavior borders on caricature, and a king that makes laws but cannot change them, scholars plaster this nonexistent king with historical factoids. For example, Hartman and Di Lella argue Darius is sixty-two years old by combining Psalm 90:10 with Daniel 6:2 to "suggest that he had a life expectancy of eighty years at his succession."[7] Stephen Miller makes a considerable historical leap and claims that Darius is actually the Babylonian governor Gubaru or King Cyrus, then creates an argument built upon hopes for nonexistent historical evidence to support his belief that Daniel 6 is factual.[8] This kind of apologetics underlines the sophisticated lengths readers take to prove something that needs no proving: Daniel 6 is fiction, nothing more and nothing less.

Verses 2 and 3 lay out Darius' governing structure to show us where Daniel fits into this system. He appoints superintendents and provincial governors, including Daniel as one of the king's superintendents, making him deeply embedded in the imperial apparatus. Not only is he part of the system, but, according to verse 4, Daniel is an exemplary cog who "distinguished himself over the superintendents and provincial governors because a remarkable spirit was in him." The word "spirit" here is the Aramaic רֽוּחַ, which carries spiritual or metaphysical connotations as well as describing one's capacity for knowledge. Thus, this "remarkable spirit" does not exclusively mean divine intervention or God's hand in Daniel's success.[9] Daniel might just be really good at his job. Either way, the point remains that Daniel ingratiates himself to the point of sparking jealousy among his peers.

Daniel's considerable devotion to this foreign empire defies biblical prophets and their position toward Israelite leadership. Biblical prophets openly decry political relationships between Israelite and non-Israelite powers, describing those who do so as immoral and an affront to their God. But these rules do not seem to apply to Daniel. According to the rest of chapter 6, the king clearly likes Daniel and wants to ensure his safety, so much so that he, the king, tries to change a law that he knows will directly affect his prized Israelite subordinate. Verse 4 tells us Daniel is so good at his job of enforcing the king and empire's will that Darius wants to appoint him over the entire kingdom. The fact of the matter is Daniel becomes the very thing Nebuchadnezzar wanted him to be in chapter 1: someone versed in the language and mindset of Israelite enemies. One would think Daniel's endearment toward imperial power would prompt interpretive backlash: Why does Daniel behave without question or defiance?

We must address the profound lack of scholarly critique against Daniel's imperial appeasement. Daniel 6's interpreters display little concern about Daniel's rise to and sustenance of imperial power. In some cases, the avoidance is downright flippant, or, worse, readers hold Daniel as a model citizen guided by his deity. For example, Miller admires Daniel's ability to appease Darius and credits it as evidence for God's working in and through the Israelite.[10] Likewise, Portier-Young makes Daniel an ideal for "not only the importance of prayer in time of religious oppression, but also the courage to worship God openly and in defiance of the king's law, whatever the cost."[11] Daniel does take a bold stance in practicing his religion, but the motives behind his actions remain opaque and solely his. Further, he does not seek to overthrow his oppressors. Everything Daniel does only grants him additional power.

Verse 5 describes the efforts of the superintendents and provincial governors to sabotage Daniel's success, but their efforts initially prove fruitless, as "no negligence and fault could be found in him." They hatch a plan to use Daniel's religious convictions against him. They urge the king to "enforce an injunction" preventing any person "a petition from anyone" other than the king for thirty days. Breaking said injunction is punishable with death by lions. This "plot" that Daniel's competitors hatch is foolish at best and pointless at worst. It is foolish because it is thoroughly unenforceable: Is someone to supervise every person in the kingdom from the moment the edict takes effect? Who gets to decide if someone broke the law, and on what grounds? It is pointless because the law is so unclear that it basically means nothing: What exactly does "requesting a petition" mean? The text itself lacks specificity, as the Aramaic here stems from the verbal root בעה. It simply means "to petition" or "to request." Theoretically, the king's appointed advisors could be asking him to prevent people from seeking assistance from anyone other than the king. Aramaic simplicity does not prevent translators from theologizing this word, as the Message translation, NRSV, CEB, NIV, and NLT erroneously render it as some form of "pray" or "prayer."[12]

Darius signs the injunction despite its considerable unintelligibility. Here again we return to the ongoing theme of incompetent kings in Daniel: Darius rubber-stamps a binding law that affects everyone, without any apparent thought toward its enforcement or its implications. Further, at verse 9 those pressing for the law's inception remind Darius that once signed the document "cannot be changed in accordance with the laws of the Medes and Persians." This comes up again later in the chapter, as Darius expresses anguish over Daniel falling victim to an edict that he, the king, cannot change. So, the real question is this: Who is in charge? Who runs the kingdom? One could argue the king's advisors run things, as their word carries power and compels Darius' decision. Yet they claim that once Darius sets the law no changes may come to it "in accordance with the laws of the Medes and Persians." This claim has no historical merit, though that does not stop scholars from trying to make it so.[13] From a narrative standpoint, either the advisors lack general legal competence, or they fabricate this position. Either way, the king is foolish for allowing it to happen.

The king's edict takes effect, and, according to verse 11, Daniel knows of its creation and implementation but responds by praying as usual and not in secret. Continuing his normal religious ritual practices is an act of defiance, but stopping his opposition there underlines Daniel's individualist passivity. Why does he not defend his faith even further by defending his people? Why not do more? Why not use the considerable power at his disposal to change the Babylonian system? If Daniel, as scholars claim, finds favor in God's eyes, why not use that divine favor to make real change?

Darius' officials predictably "catch" Daniel in prayer and scurry to Darius, like playground tattletales.[14] They share that Daniel broke the king's edict and should face punishment, giving the king "much distress." The text is unclear as to why Darius is anxious about Daniel's fate, but, if we strip away any theologizing behind the king's motives, his affection for Daniel stems from how much Daniel helped him and his kingdom. We have no reason to think the king frets Daniel's predicament beyond what Daniel did for the kingdom, as Daniel's faith and piety are unrelated to the king's anxiety. There is an interpretive strand that backs this approach, with readers like seventeenth-century Christian thinker John Mayer arguing, "[Darius'] grief for Daniel therefore was not because he was so godly . . . but because he was so wise a man, and so he thought that he should have more loss of him than of all his princes besides."[15]

Realist positions like Mayer's gained traction, with Goldingay arguing Darius is angry at Daniel for ignoring the edict, the king's inner circle that crafted the law, and even himself "for being manipulated by them into becoming the victim of his own power and authority."[16] Yet still others favor more apologetic and theological orientations. S. Miller claims Darius "understood that he had been duped by these evil men," and Duguid paint Darius as "sorry to lose a faithful and honest servant."[17] And yet Daniel 6 says nothing to support any of these claims. No interpreter knows why the king experiences distress. Anything beyond that is merely speculative.

Speaking of speculative, the boldness with which Christians approach Darius' words at verse 17 once again uncovers palatable theological assumptions. Dale Davis makes Darius' plea of "May your god, whom you serve continually, deliver you" into an assertion of theological certainty, saying it underscores "that Daniel's God is the only one who can—and will—deliver him."[18] S. Miller projects his assumptions onto the text itself:

> Nevertheless, the fact that Darius believed it was even possible that Daniel could be saved indicates that the prophet must have been telling the king of the great miracles the God of Israel had performed. Daniel's testimony not only would have included Yahweh's miracles in Babylon but also wonders from Israel's past like the dividing of the sea when Israel escaped from Egypt.[19]

Goldingay's approach to the king's wish is much more nuanced and accurate to the text: "The lack of clarity over whether Darius offers a challenge to God, or a statement of faith, or a wistful hope functions to invite the hearer to decide what he or she would mean in a situation of this kind."[20] This reading is indeed much truer to the text, as Christian interpreters tend to overlay their interpretation as normative and operative, leaving no space for interpretive possibility. Because the reality is, like Daniel, Darius had no clue that Daniel would survive the night; he may just be bidding his loyal servant farewell. If Darius has any inclination he will see Daniel again the next day, he does not show it here. We can know only what Darius says. Claiming to know what he means moves the reader beyond the role of interpreter and into that of a psychic, capable of discerning the thoughts of characters on the written page.

Daniel 6 offers nothing by way of Daniel's thoughts or inclinations about his current predicament. In fact, Daniel does not speak until verse 22, and even then he lavishes praise upon the king that just tried killing him. We only see Daniel's silent ritual and hear others discussing Daniel in verses 1–21, which again raises the question: Whose chapter is this? Based on space dedicated to words and thoughts, it is certainly not Daniel. Thus far, Daniel's place is like that of an extended cameo, making him merely a means to talk about the political interplay between a king and his subordinates that dominates the narrative. Readers learn more about the king's thoughts than any other character, so it seems yet again the book's narrative cannot help but make the king its central focus.

We stand wondering if we are meant to sympathize with the ruler that can barely run his kingdom, but this connection seems odd, as the likelihood of any reader being a monarch is highly unlikely. Such narrative ambiguities pit Daniel against interpretive strands that read the book as denouncing imperial power, as chapter 6 paints yet another affectionate picture of its non-Israelite despot.[21] Newsom argues we get Darius' perspective instead of Daniel's for added suspense and dramatic effect.[22] Yet the claim of increasing suspense still makes us again wonder why we should care about the king in general, much less how he thinks and feels. Chapter 6 is overtly sympathetic toward Darius, making him the hero determined to save Daniel even though Daniel is in a quite literal death pit because of a foolish law Darius enacted.

Despite his hesitations, Darius seals the den's entrance in verse 18. The text does not say why he seals the entrance, but such absent textual evidence only leaves space for readers to insert motive where there is none. Jerome argues the king "wanted to deliver Daniel from danger by ingenuity and strategy rather than by exerting his royal authority."[23] Ephrem argues Darius sealed the den to avoid the spread of fraudulent rumors of Daniel possibly sneaking out or receiving additional aid.[24] The text says nothing of this. However, Ephrem's position pales compared to Towner's citations of detailed "parallels" between Jesus' death, burial, and resurrection, going as far as to say in both stories that "the presumed dead reappears from the tomb, vindicated by God's saving power."[25] Modern interpreters follow this trajectory, like Hartman and Di Lella, who argue, "A parallel for this can be found in this sealing of the stone at the entrance of the tomb of Jesus."[26]

Once the king seals the den, we get more of Darius' whereabouts. We learn he goes to his palace, fasts through the night, and cannot find sleep. Verse 19 doubles down on Darius' fasting, saying that "no food was brought to him, and sleep fled from him," making sure the reader knows Darius ate nothing (and thereby implying that simply saying he fasted is insufficient). Verse 20 says that the king, despite not sleeping, "arose in the daylight and in haste" went to check Daniel's condition. One cannot help but consider how genuine the king's anxieties toward Daniel are, as he waits an entire night before checking in on his prisoner. These verses present the king as powerless and in a situation beyond his control, but the opposite is true: the king carries complete control by virtue of being king. As stated earlier, nothing (and no one) can stop him from changing the slipshod edict he made. Why does the king not stop the madness to prevent bloodshed and loss, as he clearly resents Daniel's current situation.

Interpretations and receptions of the king's anxieties highlight the overly apologetic nature of Christian readings. Goldingay suggests Darius may be "praying against the effectiveness of his action," a position that he buttresses by citing Otto Plöger's *Das Buch Daniel*.[27] Goldingay's use of Plöger is curious because Plöger argues the king makes an indirect wish on Daniel's behalf without any direct reference toward Darius engaging in prayer. Towner takes the king's unease to make connections between Daniel and Jesus, claiming that just as Pilate skirted responsibility for Jesus' death so too does Darius neglect his role in the situation.[28] Such Jesus-focused apologetics on Darius' behalf reflect a more modern evangelical interpretive stream, as earlier readers like Theodoret argue that Darius' behavior throughout the chapter is "a mark of cowardice that he was not so affected as to counter the accusers and invoke his royal authority and power to save the wronged."[29]

Verses 21–22 are quite odd. The king runs to the den and immediately cries out to Daniel, prompting Daniel's immediate response. Yet the story neglects one major detail: How does the stone get moved? How can Darius speak to Daniel, and how can Daniel respond if the stone still blocks the entrance? Gone is the seal so intricately described in verse 18, leaving open the possibility of someone having tampered with the seal and removed the stone. Based solely on what the text says, Daniel could have gotten out, spent the night elsewhere, then returned to the lair just in time for Darius' arrival. What is more bizarre is how neither Darius nor interpreters question how this conversation happens.[30] One could argue for a possible redaction and claim the stone's removal became inconsequential to the larger narrative, but no evidence exists to support that position.[31] Either this stone was far from impressive in terms of size and weight, or Daniel and the king can converse through solid matter.

Despite the glaring narrative gaff, Darius cries with anguish at verse 21 and calls Daniel's deity "the living god." Daniel responds like a textbook sycophant with "King, live forever!" There is much to unpack here. Darius' declaration is a profound power display, as he uses this moment with Daniel to make a theopolitical statement by paying respect to Daniel's God. Many interpreters see this as justification for everything that precedes and proceeds the declaration, as this foreign non-Israelite king now believes in Daniel's god. But we must remember this is the same king who issues a degree with such flippancy that it got Daniel into this situation in the first place. What makes us think we can now trust Darius' words as binding and trustworthy? Previous kings in chapters 1–5 swore allegiance to Daniel's god as their stories concluded, only to have the situation reset with each proceeding chapter. What, if anything, has changed? And considering what the king says pales in comparison to Daniel's response. In verse 22, Daniel greets Darius, who sent him to death, by exalting monarchical power. Only after he praises the king does Daniel describe in verse 23 the divine protection used to save his life. This establishes a dire and problematic hierarchy as Daniel praises Darius, an earthly king, before crediting his deity for his safety and survival. Once again, the king and his rule get narrative priority.

Daniel argues his survival confirms his innocence, which sets an odd precedence. Daniel broke a law, which is radically different from being entrapped by an unjust law, prompting readers to reconsider the very notions of innocence, guilt, and the nature of law itself.[32] On top of this, Darius' response in freeing Daniel shows that Darius can change and bend laws as he sees fit. Why did he not do this earlier? Just because Daniel survived one night with the lions does not change his legal status. The edict did not say, "Throw him in for a night and see if he survives," like some bizarre Salem witch trial scenario.

This behavior further highlights the king's weakness. Instead of changing the law to avoid possible bloodshed, Darius uses Daniel as a pawn in a divine "High Noon" style standoff. Darius is not determined to save anything or anyone; he simply awaits an outcome. If Daniel survives,

Darius knows to respect Daniel's god. If Daniel dies, then the king knows Daniel's god is absent and ineffective. Interpreters flock toward reading the scenario as joyous and vindictive of God's power and Daniel's piety. Chrysostom makes Daniel's survival a proof of concept for faith: "When things are turning out adversely, then we ought to believe nothing adverse is done but all things in due order."[33] Cyril's faith-soaked response supersedes Chrysostom: "[Daniel 6] affirms that without faith it is impossible to please [God]. For when will an individual resolve to serve God, unless he believes that 'he is a giver of reward.' . . . Faith is an eye that enlightens every conscience and imparts understanding."[34] Calvin, Heinrich Bullinger, Mayer, and Melanchthon all follow this kind of interpretive trajectory and read chapter 6 as a reward for Daniel's faith. These past Christian perspectives are only a drop in the bucket compared to how many contemporary Christians read Daniel 6 as a sort of faith manifesto.[35]

The most alarming thing that happens in chapter 6 is its conclusion. Daniel 6 pivots from an apparent celebration of monarchical piety and divine sovereignty to a soulless massacre. At verse 25, the king speaks, and the men who concocted the scheme are thrown to their deaths, along with their sons and wives. The lions kill entire families, and the text celebrates their deaths by highlighting this act of sheer brutality in saying that "they did not reach the den's bottom before the lions overpowered them and crushed their bones to pieces." Darius' behavior in verses 26–28 underscores the chapter's bitter sense of irony as he writes to all peoples, nations, and languages with wishes for abundant peace under Daniel's god because Daniel's god "delivers and recuses, and he does signs and wonders in the heavens and the earth, for he saved Daniel from the lions' hand." Darius takes the time to praise God and God's power immediately after slaughter.

Such horrors are sufficiently terrible, but how Christians overlook and outright reject the chapter's ending is more shocking. Children's Bibles present Daniel's removal from the pit as the story's ending and ignore what happens next. For example, *The Early Reader's Bible* ends its version of Daniel 6 with Daniel and his accusers standing happy arm-in-arm.[36] A more tween- and teen-friendly text called *The Action Bible* presents selected biblical stories with animation in the style of a comic book, and it too takes a creative misstep as it presents the king sending just the nobles to their deaths without their sons and wives.[37]

These tactless revisions to Daniel 6's conclusion speak to the romanticized interpretive lenses Christian readers employ. Instead of engaging what the chapter's end means for the rest of the narrative, Christians actively avoid it. We read Daniel 6 how we want it to be rather than engaging the theological and ethical considerations it carries. We know nothing more about the people the king sends to their death beyond their wanting this edict to be decreed. One could argue the king wants them dead for manipulating him, but this fails to condemn killing their wives and sons, too. On top of that, the king sidesteps his responsibility and culpability in enacting and enforcing the decree. This law never takes effect without Darius' approval, making him far from passive. Further, Daniel fails to stop these thoughtless and needless deaths. But reading how Christians celebrate this moment as a show of divine power moves their deaths beyond tasteless and into the realm of wanton cruelty.

Joe Sprinkle cites Romans as justification: "This punishment is an appropriate expression of God's judgment through human government and is poetic justice."[38] Tanner takes up a similar position, arguing that their deaths are "miraculous" because the lions "were hungry killers, and Daniel's survival underscores the miraculous nature of God's intervention."[39] Seow, like Tanner, says the slaughter proves Daniel's "divinely wrought miracle," and Smith-Christopher cites it as "the thoroughness of the miraculous acts of God."[40] Smith-Christopher rightfully associates these deaths with "oppressive, evil actions" but leaves the conversation without really pressing this observation. Contemporary apologetic Christian readings diminish against the background of earlier Christian readers like Jerome who argue that everything in Daniel 6 happens "amid barbarian peoples" so "that the worship and religion of the only God may be proclaimed."[41] This thorough dehumanization continues throughout Christian receptions, and I could list many, many other scholars with congruous theological positions. But that list would erroneously move our focus away from the reality of what happens in the text: innocent people die thanks to the king's ineptitude and Daniel's silence.

Chapter 6 ends as it began, with Darius making a decree, except this time the decree praises Daniel's god as "living," "enduring," and ruling an indestructible dominion. He orders everyone throughout the kingdom "to tremble and fear Daniel's God" because of Daniel's deliverance. Like preceding chapters, Daniel finds prosperity in this foreign kingdom. Darius' words are exactly what any God-fearing reader wants to hear, as it ties the story into a nice, neat bow. We must remember this is the same king whose fickle words led to the unjust murder of innocent civilians. Daniel 6 leaves us with the brutal realities of one king's power going unchecked, but one could argue that Daniel survives thanks to his steadfast faith. Such a reading undercuts the lives lost and the striking absence of the deity throughout the chapter. Yes, people talk about God in these verses, but, beyond that, God's absence stands marked. Daniel survives, but at what cost?

6.3 So What?

The many theological and ethical difficulties in Daniel 6 make it ripe for preaching, teaching, and ministerial consideration. A most pressing theological issue is God's absence. Darius talks about Daniel's god and lavishes considerable praise upon the deity, and Daniel attributes his survival to being "found blameless before [God]," but, despite this effusive praise, God does nothing in this chapter. Gone is the God of Exodus who intervenes and commands an imperial ruler liberate God's people. Nowhere is the deity in Genesis 1–3 who speaks creation into being and uses God's own hands to mold the first humans. This chapter talks about God without ever letting God speak or act, and yet Christian receptions would make readers believe God has an active and vibrant presence throughout. Every commentator mentioned above talks at length about God's sovereign saving power, using Daniel's life as an example of God's willingness to reward devout faith. But they fail to articulate how they project their understanding of God into the text to fit their larger theological worldviews. As stated above, characters in chapter 6 talk about God, leaving us to wonder what God may be thinking and feeling in the moment.

This narrative absence paired with interpretive injection highlights a deeply felt question: Where is God in the silence of everyday life? Christians frequently wax poetically about God's eternal presence and looking for God where it seems God is not. Such theological inclinations sound good in theory but fall apart in practice. Christians use language of "trial and testing" to explain circumstances like the ones Daniel faces, arguing it can motivate us in our struggles. Duguid's theological assessment summarizes this perspective with succinct accuracy:

> Daniel endured the test of the lions' den, emerging safely out the other side, because God judged him and found him not guilty; as a result, the lions, which acted as God's agents of judgment, did not harm him. However, the unbelievers who plotted against Daniel were found guilty and crushed by God's judgment.[42]

In similar fashion, Heinrich Bullinger's theological flippancy about these deaths is disturbing: "God next, by his own power, brought about the condemnation of Daniel's enemies to the lions, where they were torn to small pieces along with their families."[43] Ephrem the Syrian is overtly vindictive:

> Since a simple punishment was not sufficient for those culprits, in order to balance the offense they had brought against a righteous man, after being condemned to the same punishment, they were thrown to the beasts together with their wives and children.[44]

Thought not quite as direct, modern interpreters follow Ephrem and tread closely toward celebrating these deaths and attributing them to God as divine success.[45] None of these theological statements have textual merit. Innocent people died because of the king's orders; God's judgment has nothing to do with it. Daniel survives the lions' den and attributes that to God, but nowhere in the text does it say it is a test, much less one divinely ordained as a measure of piety. Chapter 6 is merely a sequence of unfolding events to which people ascribe divine purpose and meaning.

We Christians are just as quick to attribute successes to the divine as we are great tragedies. For example, in 2010 after the devastating earthquake that rocked Haiti and killed over one hundred thousand people, popular evangelist Pat Robertson claimed it was God's punishing the country for making a "pact with the devil" in exchange for independence from the French in 1804.[46] Robertson, a known political and theological firebrand, is not alone in this approach to history. In 1845, according to journalist John O'Sullivan, the United States colonized what would become the American West according to "our manifest destiny to overspread the continent allotted by Providence for the free development of our yearly multiplying millions."[47] Stretching back further, the idea of Christianity and the United States being directly in line with "God's Plan" precedes the country's establishment. Christopher Columbus spoke to his colonizing motivations in 1492: "It was the Lord who put into my mind (I could feel His hand upon me) the fact that it would be possible to sail from here to the Indies." And these snippets do not even begin to reckon with the horrors of enslavement and war that this supposedly "Christian" nation wrought upon the world.

We Christians in America believe everything that benefits us is God's will. We throw anyone and anything else down into the lions' den of history, leaving them to die in the wake of our successes. Just because someone says something is part of "God's will" does not make it so; in fact, one could argue the opposite, as an estimated fifty-six million people died from 1492 to 1600 due to European Christian-driven colonization.[48]

Slavery and the transatlantic slave trade killed fifteen million adults and children.[49] Knowing the reality of these and many other Christian-motivated atrocities, then claiming stories like Daniel 6 reinforce God's sovereign control of history, is dangerously naïve and myopic.[50]

Particularly damning about the atrocities perpetrated in Daniel 6 and by Christians in Europe and United States is it was all legal. Darius attempts to dodge responsibility by saying the law is the law but just because someone codifies something into law does not make it just. Further, sometimes the people who conceive of, make, and then enforce laws are corrupt and evil at worst or incompetent at best. Far too often, laws stand in direct opposition to that which is right and just, and that is exactly what happens in Daniel 6. Daniel's punishment and the destruction of his accuser's families are painfully legal. One cannot help but hear echoes of former president Richard Nixon's infamous words, "Well, when the president does it, that means that it is not illegal." Many Americans still (rightfully) get angry at Nixon's words, but far too many American Christians default to divine justice that benefits very few. Just as Darius traps himself in laws of his own making, we Christians trap God by our own rules and our laws, making God immoveable and stagnant.

Finally, we must engage the profound human inaction in Daniel 6. The king does nothing when he could do something, anything, to prevent Daniel's predicament. Instead of using the considerable means at his disposal to nullify the spurious law, the king commands that Daniel be thrown into the lions' den. Darius then retreats to his chamber and thinks about how he hopes no harm befalls Daniel. Similarly, Daniel, fresh off surviving the night in such a way that makes Darius praise the Israelite's god, stands back and does nothing while lions eat families alive. Both Darius and Daniel are guilty of doing nothing when they could and should have done something. Yes, the king experiences considerable distress at Daniel's punishment, and, yes, Daniel gives praise to God for his protection, but stopping there rings like the hollow sentiment expressed when contemporary Christian circles respond to tragedy with "thoughts and prayers."

The modern Christian landscape, especially on social media, seems to live and die by using "thoughts and prayers" as the solution to all our problems. We "pray," and we "think" about what a better world might look like, but far too many Christians do nothing to bring about actual substantive action. News of school shootings and countless deaths at the hands of gun violence inundate American Christians, yet we allow political and religious leaders to pacify our pain with quotes and comments about "thoughts and prayers" for affected families. Such inaction points to one of Daniel 6's most compelling messages: we sit back and read of the king being tricked and duped into crafting a fallacious, baseless law but never ask if we are the ones being tricked and duped by the limitations we put upon God and ourselves. Like Darius sealing the den with his ring to prove that he was there and authorized it, if we Christians fail to act when called upon we leave behind only the silent complacency that prayer without action unveils.

7
Daniel 7 Reconsidered

7.1 Translation

1 In the first year[1] of Belshazzar, king of Babylon,[2] Daniel saw a
dream and visions of his head[3] while upon his bed; then he wrote
down the dream.[4] The beginning of the account:
2 Daniel responded and said, "I was watching in my vision in the
night, and lo! Four winds of heaven were stirring up the great sea.
3 And four great beasts, coming from the sea, each one different
from the other.
4 The first is like a lion with wings of an eagle. As I watched, its
wings were plucked off, and it was lifted from the ground and was
made to stand[5] upon its feet like a human, and the mind of a man
was given to it.
5 And behold! Another beast, a second one, that is like a bear,
raised on one side with three ribs in its mouth between its teeth, and
thus was said to it: 'Arise! Consume much flesh!'
6 After this, behold! I saw another,[6] like a leopard, and the beast
had four bird wings upon its back and had four heads, and dominion[7] was given to it.
7 After this, I saw in the visions of the night, and behold! A fourth
beast, fearsome and frightening and exceedingly strong, and it had
great iron teeth,[8] devouring and crushing, and trampling the remnants under its feet, and it was different than all the other beasts
before it, with ten horns on its head.
8 While I was considering[9] the horns, behold! Another smaller
horn emerged[10] between them, and three of the former horns were
eradicated before it. And behold! This horn had eyes like the eyes of
a man along with a mouth, speaking great things.

9 I was looking when
thrones were set down
and the Ancient of Days was seated;
his garment was white as snow,
and the hair of his head was like pure wool.
His seat was flames of fire.
And its wheels were burning fire.
10 A river of fire was proceeding
and going forth from before him.
A thousand of thousands served him,
and ten thousand times ten thousand attended to him.
The court was seated,
and documents were opened.

11 I watched at that time because of the sound of the great words which the horn was speaking; I was watching until the beast was put to death and its body perished and it was given to the burning fire.

12 As for the rest of the beasts,[11] their dominion was taken away, and a prolonging in life was given to them until a season and time.

13 While I was watching in the visions of the night
and behold, coming with clouds of the heavens,
I saw one like a human being.
And he came to the Ancient of Days
and was presented before him.
14 And dominion was given to him, along with
glory and kingship,
that all the peoples, nations, and languages
should serve him.
His dominion is an eternal dominion
that will not pass away,
and his kingship
will never be destroyed.

15 As for me, Daniel, my spirit was distressed within me, and the visions of my head alarmed me.

16 I approached one of the attendants and asked him the truth concerning of all this.[12] And he said that he would disclose to me the interpretation of the matter:[13]

17 'As for these four beasts, four kings shall arise from the earth.

18 And the holy ones of the Most High shall receive the kingdom, and they shall possess the kingdom forever and ever.'

19 Then I desired to know about the fourth beast which was different from all others, exceedingly terrifying with iron teeth and bronze nails,[14] eating, crushing, and trampling the remnants under its feet.[15]

[20] And about the ten horns on its head and concerning the one that came up and to make room for which three fell, this horn with eyes and a mouth that spoke arrogantly for this one seemed greater than the others.

[21] As I looked, this horn made war against the righteous ones and was prevailing against them,

[22] until the Ancient of Days came and gave[16] judgment on behalf of the righteous ones of the Most High. And the time came, and the righteous ones gained possession of the kingdom.

> [23] He said thusly: 'As for the fourth beast,
> there shall be a fourth kingdom on the earth
> that will be different[17] from all other kingdoms;[18]
> it will devour all the earth
> and will trample it and crush it to pieces.
> [24] As for the ten horns,[19]
> from this kingdom ten kings will arise,
> and another will arise after them.
> This one will be different[20] from the former ones
> and will put down three kings.
> [25] And he will speak words against the Most High,
> and he will wear out the righteous ones of the Most High,
> and he will attempt to change the sacred time and law;
> and they shall be given into his hand[21]
> for a time, times,[22] and a half a time.
> [26] Then the court will be seated,
> and his dominion shall be taken away;
> it shall be consumed and completely destroyed.
> [27] The kingship and dominion
> and greatness of kingdoms under the heavens
> shall be given to righteous people[23] of the Most High;
> their reign shall be an eternal reign,
> and all dominions will serve and obey them.'

[28] Here is where this account ends. I, Daniel, my thoughts greatly alarmed me, and my countenance changed within me, and I kept this matter in my heart."

7.2 Reading against the Grain

The common Christian approach to Daniel 7–12, regardless of theological and denominational orientation, argues that these chapters shift in genre from Daniel 1–6's general narratives to an apocalyptic orientation. My reading very much agrees with labeling Daniel 7–12 as apocalyptic, as each chapter's tone, content, structure, and execution reflects the genre's fundamental elements.[24] Where my approach differs lies in what these apocalyptic chapters can mean for Christians and the church in general. To start, we must dig through and call out Christian assumptions projected upon Daniel as an apocalyptic text. Such assumptions severely limit interpretations, as Christian readers manipulate Daniel 7–12 to fit their circumstances and agendas. Simply put, we Christians make Daniel 7–12 about us. Pushing against such Christian self-aggrandizement lets divergent readings surface and illuminate possibilities for a renewed sense of how apocalyptic biblical texts can function. Because as the dominant readings show, Daniel's second half is in dire need of reconsideration.

The Christianization of Daniel through Christian interpreters happens early and often with striking consistency. Hippolytus wrote one of the oldest extant Christian commentaries on Daniel, and he makes the apocalyptic chapters especially Christian-centric when he uses Daniel 7–12 to chart a trajectory of the antichrist leading to Jesus' second coming. Cyril of Jerusalem, Theodoret of Cyrus, Justin Martyr, Andrew Willet, Martin Luther, John Calvin, John Mayer, and many, many other early Christian interpreters follow that same path. Making Daniel 7–12 about Jesus' return gets baked into Christian reception histories and continues through the work of scholars like Sharon Pace, Tanner, Towner, Duguid, S. Miller, Goldingay, and other contemporary Christians. Reading the works of these scholars makes one think Jesus is central to Daniel, but, despite Christian projections, Daniel 7–12 says nothing of the Christian Messiah. This reading pushes against and rejects Jesus-centric approaches.

Turning to the text itself, Daniel 7:1 opens like Daniel 1–6 and introduces the ruling king. In this case, Belshazzar is in his first reigning year, and Daniel experiences "a dream and visions of his head while upon his bed." Right from the start we have another literary signpost: the last we heard of Belshazzar is at his death in Daniel 5. But at Daniel 7:1, the Babylonian king is alive and well. Unlike Daniel 1–6, Daniel 7's king plays no role in what unfolds. He never speaks, nor does he have sway over the proceedings; he appears in the first verse, then disappears until Daniel 8. So, why does Daniel 7 mention him? Workable solutions lie in how verse 1 notes the chapter unfolds in the first year of Belshazzar's reign, making Belshazzar a demarcation of time. Unlike the more flexible timetables in Daniel 1–6, mentioning Belshazzar offers a much narrower window for Daniel 7's literary historical context.

Like all things related to historical chronologies presented in the Bible, there is much controversy around whether Daniel 7 was written and actually takes place in the first year of Belshazzar's reign. This is highly unlikely. For starters, according to nonbiblical historical sources, Belshazzar never received the title of king. His highest formal title was vice-regent for his father, Nabonidus.[25] Mindful of this, we have two possibilities for why Daniel 7 calls him "king": the author thought Belshazzar was at one time a king and is incorrect, or the text is doing something else with its use of history. Let us consider both, as doing so highlights how dominant interpretive strands reconcile this historical inconsistency.

Evangelical receptions reject, ignore, or sidestep Daniel 7 misidentifying Belshazzar as king. Duguid simply avoids the issue, while S. Miller, Towner, and Goldingay argue Belshazzar's first year in power was 553 BCE because Nabonidus' third year was 556 BCE. What makes such conclusions peculiar is how scholars supporting this 553 BCE argument use the same evidence other interpreters use to claim Belshazzar was never king.[26] How can the same evidence produce two contradictory conclusions? It is possible through yet another case of interpretation, only this time the thing interpreted is archeological evidence. Such interpretive inconsistencies do not change the fact that, according to widely accepted historical evidence, Belshazzar never ruled Babylon. This means regardless of where one lands in relation to Belshazzar, biblical chronology, and historical evidence Daniel 7 is incorrect in making Belshazzar king.

Despite never ruling Babylon, Belshazzar did exist according to historical records. Belshazzar lived and worked in Babylon during the sixth century. Thus, making Belshazzar king in Daniel 7 gives the chapter a specific sixth-century Babylonian literary orientation. This means when Christian interpreters make Daniel 7 fit their contemporary circumstances, they neglect the text's presented context. Daniel 7 does not describe historical events connected to the United States or current political powers; claiming that it does is blatant interpreter projection. Reading Daniel 7 in line with this Babylonian literary context makes ideas and images that Christian readers deem mysterious and cryptic quite the opposite. A Babylonian backdrop lifts Daniel above Christian-centric eschatological parameters and makes it something more. Despite such interpretive possibilities, we need not look far into the chapter to see just how quickly and consistently we Christians project our circumstances onto Daniel 7, Babylonian narrative context be damned.

Unlike Daniel 2 and 4 with Nebuchadnezzar, Daniel, not the king, experiences dreams and visions. Verse 1 says Daniel writes down what he sees in "a dream and visions of his head while upon his bed." Daniel not only dreams, implying he sees things as he slept, but he also experiences visions. What he writes down is a combination of what Daniel saw when he slept and when he was awake. Dreams and visions in Babylon and throughout the ancient Levant were common vehicles for deity-to-human communication. Babylonian cosmology operated in a hierarchical sense, in that humans could not transgress the divine realm, but deities can (and often did) communicate or step into the human world. So, in short, dreams and visions were methods of communication between the gods and humans.[27] Biblical dreams and visions are no different, as the Bible reflects the social, cultural, and religious contexts of the people who produced it. Thus, contemporary Christian interpreters would be wise to consult and consider ancient Levant literature in interpreting Daniel's dream-visions within the book's larger context. But this is not the case, as Christian scholars and pastors situate the contents of Daniel 7 within our respective contexts with considerable regularity. Reading Daniel 7 alongside Christian interpretations highlights these interpretive projections to emphasize that we Christians talk more about what we want this text to say as opposed to reading the text itself.

Verses 1 and 2 flow together with a nice interplay between the chapter's use of "dream" and "vision." Verse 1 lets us know Daniel saw both the dream and visions "while upon his bed," followed by verse 2 saying Daniel watched his "vision in the night." The narrative doubles down on Daniel experiencing these things during the traditional evening sleeping period, telling us this was not something that struck Daniel during the daylight hours. Interpreters, both ancient and modern, build their readings around what Daniel sees, but the text speaks to the importance of the divine using night dreams and visions to convey some sort of message. Daniel did nothing to receive or channel what he sees. God chose Daniel, not the other way around.

The first thing Daniel sees in verse 2 is "four winds of heaven" that "were stirring up the great sea." The "four winds" and "great sea" introduce plentiful literary similarities between Daniel 7 and Babylonian literature, as these images and others scattered throughout the chapter are rife with symbolism. The "four winds" is a widespread literary image in Levant literature, like in *Enuma Elish* when the Babylonian god Marduk corrals the four winds to subdue the water-chaos goddess Tiamat. This kind of Levant chaotic sea imagery symbolizes political chaos, social disorder, and the metaphysical unknown.[28] Biblical wind-and-sea imagery carry this symbolism as well when we learn the monsters emerging from Daniel's sea are agents of chaos and destruction. This is not to suggest that Daniel's authors/compilers intentionally used such imagery as a direct callback to nonbiblical literature. It does, however, highlight intersections of biblical and Babylonian themes.

A basic understanding of these themes makes Daniel 7's imagery shockingly common, but, despite this commonality, Christian receptions fail to do more than acknowledge the Bible's surrounding cultural milieu.[29] There is no particular reason why Christians neglect how surrounding cultures shape a text and traditions therein, but it is possible such disregard reflects ongoing interpretive streams. Jerome, Theodoret, Hippolytus, Tertullian, and Origen cite Daniel's Babylonian connections, but their readings make Daniel neutral, coasting spotless and without blemish through that environment. Later, Calvin, Luther, Bullinger, Mayer, and Melanchthon follow similar tracts as, in their eyes, Daniel unfolds in Babylon but carries no markers of Babylonian ideas and images.[30]

What unfolds in verses 3 through 14 is the bulk of Daniel's vision as "four great beasts" emerge from the chaotic, primordial sea. A winged lion precedes a bear with grotesque teeth, followed by a multiheaded winged leopard, then a "frightening and exceedingly strong" fourth beast with iron teeth. These images shock Daniel and cause him great fear and confusion. We cannot fault Daniel for his fear, as these four beasts prompt similar responses from Christian interpreters. Nothing about these beasts is what one could call "normal," as, for starters, each one emerges from the sea. To state the obvious, lions, bears, and leopards are not sea creatures, and nothing about the fourth beast suggests it calls the sea waters "home." So, seeing these land creatures emerge from water immediately disorients Daniel. On top of that, the physical composition of these animals highlights a world thrown into chaos, like Babylonian stories of warring chaos monsters fighting for the power to rule creation. The lion and leopard have wings, meaning they are capable of flight. The lion morphs into a human-animal hybrid, as it stands upright and receives "the mind of a man." The bear lounges on its side and has three ribs in its mouth among its teeth, perhaps to indicate it recently finished eating a large animal or that its teeth are so large and so numerous, it is as if bones fill the bear's mouth. Not only can the leopard fly, but it has four heads, each with a mouth capable of consumption and destruction. But nothing compares to the fourth beast, a being that prompts Daniel to forgo describing what kind of animal it is in favor of simply calling it "fearsome and frightening and exceedingly strong." Each beast brings pain, suffering, and death, as it seems their only purpose is to reign with terror, consume flesh, and destroy.

Daniel's macabre scene lodges itself in the reader's memory, opening seemingly endless interpretive possibilities. If, as many Christians claim, Daniel reflects the might and power of divine sovereignty, the theology of this scene raises more questions than it answers. Verse 2 tells us the "four winds of heaven" stir up the great sea, making the sea produce these monsters. The beasts themselves do not manifest the winds, meaning that an outside force pushes the first domino that makes the rest fall. So, this "first mover" is either God or some unknown, unnamed source. This entity's identity is crucial, as the use of passive Aramaic verbs throughout the chapter suggest ongoing intervention and interaction.[31] The problem here lies not with the notion of sovereignty itself; what matters is this unnamed intervener's actions cause much destruction so that Daniel stands shocked and terrified. Is Daniel's god the one responsible for such wanton destruction? Or is it another deity? If it is Daniel's god, what does that mean for the divine's role in history as Daniel presents it? If it is another deity, does it contest with Daniel's god for supremacy? Such theological hesitations do not stop Christian justifications that render the surface problem moot without reckoning with the consequences therein.[32] We may want to project a sense of divine control on what Daniel sees, but doing so only ignores the considerable suffering these creatures bring.

Dissecting how Christians read these beasts uncovers a considerable lack of critical theological engagement, especially regarding the beasts' actions and their repercussions. Modern interpretations follow a historical paradigm to identify each beast with a particular ruler or kingdom: the first beast is Babylon/Nebuchadnezzar, the second is Persia/Cyrus, the third is Alexander the Great's Greece/Alexander himself, and the fourth is an otherwise unknown, unspecified entity. Before we dig into the quagmire that is Christian receptions of the fourth beast, let us first wrestle with the origins of this "animals = historical kingdoms" paradigm. This "four beasts, four kingdoms" approach is the unquestioned gold standard in mainline biblical scholarship, both ancient and modern. But like all receptions and interpretations, the four-kingdom approach takes the text and ties it to specific historical circumstances without factual support beyond a given interpreter's particular political agenda. One might balk at questioning the Babylon, Persia, Greece, and unknown fourth kingdom approach, but the reality is Christian readers following this interpretive path are merely using precedent established by Hippolytus' *Commentary on Daniel* from the third century CE. This means contemporary Christian readers who perpetuate this interpretation limit Daniel 7 to the historical politics of a man that died nearly eighteen hundred years ago.[33]

Verse 7 describes the fourth beast as "fearsome and frightening and exceedingly strong" with "great iron teeth." This beast brings rampant destruction and has ten horns on its head, differentiating it from the preceding three. That is as far as Daniel goes in describing the creature, but Christians make the fourth beast into whoever or whatever our current adversary happens to be. For example, Jerome and Theodoret argue the fourth beast is the Roman Empire out of a misguided belief that Christians experienced persecution at the hands of the Romans (despite both men being born and educated in the Roman Empire). Aphrahat reads it as "the sons of Shem," which carries distinct anti-Semitic tones, considering later German readers who use Daniel 2 and 7 to read Jewish people as the antichrist. Luther claims it is the Roman Empire controlled by Pope Leo X, to which Leo X's supporters retorted by claiming Luther himself is the fourth beast. Calvin and Mayer also claim the fourth beast is the Roman Empire in a not-so-veiled jab at the Roman Catholic Church. These men are as petty as they are political, as their readings make the Catholic Church the preeminent "bad guy" of history to buttress their own religious reformations.

The rest of this chapter could focus on us Christians projecting our enemies on the fourth beast, but such an exercise would be futile. What matters is acknowledging how Daniel does not identify any of the beasts with a specific kingdom or ruler. Even after Daniel asks for more information about the fourth beast in verses 19–23, the text offers no specifics. Nor does it offer specifics about the ten horns on its head, but, like the beast itself, Christians run wild with identifying each of the horns. We put much interpretive weight on verse 8 and the smaller horn, with the dominant narrative claiming this horn is Antiochus IV. And yet despite the layered and complex arguments interpreters present, the text itself says nothing about what these beasts and horns symbolize. What is truly remarkable about each Christian approach is how we always arrange the ones doing the interpretation (Christians) as the people redeemed and saved by the Ancient of Days at verse 22. This approach severely limits Daniel 7, as no Christian readers take the time to consider which side of the vision they are on: the side to be saved or the side to be destroyed.

It seems that, in rushing to identify who and what these beasts are, Christians fall into a self-reinforcing interpretive trap that neglects the text's bold simplicity. Amalgamated monstrous animals are staples of Babylonian and Mesopotamian literature. They bring chaos and doom wherever they tread. The horns adorning the fourth beast's head convey strength and power, and the more horns an entity has, the more powerful, capable, and authoritative that being is. Seeing four cacophonous creatures, with one bearing ten horns, shows Daniel, and in turn us, a catastrophe that prompts divine intervention.

Contemporary Christian interpreters read Daniel 7's sea as symbolizing the chaotic and evil nature of humanity, meaning that we (humans) create these creatures and give them power.[34] But none take responsibility for our role in perpetuating and enabling such controlling dominance. Further, in claiming these beasts represent certain kings and kingdoms in and around the Mediterranean Sea, Christians severely limit the chapter's global and cosmic theological significance. Ancient Rome or the Levant cannot lay sole claim on God, as God transcends geographic political boundaries with extreme prejudice. These beasts can symbolize ancient empires, but that is not their only possibility. The images in Daniel 7 are ahistorical and are not limited to one time or place for interpretation. Yes, they carry Babylonian literary influence, but such influence does not ensnare Daniel in that time. This is not to oppose reading Daniel 7 against a reader's given historical background—quite the opposite. Reading Daniel's four beasts in our time alongside Daniel's cultural milieu beckons us to consider on which side of the vision we stand: the redeemed victors or vanquished foes?

The Ancient of Days arrives at verses 9–15 in judgment, seated on a flaming throne equipped with "burning fire" wheels. Some translations gloss the Aramaic at verse 13 and call the deity "the Ancient One," rejecting the more literal "the Ancient of Days."[35] Daniel 7 is the only place in the Hebrew Bible that calls the deity the Ancient of Days, and there is considerable scholarly discussion around it.[36] Some try connecting it to ancient Levant literature to no avail, while others simply mark it as one of many names or titles given to the deity.[37] The throne upon which the Ancient of Days sits echoes Ezekiel 1 and the vision of the amber throne surrounded by fire, moving about on wheels. Like Daniel 7, Ezekiel 1 also discusses four amalgamated creatures bearing human and animal features. Paired with Babylonian and Mesopotamian images, such intertextuality shows how thoroughly unoriginal the Daniel 7 vision is. On the surface, this vision is nothing more than a repacked blend of familiar stories and images. But what makes Daniel's reuse compelling is how it helps consider the connection between the four beasts and the Ancient of Days: they work in conjunction here, not opposition. Without the four beasts, there can be no Ancient of Days.

No other spot in our discussion warrants deconstruction of Christian receptions more than verse 13 and the "one like a human being." The Aramaic phrase here כְּבַר אֱנָשׁ translates literally as "like a human being." There is considerable scholarly discussion around the phrase, its meaning, and subsequent implications for interpretation.[38] For our purposes, we focus on how Christian readers either make this unknown figure into Jesus himself or claim the phrase is a harbinger for the eventual Christian Messiah. Daniel presents this figure as one of many ambiguous entities scattered throughout this apocalyptic dream-vision. Nothing in Daniel 7 even hints at the possibility of it being Christian. But before we deconstruct this "the Son of Man is Jesus" approach, I want to expand upon why my translation renders the phrase as "like a human being" instead of the conventional "Son of Man." My reasoning is twofold. First, at a scholarly level, "like a human being" is quite common. Collins, Seow, and the NRSV accept this translation, and others like Newsom, Hartman and Di Lella, and Goldingay accept a slight variation of "one in human likeness." Scholars who insist on the "Son of Man" reading either depend too much on the King James translation, rely on the Old Greek, or let Christian biases interfere with the very language itself.[39]

Which brings me to the second reason I argue "like a human being" is more accurate than "Son of Man": the Aramaic כְּבַר אֱנָשׁ quite literally means "like a human being." The first word, כְּבַר, is actually three words in English. The first letter is a preposition that means "like" or "as," and the corresponding two dots under it denote the indefinite article. Thus, it reads "like a" or "as a." The next two consonants translate to "son" or "child" in the sense of being some sort of offspring. This word does not pertain only to humans within and beyond the biblical text, and it can mean the offspring of an animal.[40] אֱנָשׁ is the common Aramaic word for "human," and it is not a proper noun in this construction. This means scholars who capitalize "Son" and "Man" in their translations do so at their own discretion. A prominent Hebrew cognate example is in the book of Ezekiel when the speaker calls Ezekiel a בֶּן־אָדָם, commonly translated as "mortal" or "Son of Man." No Christian scholar would claim that Ezekiel's בֶּן־אָדָם is Jesus or a reference to Jesus; it simply shows us that Ezekiel is a human being, or "the offspring of a human." Similar phrasing appears throughout the Hebrew Bible with titles like "son of David" or "son of [Hebrew name]" to demarcate from which household or tribe one lays claim. So, in short, saying this figure in verse 13 is "like a son of man" means that the figure is "like a human being." It does not mean the figure is some sort of deity or divine being; he is something the narrator describes as looking like a human.

Despite the phrase's simplicity, Christian scholars make this commonplace human into the Christian messianic figure Jesus of Nazareth. Tanner spends twenty single-spaced pages dissecting arguments and laying out perspectives for and against this phrase being a foreshadowing for the Christian messianic figure Jesus. Despite such thorough yet accessible work, Tanner defaults: "the Son of Man" is "the Lord Jesus Christ."[41] Other Christian readers follow paths similar to Tanner's, ending with the Son of Man being Jesus himself.[42] But, as with all Christ-centric readings thus far, these "the Son of Man is Jesus" readings find roots in Christian readings dating to the second and third centuries BCE.[43] To read the Israelite Son of Man as Jesus is a shocking norm throughout Christian history, one that places severe limitations on how contemporary Christians may preach, teach, and learn from these texts. Furthermore, projecting Jesus onto a place where Jesus is not is anti-Semitic supersessionist replacement theology of the highest order that we must reject as often as we encounter it.

More happens in verses 9–14 than the arrival of one like a human being and the Ancient of Days. According to verse 10, a river of fire comes from the Ancient of Days and his throne, with a court of "a thousand of thousands" serving him and "ten thousand times ten thousand" attending to him. This celestial cadre gathers and takes their seats to witness the opening of what the Aramaic says is סִפְרִ֖ין, meaning "books" or "documents." Verse 10 and the rest of the chapter tell us nothing else about these documents, nor does it disclose the contents therein. The image calls to mind a judge entering a courtroom, with servants and gallery attendees standing at attention before the court comes to order. It is a profoundly direct image conveying the Ancient of Days as the one in charge of proceedings, with his attendants hanging on every word.

It is shocking to see that death is the first judgment rendered when the talking horn and the fourth beast itself are "put to death," with the beast's body burnt to ashes. This judgment renders no trace of the horn or the beast, offering a final and decisive end to the beast's reign. The other three beasts receive murkier and more ambiguous fates. Verse 12 says the

Ancient of Days "made their dominion to pass away," implying each beast loses its reign and ruling power. But they do not face death and cremation; instead, the Ancient of Days extends their lives until "a season and a time." So, in an incongruous twist, the last beast dies while the rest get to live longer. None of this happens by happenstance, as the text is clear about the deity's role: everything happens because he makes it so. Everything leading up to the court's procedures, including the inception of the beasts and their destructive reigns, falls under the celestial judge's auspices. The Ancient of Days controls everything, for better or worse.

Distress and alarm overtake Daniel at verse 15. This vision scares and confuses Daniel so much that he seeks an attendant in verse 16 for "truth concerning all of this." Note the switch chapter 7 brings: unlike chapters 1–6, Daniel no longer interprets the dream. He now needs interpretation, which he receives with minimal clarity. The curt, borderline flippant, attendant says what one can infer from the vision itself: each beast is a king, but only the "holy ones" of the Most High will receive and possess the eternal kingdom. But what exactly is this kingdom, and who are the "holy ones of the Most High"? The text lacks specifics about both, but we Christian readers hastily read ourselves as these "holy ones." We fail to entertain the possibility that the holy ones would be anyone but Christians, as readings paint this kingdom as a sort of Christian utopia designed to reward steadfast faith.[44] Such an assumption is as cavalier as it is textually unfounded.

Daniel presses the attending interpreter at verse 19 for more information about the fourth beast. It scares Daniel more than the preceding three, as he describes it as "exceedingly terrifying." Daniel's fear makes him misremember or expand on the vision when he says it has "iron teeth and bronze nails." Referencing nails, which the vision itself lacks, shows just how shook the vision has Daniel, as his fear-driven imagination makes him recall things not in the original dream-vision. Daniel's fear is genuine, and he presses for more information to better understand what it all means. Repetition does not stop there: Daniel tells the attendant about the horns and the war they waged among themselves, followed by the Ancient of Days' judgment. Daniel presses the issue and wants the interpreter to know his initial succinct response will not do. Daniel's fear makes him need more, but, as the chapter's conclusion shows, he does not get it.

In reading verses 23–27, we see the interpreter offer Daniel little by way of concrete understanding; he basically recounts everything Daniel already saw. The fourth beast is a kingdom, just as the other three are kingdoms. The horns represent rulers vying for power, with one coming that will kill three "horns" and then speak out directly against God the Most High. He will rule for an unknown, unspecified time, as underlined with the wordplay of "a time, times, and a half a time." Dispensationalist Christians labor and strain to make this Aramaic play on words into a specific chronology, with some like William Miller or Harold Camping providing definite dates that never come to fruition. This "time, times, and a half a time" is intentionally vague, like the beasts that come before it. It seems that, like Daniel 7 itself, these words reveal more about the person doing the interpretation than the text. The attendant offers what he wants to Daniel, which is extraordinarily little specific transparency.

But perhaps that is the point. Perhaps this lack of specificity is at the heart of the chapter. Verse 28 shows us Daniel's reaction is not one of comfort; he is "greatly alarmed." He is so scared his "countenance changed" and he kept "this matter" in his heart. The NRSV renders זִיוַי֙ יִשְׁתַּנּ֣וֹן (which I render as "countenance changed") as "my face turned pale." It suggests the attendant's response makes Daniel's fear worse, but we stand wondering why. Is it because Daniel does not understand the vision? Or does his countenance change because he does understand the severity of the vision, prompting him to hide it? One could ask why Daniel hides this vision and interpretation, but fear is a powerful motivator. And, to state the obvious, Daniel 7 shows us the message is not hidden. We experience the dream-vision and interpretation as Daniel does. Daniel's fear indicates that the message of this dream-vision is not peace or harmony; it is distress and uncertainty. He does not walk away from what he sees relieved, and nor should we. For Daniel has seen the future, and it is one of destruction and death. So now the question becomes this: Will we as readers hide this message in our hearts out of fear? Or will we spread it with great urgency? What are we to do with Daniel 7?

7.3 So What?

There are two major points of consideration when engaging Daniel 7 and its Christian interpreters: anti-Semitic supersessionism and neglecting the chapter's overt ancient Levant roots. Let us start with anti-Semitic supersessionism, the proverbial elephant in the room with Christian interpretations of Daniel 7. The widespread supersessionist replacement theology in Christian readings is shocking. I want to offer several examples here, because merely mentioning that this is something Christian do is insufficient; one must see it to believe it. Tanner is not even subtle in making his reading anti-Jewish: "Yet even to this day the grand saga of Israel's blindness continues, her sin compounded by her rejection of Messiah Jesus."[45] Tanner is not alone, as this reading merely regurgitates an established line of Christian interpretation that dates to before the Protestant Reformation. Theodoret outright says the antichrist comes from Jewish people, claiming the little horn is the antichrist, "springing up from the little tribe of the Jews."[46] Tertullian reads the human being in Daniel 7:13 as Jesus and ties that to being critical of the Jewish people for looking "at him as merely a man" and not "the Son of God."[47] Cyril reads the Jewish people as worshiping the antichrist as messiah at Daniel 7:21, claiming the antichrist will be Jewish because he will be a man from the "house of David destined to rebuild the temple erected by Solomon."[48] Christian reformers continue this trend, including John Mayer, Calvin, and Luther.

This anti-Semitic approach is dangerous and wrong. It also does not make sense given the fact Daniel was written by Israelites for Israelites. Any claim to Daniel 7 being anti-Jewish comes from individual and communal anti-Semitism, the kind that is deeply embedded in much of Christianity. Highlighting rampant interpretive anti-Semitism brings another shocking reality to the fore: much of contemporary Christian practice and doctrine is still unapologetically anti-Semitic. For example, any sermon that preaches Jesus as the fulfillment of Old Testament scripture undercuts Israelite connections to their own scripture. Further, Christians frequently preach and teach about Jesus coming to "fix" Israelite religion and the faith practices that would become Judaism. But none of that makes sense given the fact that Jesus was Jewish. Jesus is critical of religious leaders in the New Testament, but that is because he is speaking to problems he sees in his own religious group. Claiming Daniel 7 makes Israel and Jewish people adversarial underlines unchecked, unquestioned anti-Semitism inherent among many contemporary Christians. Neither Daniel nor Jesus opposed Judaism, and calling out these anti-Semitic readings is a much needed first step toward us Christians accepting responsibility for the ongoing role we play in perpetuating modern-day anti-Semitism.

The Christianization of Daniel 7 does not stop with rampant anti-Semitism. We neglect and ignore the chapter's clear connections to Babylonian and Mesopotamian religious literature. This is not to say Christian scholars stand unaware of or do not mention the images and narratives that Daniel 7 echoes. It is quite the opposite. They neglect what the presence of this imagery can mean for interpretation. Many scholars, like J. Collins, Newsom, Seow, and Goldingay, mention the considerable similarities between Daniel 7 and ancient Levant images of the sea, four winds, four beasts, one like a human being, and the Ancient One. Still others, like Towner, Duguid, Sprinkle, and Tanner, acknowledge the existence of Mesopotamian cultures to proof-text Babylonian kings and practices like lions' dens and fiery furnaces, but the interpretive work stops there.

Despite widespread availability and accessibility of ancient Levant resources, Christian interpreters do not reckon with what these narrative echoes and mutual images can mean for interpretation. It also highlights how selective Christian interpreters are with historicity and the Bible, as we have considerable historical evidence that confirms the Babylonians invaded and conquered Israel. Thus, it makes sense that Babylonian culture and religions would affect Israelite religious practice and literature, since the Babylonians and then the Persians quite literally subjugated the nation and its people. We Christians do not like the idea of our sacred texts being influenced by non-Israelite, non-Christian cultures. Despite such hesitation, Daniel 7 is very much a product of the environments that produced it. Ignoring the worlds of the people who made it ignores and silences those people, subjugating them to a "lesser than" status. These Babylonian images make a bold political and apocalyptic statement, while also delicately showing how profoundly human the book is. We have much to learn from the people who wrote these stories and images down, and respecting them for being living, breathing people can usher in an era of revitalized biblical interpretation.

Just as chapter 7 ushers in Daniel's apocalyptic section, so too do we interpreters use Daniel 7 as another chance to double down on our notions of historical divine sovereignty. We Christians project our anxieties onto the text, only to dilute genuine concerns about issues of war, famine, and climate change with vague aphorisms like, "If people want to know how the world will end . . . what better place to turn than to the Word of the sovereign God, who controls all history?"[49] But does Daniel 7 actually present a deity controlling history? Or is that what Christians want it to say? And if the deity is in control throughout Daniel 7, that makes God responsible for the wanton death and destruction spread throughout the chapter.

The reality is many of us Christians, Americans in particular, are too comfortable with accepting war, death, and famine as divinely controlled, and we use Daniel 7 to support this theological orientation. But such an orientation is as selfish as it is textually unfounded. In February 2023, a 7.8 magnitude earthquake rocked Syria and Turkey. Over fifty thousand people died, and, at the time of this writing, over four million people rely on humanitarian aid because the earthquake destroyed food production and distribution systems across the two countries. An earthquake hitting Syria is yet another tragedy to befall the already war-torn country, but, to read this situation from a Daniel 7–style Christian perspective, this is what God wants. Daniel 7 does not say that. Christians make it into such a manifesto and drastically dehumanize the millions who still suffer. And this is just one example.

What, then, are we Christians to do with Daniel 7? How can we teach and preach it? The possibilities are endless. The first thing we must do is break these cycles of anti-Semitism and passivity. Daniel experiences profound fear through the chapter, as he sees the world he calls home falling into utter ruin. When he asks for an interpretation of what he sees, he stands unfulfilled. Our discomfort and fear should mirror Daniel's, as the world God has given us continues to fall apart. We cannot control everything, but Daniel 7 beckons us to do something. We cannot hide what we know to be true, that our world and the people in it are in dire need. Only when we accept the human realities portrayed in this chapter can we move toward the final kingdom of God in Daniel 7. It is plain to see that unless we fight, act, and change, our world will be like the fourth beast: consumed and completely destroyed.

8
Daniel 8 Reconsidered

8.1 Translation

[1] In the third year of the reign of King Belshazzar, a vision appeared to me, I, Daniel, after the one that appeared to me first.

[2] And I saw the vision, and I was seeing myself, and I was in Susa the citadel, which is in the province of Elam. I saw in a vision, and I was above the canal of Ulai.

[3] And I lifted my eyes and saw. And lo! One ram standing beside the canal, and it had horns. And the horns were high, and one was higher than the other, and the higher one came up last.

[4] I saw the ram goring westward, and northward, and southward, and all the beasts were unable to stand against him. And there was no one rescued from its hand. And he did as he pleased and became strong.

[5] And I was considering, and lo! A male goat coming from the west over the face of the entire land, and it did not strike the ground, and the goat had a conspicuous horn between its eyes.

[6] And it came as far as the lord of horns[1] ram that I saw standing before the canal, and he ran toward him with wrathful strength.

[7] And I saw him coming beside the ram, and he was enraged toward him, and he struck the ram and broke two of his horns, and there was not strength in the ram to stand against him. And he threw the ram down to the ground and trampled him, and there was no one to rescue the ram from his hand.

[8] And the male goat became very powerful, and when it was strong, the great horn was broken and four conspicuous horns came up beneath it, toward the four winds of the heavens.

9 And from one of them there came a little horn, and it grew exceedingly great toward the south, and toward the east, and toward the beautiful land.

10 And it grew until the host of the heavens, and it threw to earth some from the host and some from the stars, and it trampled them.

11 And it grew as far as the ruler of the host, and it took away the regular offering and overthrew a sanctuary place.[2]

12 And the host was given over with the regular offering on account of a transgression, and it threw truth to the earth, and it succeeded in its act.

13 And I heard a holy one speaking, and another holy one speaking to the one that had spoken, "How long is the vision about the regular offering? And the transgression that desolates? And the giving over of the holy place and the host being trampled?"

14 And he said to me, "Until two thousand and three hundred evenings and mornings; then the holy place will be restored."

15 And I, Daniel, had seen the vision. And I sought to understand it, and lo! Standing before me was one with the appearance of a man.

16 And I heard a human voice between the Ulai, and it was calling, and it said, "Gabriel, make this one understand the vision."

17 And he came near where I stood, and as he came I was frightened. And I fell upon my face, and he said to me, "Understand, human, that the vision is the time of the end."

18 And as he was speaking with me, I slept upon the face of the earth, and he touched me and caused me to stand upon my station.

19 And he said, "Lo! I will make known to you what will be after the indignation of the appointed end time.

20 The ram which you saw, the lord of horns, are kings of Media and Persia.

21 And the hairy male goat is king of Greece, and the great horn between its eyes is the first king.

22 And it was broken, and four replaced it. Those are four kingdoms that will arise from its nation without its power.

23 And at the end of their reign, when their transgressions are complete, a bold-faced king will stand and be skilled with intrigue.

24 And he will be great with power, and not his power, and will cause fearful destruction, and it will be done. And he will destroy the mighty and people of the holy ones.

[25] And because of his cunning, he will succeed deceitfully by his hand, and he will be great in his own heart, and in prosperity he will destroy many, and he will stand again a prince of princes. And without a hand, he shall be broken.

[26] And the vision of the evening and the morning which has been told, it is true. And you, seal the vision because it is in reference to many days."

[27] And I, Daniel, was overcome and was sick for days. And I arose and did the business of the king, and I was appalled by the vision and was without understanding.

8.2 Reading against the Grain

Daniel 8:1 unceremoniously switches back to Hebrew from Aramaic. The text makes no note of the switch, nor does it provide justification. Chapter 7 simply ends in Aramaic, and Daniel 8:1 begins in Hebrew. No one knows why the language shift happens, and we should treat any claims about the "why" surrounding the Hebrew-Aramaic language interplay as speculative at best. In terms of engaging the text, Christian approaches to Daniel 8's content are shockingly consistent in two ways. First, Christian readers lump chapters 8–12 together, making the five chapters into a single unit. Commentaries and analysis engage specific sections and verses of these chapters, but each veer toward a monolithic understanding of chapters 8–12. Second, Christians are quick to ascribe specifics about history, chronology, and identity to Daniel's visions. I give each of 8–12 its own chapter in this book to highlight details that can otherwise go glossed over or neglected. Though Daniel's visions in these chapters blend and form a narrative unit, there is much to learn and consider by moving through Daniel 8–12 slowly and with intent. With each chapter I highlight the Christian interpretive trends, with a particular eye for how readers tie Daniel 8–12 to their specific histories. This twofold approach lets each chapter shine independently, while also creating space for the reader to reconsider how Daniel 8–12 fit together. With this in mind, let us turn to the text itself.

Daniel 8:1 opens two years after Daniel 7, "in the third year" of Belshazzar's reign. Like chapter 7, the monarch never speaks and has no effect on what precedes. Also, like Daniel 7, making Belshazzar king situates chapter 8 in a particular narrative time and place. Daniel 8's literary setting is the Babylonian exile. However, like the rest of the book, Daniel 8's composition date is uncertain. And yet, despite considerable historical evidence to the contrary, many Christians default to Daniel being written during the Babylonian exile.[3] Such insistence reflects the penchant to take the Bible at historical face value, which presents a blatant disregard of the apocalyptic literary form and the very nature of apocalyptic literature itself. The fundamentalist approach of binding the Bible's theological validity and veracity to historical chronological certainty underlines a shallow understanding of what we Christians call "sacred." When the text was or was not written stands inconsequential compared to what we, the readers, do with the text as it stands before us.

The narrator, Daniel, speaks in the first person throughout the chapter. This means we get his perspective and only his perspective. One could argue this approach makes Daniel's read on the vision unreliable because we get the vision as only Daniel experiences and feels it. Daniel says this vision appears "after the one that appeared to me first," suggesting what proceeds happens immediately after the vision in Daniel 7. What Daniel sees is quite literally an out-of-body experience, as he seems himself in verse 2 at the citadel in Susa in the province of Elam by the river Ulai. Susa was a real place, situated by the Zagros mountain range close to the modern-day Tigris River. It was the capital of an Akkadian province until a rogue governor rebelled and made it the independent state known as Elam. Elam was situated in the southwest portion of modern-day Iran next to the Persian Gulf. Historical evidence suggests this was a hotly contested area, changing hands according to the whims of who was in charge.[4] Such political and military tumult makes Susa a fitting location for this vision to unfold. But it is remarkable that Daniel sees himself in this location, as he does not say he is in Susa when he sees the vision. According to verse 2, he sees himself "above the canal of Ulai," meaning he watches himself participate in the vision. Daniel simultaneously views and participates in what he sees. He cannot claim innocence of a bystander, as his inclusion highlights his effect on the vision.

Daniel continues his gaze and sees a multi-horned ram standing by the canal. As stated in previous chapters, horns in the ancient Levant symbolize power and authority. Rams also become aggressive and territorial in fights, so the use of a ram conveys a deceptively simple point confirmed by its behavior in verse 4: it behaves erratically, attempting to destroy anything it sees. Ancient and contemporary Christian readers are quick to read the ram as metaphorical for some historical leader or empire. For example, Theodoret builds off the text and concurs that the ram is "the Persian empire," while Ephrem narrows his position to claim it "signifies

Darius the Persian."[5] Christian receptions build on this Mede and Persian connection to make specious claims about the history and lineage of the Persian Empire as laid out in Daniel 8. These same readers also take considerable liberties in tying the chapter's unnamed and unknown ram and goat to specific historical figures.[6]

Across the entire chapter, we have only vague, nondescript references to kings of Media, Persia, and Greece. Skillful use of specific kingdoms like Media, Persia, and Greece orients the reader to where and when the political intrigue occurs. One need only study history to learn that multiple kings and leaders held the throne in each of these empires, so limiting Daniel 8 to specific kings does a disservice to the text's potential. And the interpretative potential of this chapter and chapters 9–12 is significant. Despite the chapter's overt political machinations, Christians again default to making chapters 8–12 a display of divine sovereignty over and against human power. These readings fall into the trap of projecting narrative certainty where there is none. Daniel 8's understanding of history is far from certain. Daniel's response to what he sees at verse 27 highlights this uncertainty, as the vision overcomes Daniel, makes him sick, appalls him, and leaves him without understanding.

But before we dig into Daniel's visceral reaction, let us consider what he sees. The ram at verse 4 gores west, north, and south, suggesting it hails from the east. The text does not say why the ram spares the east from its wrath, as it wreaks havoc so great that "all the beasts were unable to stand against him."[7] No one escapes the ram's hand as his power goes unchecked, until verse 5 and the male goat's arrival. This goat does not touch the ground as it travels, and, if that was not peculiar enough, it has a horn between its eyes. A brutal battle unfolds, resulting in the goat breaking two of the ram's horns and trampling the once mighty creature into the ground. Note verse 7 uses language paralleling verse 4 with "there was no one to rescue the ram from his hand." This goat's victory over the ram is not a fluke: the once powerful and unstoppable ram met his match.

The political metaphor here is straightforward: the goat's destruction of the ram's horns symbolizes destruction of power and authority. Verse 8 shows us the goat's fate as its single horn is broken and replaced by four horns. Unlike the ram, we do not know how or why the goat's horn breaks, but we do learn the four replacement horns move "toward the four winds of the heavens." This "four winds" image echoes similar imagery from Mesopotamian and Egyptian literature, in which winds from the four cardinal directions are personified as divine figures.[8] Thus, such imagery highlights the goat's intent, as he tries to extend his reign toward the heavens.

One of these horns sprouts another horn that grows physically, symbolizing a significant growth in political power and stature. This horn is so powerful that, according to verses 10 and 11, it reaches the heavens and pulls down and then tramples some of the host of heavens and the stars themselves. Much is made of this "host of heavens" language in Christian circles and among evangelical Christians in particular. The Hebrew word rendered as "host" is צָבָא, which literally means "army," which reiterates the chapter's military focus, as the horn successfully attacks this heavenly army as an additional display of its strength and destructive capacity. Unlike the ram, the goat can cross from the human, earthly realm into the divine realm. This makes the battle between the ram and goat take on cosmological significance, as we now see the goat uses the ram as a stepping-stone toward its larger political and cosmic ends: it wants to control heaven and earth.

The horn's interference with the divine realm suggests the opposite of divine sovereign control as its power lets it strike against God's literal army. Seeing how Christians work around this narrative reality is striking: Sprinkle barely acknowledges it, while Tanner makes verse 10 into an elaborate metaphor for Antiochus IV's military aggression against Judah: "[It]was as though he made an assault 'upon the host of heaven.'"[9] One thing that transcends theological and political convictions in interpretation is the tendency to read Daniel 8 through a conclusions-based lens. Here is what I mean: Christians read the chapter with the apocalyptic culmination in mind. Indeed, the earthly forces embodied in beasts like this ram and goat do ultimately fall, but constructing their fall as the chapter's narrative heart does a considerable disservice to voices living in those political moments. Imagine telling someone living in Britain during the WWII blitzkrieg or in Hanoi amid Operation Rolling Thunder that "fifty years from now things are better." Think how much that paradigm discredits the fear, anxiety, and death that wartime brings. Daniel's response to the vision in later verses shows fear, anxiety, and uncertainty, so piling certainty onto this chapter flies in the face of Daniel's own reaction.

This thing I am calling an "apocalyptic culmination lens" finds roots in Christian receptions grounded in specific historical positioning. Christian readers, going back to some of the earliest interpreters like Jerome and Ephrem, wrestle with identifying the little horn as Antiochus IV Epiphanes, the Greek Hellenistic monarch who reigned over the Seleucid

Empire from 175 to 164 BCE. Reading Antiochus as the little horn became the standard historical ballast against which Christian interpreters measure Daniel's historicity and chronology, but historical evidence supporting this claim is specious. Ephrem reads the little horn in Daniel 7 and 8 as Antiochus because "Antiochus extended his empire especially in these two parts of the world."[10] Interestingly enough, Jerome sets up reading Antiochus in chapter 8 by saying Antiochus is not the horn of the fourth beast in Daniel 7.

Reading Antiochus IV as chapter 8's antagonist is so commonplace that pushing against it here may likely yield criticism.[11] The fact remains that Daniel 8 does not mention Antiochus, or any other ruler, by name. So, the approach of reading chapter 8 through Antiochus to establish a timeline is grounded within a specific historical context created by Jerome, Ephrem, and other Christian readers to lock Daniel into one chronology. What makes this line of interpretation demand attention and critical evaluation is how contemporary Christians continue to use it as the default historical approach to Daniel 8. Such widespread acceptance makes one think the evidence supporting such a claim is irrefutable. The reality is the opposite.[12] It stems from something called the "Maccabean Thesis," which reads Daniel alongside 1 and 2 Maccabees to reconstruct the history of the Israelite world during the second century BCE. Scholars also weigh nonbiblical histories written, in some cases, hundreds of years after the events described in Maccabees. But 1 and 2 Maccabees do heavy lifting in terms of historical and chronological alignment with Daniel, especially chapters 8–12, despite no indication toward that being 1 and 2 Maccabees' purpose. For this reason, I do not read the widely accepted but rarely critiqued Maccabean Antiochus IV paradigm onto Daniel 8–12. Trapping these chapters and their fantastical visions into one set, seemingly immovable, historical model limits further interpretive possibilities.

It also sidesteps the significant theological, ethical, and hermeneutical avenues these chapters can yield. For example, the Hebrew in Daniel 8 is quite complex and leads to considerable differences in translation. Since the average person does not read biblical Hebrew, here are five translations of Daniel 8:12 commonly used by Christians:

> And a host was given him against the daily sacrifice by reason of transgression, and it cast down the truth to the ground; and it practiced, and prospered. (KJV)

> Because of rebellion, the LORD's people and the daily sacrifice were given over to it. It prospered in everything it did, and truth was thrown to the ground. (NIV)
>
> Because of wickedness, the host was given over to it together with the regular burnt offering; it cast truth to the ground, and kept prospering in what it did. (NRSV)
>
> And a host will be given over to it together with the regular burnt offering because of transgression, and it will throw truth to the ground, and it will act and prosper. (ESV)
>
> The army of heaven was restrained from responding to this rebellion. So the daily sacrifice was halted, and truth was overthrown. The horn succeeded in everything it did. (NLT)

And this is just one verse; I could dedicate another book entirely to discussing and considering the translation variations in the chapter. Such variations might give readers pause, as we grow up learning to "read the Bible" without ever really being told how different the very Bibles we use are from one another. But therein lies the potential. Reading Daniel 8 then becomes an exercise in choices: What version will I read? Why did I pick that version? How different is the version I chose from others that someone else may choose? And what do those choices say about me as the reader?

Because as the chapter continues, the imagery becomes even more layered and complex. Verse 12 talks about a "transgression," with "truth" thrown to the earth. Two "holy ones" speak in verse 13 about a vision of a regular offering, alongside "the transgression that desolates." That does not even begin to weigh in on what is happening with verse 14 and the "two thousand and three hundred evenings and mornings." These images give scholars and lay readers fits as they try to unlock a code or secret they believe to be buried within the cryptic language. But despite their best efforts, the conclusions are often just as muddled and confusing.

Standard Christian interpretations focus on "the transgression that desolates," commonly translated as "the abomination that desolates."[13] The text itself offers no further insight into what exactly this transgression is, but the scholarly consensus theorizes Antiochus IV erected some kind of foreign alter in the Jerusalem temple meant for non-Israelite sacrifices.[14] But, here again, we see how scholars tie Daniel 8–12 to Antiochus IV, meaning that this theory about the abomination that desolates is simply that—a theory—as are any arguments for unpacking what the holy one at verse 14 means with his answer to Daniel's "how long" query. American Christian restorationist William Miller became famous in the 1840s for his proclamation that, based on his readings of Daniel and Revelation, he unlocked "the" timeline for events and conclusions foretold throughout the Bible. W. Miller claims that, according to his calculations, Jesus would return in 1843. Foundational to his argument is the "two thousand and three hundred evenings and mornings" response in verse 14, except he argues 2,300 days is actually 2,300 years.[15] Invigorated by his own readings, W. Miller built a timeline beginning at Cyrus the Great's edict to rebuild the temple, culminating with Jesus' return in 1843. This did not happen, prompting W. Miller to adjust his prediction to October 22, 1844. That date came and went without Jesus' return, which is an event that came to be known as the Great Disappointment. Many of Miller's followers forsook their apocalyptic beliefs for other religious convictions, but others gravitated toward the teachings of Ellen White, eventually forming what is now known as the Seventh-day Adventist sect of Christianity. Adventists still hold fast to their apocalyptic beliefs, with considerable emphasis on Daniel 8.

But W. Miller and later the Adventists are not the only Christians using Daniel 8 for a historically entangled argument about chronology for Jesus' return. Few Christians are as aggressively specific about Jesus' second coming, but far too many commit the anti-Semitic error of Daniel being a road map that ends when Jesus arrives. These messianic views focus on Daniel's fulfillment through Jesus, an interpretive move that severely undercuts the text's Israelite orientation in favor of a Christian supersessionist replacement perspective, making Daniel 8 into something it quite literally is not. Further, other Christians taking a less direct stance still envelope their interpretations with supersessionist anti-Semitism by claiming the "little horn" represents the antichrist. Martin Luther's work supports this claim to argue Antiochus is the antichrist, but Calvin and Melanchthon push back, with Calvin outright saying Luther is guilty of "indulging his thoughts too freely."[16] That said, Calvin, Melanchthon, and Oecolampadius do argue that the antichrist figures into and appears in Daniel 8; their disagreement stems from Luther's attributing the antichrist to Antiochus. We modern Christians take similar stances, making Daniel 8's unspecified dates, times, and characters into our very own self-fulfilling prophecy, with us always the victors.

Jesus does not appear in Daniel 8, nor does the antichrist. Daniel 8 weaves a complex apocalyptic tapestry that befuddles Daniel himself.

Verses 15–27 comprise Daniel's attempt to get the new character Gabriel to help him understand what he just witnessed, as verse 17 shows Daniel finds no comfort in what he sees. A human voice told Gabriel to help Daniel at verse 16, and Daniel experiences such fear that he falls on his face before Gabriel. The text says Gabriel has "the appearance of a man," and nothing about Gabriel denotes his possibly being some kind of angelic figure. This brings us to the Gabriel conundrum: Daniel 8 is the first time Gabriel appears in the Bible. He appears again in Daniel 9 and in the New Testament in Luke 1. Luke describes Gabriel as an angel, but Daniel 8 and 9 do not. Daniel 9:21 describes him as "the man Gabriel," and pairing that with the "appearance of a man" description at Daniel 8:16 calls into question the prevailing theory of Gabriel being an angel. Yes, Luke describes him as an angel, but I do not want to project an overtly Christian text like Luke back onto Daniel as a form of Christian proof-texting. Using Daniel and only Daniel, Gabriel is just a man. He may be some kind of holy man, as the disembodied voice at verse 16 calls him to interpret for Daniel, but he is still just a man.[17]

Christians use Luke 1 to justify making this man an angel, with little to no serious questioning of that label. The issue of angels themselves gets repeatedly glossed in Christian circles, as a considerable majority of Christians believe in a monotheistic, singular deity: there is no other God but God. Christians read this monotheism into the Hebrew Bible and across the New Testament, but the existence of angels calls the very concept of monotheism into question. This is another discussion for a different book, but the point still stands: If God uses inhuman, divine messengers to run errands and speak on God's behalf, is that not the basis of a Levant-style polytheistic pantheon? On top of this mono- and poly-uncertainty, reading Gabriel's appearance through Daniel 8 shows us he responds to a human voice, not God's (or any other deity for that matter). Who is the human voice at verse 16? And why does the disembodied voice select Gabriel instead of asking Daniel himself to interpret like he did in chapters 1–6?

Confusion continues to mount with Gabriel's interpretation itself. Gabriel tells Daniel (and in turn us) "the vision is the time of the end." Oddly, Daniel slips into sleep when listening to Gabriel, who apparently awakens him to "make known" what will unfold "after the indignation of the appointed end time." Gabriel does not identify the ram; he identifies the two horns as "kings of Media and Persia." The goat is "king of Greece," and its great horn is the ambiguous "first king." The four horns represent four inferior kingdoms that will be replaced with a bold, powerful, and skilled monarch. Again, Gabriel offers no further specifics regarding these rulers and their identities. The Median dynasty thrived from the seventh century BCE until the mid-sixth century BCE, and four kings ruled during this time, so does the Media horn represent one or all the kings? Cyrus the Great brought the Persian Empire to prominence in the mid-sixth century BCE, but twelve more kings ruled after him. Christian readers default to making this "king of Greece" into Alexander the Great, while others say the horn atop the goat's head is Alexander to align their understanding of history with the four horns that replace the first.

Interpretive madness ensues when trying to consider the identity of the king at verse 23. Some present him as Antiochus with considerable gusto, while others label him the antichrist. Still others, like Seventh-day Adventist scholar Uriah Smith, claim things like this unknown king represents the Roman empire and therefore the Roman Catholic Church.[18] And yet, at the risk of redundancy, Daniel again offers no specifics around this king's identity. Verse 24 does, however, tell us this king's power is "not his power," meaning the trope of all political power stemming from God makes another appearance.[19] If this is the case, why not be more explicit? Further, if God bestows power upon this man, then God is responsible for the havoc and destruction he brings. Daniel 8 gives three verses to Gabriel's interpretation of this king and his actions, setting him beyond the horrors of those who precede him. Verse 25 describes the king's arrogant self-aggrandizement, but he still destroys many people "without warning," making him dangerous and capricious with his power. The verse ends with something resembling assurance, telling us with a clear allusion back to Daniel 2 and the statue that "And without a hand, he shall be broken." This destruction implies that at an unknown time, inhuman forces will overtake the king. It can also imply something like sickness or some other means will break the king. Gabriel does not tell us how it will happen; we just know that eventually it will.

Gabriel's final instruction for Daniel is to "seal up the vision," which Daniel clearly does not, as we are reading and considering the vision in question. Like chapter 7, Daniel finds no peace in what he sees and hears. He is so overcome that he becomes physically ill, as the vision dismays him because he does not understand what it contains. Gabriel's interpretation offers Daniel no solace or comfort. What then is the purpose of his man and his interpretation if Daniel does nothing with it and gets nothing from it? But what is more concerning is, despite Daniel seeing a vision about the future destruction of known human governments, at verse 27 he "did the business of the king." He warns no one and makes no attempt to make changes or preparations for the coming destruction. To the outside world, it is as if Daniel simply was sick. This vision and interpretation change nothing.

8.3 So What?

The most pressing theological issue in Daniel 8 is familiar: God is strikingly absent. God does not speak in chapter 8, nor does the narrative indicate that anything that happens is the result of God's choices and God's actions. The chapter uses passive voice in certain instances, but the text attributes nothing to Daniel's deity. Characters talk about God, and one could argue they speak on the deity's behalf (Gabriel talking to Daniel), but nothing that unfolds connects explicitly to God. Yet Christian receptions are quick to claim history in Daniel 8 goes according to an unknown, unseen, and unquestionable divine plan. For example, regarding verse 13, J. Collins argues, "The antecedent is God, who has not been mentioned directly but whose control of the course of events is assumed throughout."[20] Others take a similar approach despite God's aforementioned absence, watering this vision down to another extended "God is in control" analogy.[21] As romantic and idealistic as this thought might be, placing this theological understanding into contemporary contexts is dangerous and elitist. It makes the unimaginable suffering and pain endured at the hands of ruthless tyrants and inept politicians into an act of selfish and myopic hubris. For some, reading history as a divine road map offers comfort during times of trauma, but for many it is a pathway to alienation, shame, and a belief system built on fear.

Christian worldviews define themselves on success and prosperity far too often. Countries like the United States have zealous Christian supporters who pride themselves on living in a "Christian" nation and make claims like America being a "nation under God." Yet the lived realities of many American citizens reflect profound and considerable political and economic instability. As an American myself, I see the scars and wounds of racism, sexism, and poverty that are the norm in this country. And this does not even begin to address the ongoing effects of American colonization and economic destabilization we wrought upon this world. For example, Americans who can trace their roots to the African continent were not granted full U.S. citizenship until the Voting Rights Act of 1965, one hundred years after the American Civil War's end. Even that legislation failed to undo the shameful legacy of American slavery, as the wealth gap between white Americans compared to black and Latino Americans is staggering.[22] On top of this, the United States has one of the highest rates of incarceration in the world, coming in with over two million people imprisoned.[23]

Stepping outside the country, what the United States did (and in some cases is still actively doing) to destabilize the governments of other countries is distressing. Contemporary rhetoric around immigration into the United States is horrifying in its dehumanization, with some politicians calling to make it legal to shoot undocumented persons like "immigrating feral hogs."[24] The reality is the United States is responsible for much of the immigration crisis, as America played a defining role in the current instability in Guatemala, El Salvador, and Honduras.[25] Some may claim a more partisan perspective and argue Republican presidents are responsible, but the atrocities transcend political parties, as Bill Clinton and Barack Obama are just as culpable as Ronald Reagan, George H. W. Bush, and George W. Bush. But perhaps what is most shocking of all is how little the country's own citizens know of America's dealings and machinations. For many Americans, the wars and rumors of war foretold in Daniel 8 are hypothetical. Many outside the country live in active war zones brought on by American plans and funded by our tax dollars.

Someone reading this may say, "What does anything about American poverty, racism, and colonization have to do with Daniel 8?" Political allegory and intrigue consume Daniel 8. It presents the rise and fall of kings and their kingdoms, making it an inherently political chapter in an already overtly political book. The chapter begins under the reign of a foreign ruler in Belshazzar, and the vision Daniel witnesses includes a brutal, violent struggle between military forces personified in the ram, the goat, and their horns. Verses 20–21 say the ram represents kings of Media and Persia, and the goat is king of Greece. Historical circumstances around the empires of Media, Persia, and Greece are bloody, merciless, and inhuman. Untold numbers died and suffered as power changed hands across centuries, with each king looking to top the ones who came before them in power and strength. So, to separate the political ramifications of Daniel 8's interpretative possibilities is to misrepresent the text and Daniel's vision therein.

We Christians have long tied our fortunes to political power, reaching back all the way to the apostle Paul using his Roman citizenship for the greatest possible benefit.[26] Constantine ensured Christianity would thrive and spread without government pressure in 313 CE with the Edict of

Milan, prompting Christian leaders to make allegiances with ruling powers for centuries. Christians' relationships became so interconnected that kings claimed their leadership came from divine right and God's mandating, with Christians in power reaping the benefits of financial and political influence. And this does not even begin to scratch the surface of connections (and outright blessings and support) between Christianity and European colonization and the enslavement of millions from the African continent. Even the most basic and cursory histories confirm this shocking and shameful reality.

So, what, then, does this mean for Daniel 8? And, if, as I claim, Daniel 8 does not refer to Antiochus or anyone specifically, who then is this text talking about? Daniel's vagueness leaves the book susceptible to various prognostications and theories. Daniel 8 and its vision is a political prism, designed to draw us readers in and see ourselves in its refractions. The text lends itself to narrower and more specific interpretations thanks to the Media, Persia, and Greece references, but constructing an entire historical timeline culminating in the world's end from such vague and broad allusions is myopic and self-centered. It also eliminates the actual historical contexts in and around Daniel, making an Israelite text about war, peace, and prophecy into a misguided Christian conduit to fulfillment in Jesus. We Christians who use Daniel 8 to map the future commit a grave mistake in centering ourselves and our contexts as "the" text's point and chronological focus. Every historically based prediction based off Daniel 8 has been wrong. The world did not end in 1843 or 1844. The pope is not the antichrist, as Martin Luther passionately argues. Martin Luther is not the antichrist, as papal supporters claimed. Jesus is not in Daniel 8, nor is the antichrist, and, as noted above, God's absence is distinct.

It is in these things we Christians project onto Daniel that we find interpretive possibility: perhaps in a modern context, Daniel 8 is meant to tell us more about the person reading the text than the text itself. Christians are not Israelites in the period of the Babylonian exile. But in knowing the exilic context, we Christians can ask ourselves where we stand in relation to Daniel 8: Are we the ones in exile, or are we those responsible for it? Does Christianity today, especially in the United States, reflect the lessons learned from war, pain, and death at the hands of political leaders that led to the exile? Or does it reflect the inhuman greed and arrogance from Israelite leadership that brought so much suffering upon the Israelites themselves? This is not to say Christians and Israelites should be seen as being the same people; such language and sentiment is supersessionist and anti-Semitic. What Daniel 8 holds for us Christians is a chance to look at ourselves and ask what kind of person and what kind of people we are. Because the words themselves are not meant to comfort. Daniel becomes sick and horrified at what he sees, and we should be just as aghast at the world we created for ourselves.

War like that between the ram and the goat, followed by lust for power of the horns, is ingrained into our cultural DNA. In 2022, the United States spent $877 billion on the military, compared to $76.4 billion toward education. At the time of this writing, Joe Biden is president, and his administration's 2024 budget requests include $842 billion for the military and $90 billion for education. These numbers should scare Christians into action, but like Daniel at the chapter's end, we stand by and let it happen. Like Daniel 8, our lack of action adds up to nothing. But it does not have to stay that way, and that is what Daniel 8 can show us. Daniel 8 shows us a world like our own, in which powers beyond most of our control determine the destiny of billions. What we do with this information is completely and totally up to us, which in itself is a challenge from the God that made us and this world. We see what happens when we make things about ourselves and build our hopes upon empires and misbegotten leaders. Despite this, we can dream about a world that is the opposite, in which we shed our selfishness and build the world that God intended at creation. That, it seems, is the mandate from this chapter: standing by and doing nothing changes nothing, and we allow ourselves to remain in this quagmire of our own making. But it does not have to be this way. Daniel 8 shows us the world as it really is; what, then, can the world possibly be?

9
Daniel 9 Reconsidered

9.1 Translation

1 In Darius son of Ahasuerus' first year, from seed of Mede, who was the king over the Chaldean kingdom.

2 In year one of his reign, I, Daniel, understood in the books the number of years, which, according to the word of YHWH to Jeremiah the prophet, was for the fulfillment of Jerusalem's seventy-year desolation.

3 And I set my face to Adonai Elohim to entreat prayer, and sackcloth with fasting, and sackcloth, and ashes.

4 And I prayed to YHWH Adonai, and I confessed, and I said, "Please, my god! The great and awesome god, the one keeping the covenant and the faithfulness to people that love him and keep his commandments.

5 We have sinned and we have wronged and we have done wickedly and we have rebelled and we have turned aside from your commandments and your judgments.

6 And we have not listened to your servants, the prophets, who spoke in your name to our kings, our princes, and our fathers and to all people of the land.

7 Righteousness is with you, Adonai, and we are in open shame this day. For the men of Judah and inhabitants of Jerusalem and to all of Israel, the ones near and the ones far away in all the lands where you have driven them because of the treachery they have committed against you.

8 YHWH, we are in open shame, because our kings, our princes, and our fathers have sinned against you.

[9] Compassion and forgiveness are with Adonai our god, for we have rebelled against him.

[10] And we have not heard the voice of Adonai our god, to follow his laws which he placed before us by the hand of his servants the prophets.

[11] And all Israel transgressed your law and turned aside from listening to your voice, and it has been poured out upon us, the curse and the oath written in the law of Moses servant of Elohim, because we sinned against him.

[12] And he has confirmed his words, which he spoke against us and against our rulers which ruled us, bringing a great evil upon us, one that had never been done under all the heavens, when it was done to Jerusalem.

[13] As it was written in the law of Moses, all this evil that has come upon us, and we did not seek favor before YHWH our god to turn from our iniquities and to find understanding in your truth.

[14] And YHWH watched this evil until he brought it upon us. For YHWH our god is righteous in all his deeds which he does, and we do not listen to his voice.

[15] And now Adonai our god who brought you, your people, from the land of Egypt by his strong hand, and made your name to this day. We have sinned and we have been wicked.

[16] Adonai, according to all of your righteousness, please turn your face and wrath from your city, Jerusalem, your holy mountain, for we have sinned, and with the iniquities of our fathers, Jerusalem and your people are reviled by all that surround us.

[17] And now, listen, our god, to the prayer of your servant and to his supplication, and shine your face upon your desolate sanctuary, for the sake of Adonai.

[18] Stretch out your ear, my god, and hear; open your eyes and see our desolations and the city that has your name called upon it. We do not bring supplications before you because of our righteousness, but for your great mercies.

[19] Adonai, hear; Adonai, forgive. Adonai, listen and do without delay! For your sake, my god, for the city that has your name called upon it, and upon your people."

[20] And as I was still speaking and praying and confessing my sin and the sins of my people, Israel, offering supplications between YHWH my god upon the holy mountain of my god.

21 And I was still speaking in prayer, and the man Gabriel, whom
I saw before in a vision, came swiftly to me during the time of the
evening sacrifice.
22 And allowed me to understand and spoke to me, saying, "Daniel
now I have come out for insightful understanding.
23 When your supplications began, a word went out, and I came
to declare it, for you are loved. Consider the word and understand
the vision.
24 Seventy weeks are decreed for your people and your holy city,
to finish the rebellion and to seal the sins, and to atone iniquity, and
bring in eternal righteousness, and to seal the vision and prophet,
and to anoint a holy of holies.
25 And may you know and understand: when a word went out to
restore and rebuild Jerusalem, until the time of an anointed leader[1]
will be seven weeks. After sixty-two weeks it will return and be
rebuilt, street and moat, and in a distressful time.
26 And after the sixty-two weeks, an anointed one will be cut off,
and he will be nothing. And people of the leader will come and
destroy the holy sanctuary. His end will come in the flood, and until
that end is war. Desolations are decreed.
27 And he shall make a covenant for many for one week, and for
half a week he will cease an offering and a sacrifice, and upon its
wing[2] desolating abominations, and until the decreed end it shall be
poured out upon the one desolating."

9.2 Reading against the Grain

Narration in Daniel 9 shifts back from Gabriel to Daniel himself, with multiple verses in which Daniel speaks as the narrator. Verse 1 opens like Daniel 6:1, with Darius the Mede as king. Chapter 9 is more specific than Daniel 6 in saying Darius "was the king over the Chaldean kingdom." This is the same narrative context as Zechariah 1 and 2 Chronicles 36, but, since Daniel 9 uses Darius as the narrative's chronological marker, the same historical issues persist here as they did in Daniel 6: Darius the Mede never existed.[3] Knowing this radically reorients how we can read Daniel 9. Instead of merely continuing constructed Christian historical road maps begun in chapter 8, it can be something altogether different. At first glance, it appears as a straightforward prayer from Daniel to his god, followed by another Gabriel appearance. But deeper consideration peels back layers to uncover the chapter's profound theological possibilities.

In the hands of Christian interpreters, Daniel 9 is either an afterthought or yet another chronological puzzle to unlock.[4] Like chapter 8, Daniel 9 offers enough specifics to prompt wild speculation among Christians while being general enough to allow those speculative conclusions to vary considerably. And, not to neglect our own biases, Christians once again make Daniel a book about Jesus of Nazareth despite a total lack of supporting textual evidence. Augustine uses Gabriel's appearance to trace Jesus all the way back to the when Moses went up Mount Sinai, claiming that "the coming of Lord Jesus Christ was arranged and foretold through the law," and Irenaeus incorporates Daniel's reference to Jeremiah at verse 2 to argue the god Daniel experiences here is "manifest by Christ."[5] Melanchthon makes Daniel's prayer "the clear testimony concerning the advent of Christ, the death of Christ, the righteousness of the New Testament, and the destruction of the Jewish state."[6] Wigand's hatred of the Jewish people is palpable when he calls chapter 9 "one of the most special in all of Daniel," as it is a "compendium of the most important articles of faith: God, sin, the forgiveness of sins, penance, faith, prayer, the Messiah, the end of the Jewish people, the antichrist, and the destruction of the world."[7] The unapologetic anti-Semitism in these readings is obvious, as they again highlight the Christian proclivity to make everything in the Bible about Jesus. This alone highlights the pressing need to reread Daniel 9 outside the boundaries of such overt hatred.

Daniel's reference to Jeremiah in verse 2 yields a noteworthy example of biblical intertextuality, meaning Daniel 9 calls back to Jeremiah 25 and the prophecy of seventy years. God narrates at Jeremiah 25:11–12, foretelling the coming destruction of Babylon and its king. Both Daniel and Jeremiah refer to Babylonians as "Chaldeans," which is a nice bit of shared cultural nomenclature on Daniel's part. Daniel 9's use of Jeremiah is an artful way of acknowledging and possibly accepting Jeremiah's prophecy into Daniel's literary context. There are many references to "false prophets" throughout the Hebrew Bible, which points to considerable competition for power and prestige among Israelite prophets leading up to, during, and after the Babylonian exile. Daniel 9's respect for Jeremiah's prophecy is a possible olive branch from one prophetic voice to another that bridges and eliminates any perceived competition between these two prominent figures. Chapter 9's use of Jeremiah does not undo or negate the prophet's work. Jeremiah is not dependent on Daniel for interpretation, nor does Daniel depend on Jeremiah. That said, reading Jeremiah alongside Daniel expands on Jeremiah's ideas by incorporating the prophet's voice into Daniel's apocalyptic framework.

And to truly consider shared interpretive connections between Daniel and Jeremiah, and the complete collection of scriptures that Christians call the Hebrew Bible, we must engage and consider the Israelite exile. I have intentionally avoided this watershed event up to this point because I want to use the raw vulnerability Daniel shows in his prayer as avenue to discuss what happened. Events leading up to, during, and after the Israelite exile are the most significant scriptural events that Christians avoid, ignore, or lack the courage to understand. The Israelite exile is the biblical event (and series of choices) that prompts those ancient peoples we call "Israelites" to write down their sacred stories, poetry, and beliefs, ultimately culminating in this thing we call "the Bible." The exilic period receives passing mention in Christian circles, mainly as a means to explain the so-called "Immanuel Prophecy" in Isaiah 7, which then becomes a conduit to read the Christian reception of that prophecy in Matthew 1. The Israelite exile is much, much more than that Christian romanticization of our shared messianic origin story.

And yet, giving earnest consideration to the Israelite exile is complicated. The first pressing issue is the matter of which sources to consider. The biblical account is a highly theologized historiographic reconstruction based on the perspectives of a select few, but this account is the one most readily available and most widely read. Therefore, using it as a "jumping off" point would seem to be the logical choice. However, historical information and resources outside the Bible exist but are quite sparse, limited in perspective, and built around retelling the exile narrative from an openly Israelite perspective.[8] And not just an "Israelite" perspective, because by the time the Israelite exile happened, Israel itself was a divided nation. Northern Israel, known as Israel, had its capital in Samaria. The capital city of Southern Israel, or Judah, was Jerusalem. According to biblical sources, Solomon's death led to a leadership crisis: Who would rule now that the king is dead? First Kings and 2 Chronicles talk of political and social discontent with Solomon's successor, his son Rehoboam. This creates space for Jeroboam, a high-ranking and well-liked official of Solomon's, to lead a revolt against Rehoboam. Ten Israelite tribes aligned with Jeroboam, eventually leading to the creation of the Northern Israelite kingdom in the tenth century CE. A once-united monarchy now stood at odds with itself. This Northern-Southern split promoted considerable political division, culminating in an event commonly known as the Syro-Ephraimite War/Crisis.

This skirmish unfolded between 734 and 731 BCE when the northern kingdom of Israel (also called Ephraim) aligned with Damascus (otherwise known as Syria) to overthrow the southern kingdom's monarch, Ahaz.[9] The goal was to install a leader more amenable to forming a coalition against the growing Assyrian empire. Damascus and Israelite plans backfired, however, as the Assyrians came to Ahaz' aid by capturing Damascus in 732 BCE.[10] According to 2 Kings 17, the king of Assyria then besieged the northern kingdom in 722/721 BCE, captured Samaria, made Judah an Assyrian vassal state, and sent its people into exile in Assyria. Christian scholars engage the Syro-Ephraimite conflict along with the Assyrian takeover/occupation of Northern Israel, but in practice Christians fail to weigh the political and social realities of these events when considering biblical Israel and the subsequent fall of Judah to the Babylonians. Trauma from the southern kingdom's Babylonian exile did not appear at random; it was a smaller piece of much more substantial Israelite trauma that began with Solomon's death.

Biblical sources claim the southern exilic period began with noteworthy events in 597 BCE and 586 BCE. Nebuchadnezzar II, king of the Neo-Babylonian empire, attacked and captured Jerusalem in 597 BCE. Nebuchadnezzar II then installed a puppet king, Zedekiah, but he rebelled against Babylon.[11] This prompted a Babylonian crackdown on Israel in 586 BCE. Nebuchadnezzar's army destroyed Jerusalem and the Israelite First Temple as a show of strength and to break the Israelite people's morale.[12] Israel's destruction, fall, and dissolution was prolonged, brutal, bloody, and deeply personal. The temple's destruction shattered any sense of normalcy Jerusalem clung to, while also making the remaining Israelites question their religious practice and heritage at an existential level. We cannot overlook the pain behind biblical voices crying out to God for salvation and forgiveness by couching our understanding in the eventual return from exile in 539 BCE. The suffering was real, and it shaped the Bible as it exists today.

It is against this exilic backdrop that Daniel offers his prayer. He begins with an outward display of mourning in verse 3, reflecting his internal anguish through "fasting, and sackcloth, and ashes." Daniel speaks in the first person and addresses his deity as both "Adonai Elohim" and "YHWH Adonai." English translations render Daniel's addresses as "the Lord God" and "the Lord God," respectively, which makes for a nice and clean rendering that simultaneously glosses over potential theological and political implications of Daniel addressing the deity as both Elohim and Adonai. There is a widely accepted scholarly approach to the different names and titles the Israelites use for God throughout the Hebrew Bible, commonly called the Documentary Hypothesis. In essence, the argument claims the different names and titles for God (YHWH, Elohim, Adonai) represent different ancient religious traditions that came together over time, creating a more amalgamated but egalitarian approach to the various religious sects that eventually come to represent Israelite monotheism.[13] This makes Daniel's addressing of God as YHWH, Elohim, and Adonai a broader blanket statement that we can understand as uniting disparate groups and possible factions. Such a move makes Daniel 9 into a bridge between different Israelite traditions, as he does not speak to one form of Israelite thought over another.

Daniel begins his prayer with an admonition followed by an admission. He highlights the deeply personal relationship with his deity with "Please, my god," followed by an acknowledgment of who God is and what God does. Daniel's deity is great and formidable, a god who keeps and has faith in those who love and keep his commandments. But all this leads to an admission that is as personal as it is communal. The shift in pronouns here is significant: Daniel starts with "I" but uses "we" from verse 5 until verse 19. Daniel has taken it upon himself to speak for the Israelite people, a bold stance considering no Israelite asked him to do this, nor was he elected or appointed by Israelites. Daniel 1 shows that Daniel gained his power and authority by Babylonian assignment. This makes Daniel's prayer paradoxical, as it is simultaneously heartfelt and sincere while also coming into existence by virtue of Daniel's complacency in the book's Babylonian regime.

It is entirely possible Daniel prays from this sense of contradiction. He does not condemn the Israelites responsible for the exile, but he also does not expunge himself. "We" have sinned, and "we" have wronged. Daniel realizes that both he and his people have become the very thing Jeremiah warns about in Jeremiah 7: people cast from God's sight. And yet, we must again ask who exactly Daniel's "people" are: Does he speak for all of Israel, or just a few? The Bible presents the exile as total and all-encompassing. When the Bible speaks of Israel in the exilic context, one gets the impression that the exile affected all of Israel. The reality is quite different, as a lack of nonbiblical sources limits what we can know about how many Israelites were forced into exile.[14] Even extant biblical evidence is marred by inconsistencies, like

2 Kings claiming two major deportations occurred as compared to Jeremiah's three deportations. What scholars do with this biblical evidence varies wildly, creating a spectrum ranging near-total annihilation to something resembling active migration with inconclusive motives.[15]

This makes the Bible's presentation of the exile into more of a series of ideological manifestos than an accurate depiction of historical events. And yet, the exile's collective trauma permeates this thing we Christians call the Old Testament. Dire prophetic warnings become cries of atonement and repentance in Daniel 9, laced with a bitter undertone of resentment toward Israel's ancestors. Verse 6 shows Daniel's frustration toward "our kings, our princes, and other fathers and to all people of the land" who disregarded the prophets and their words against political treachery and complacency. Daniel narrows his scope at verse 9 to place blame upon just "our kings, our princes, and our fathers" that "sinned against" their deity. Such a move feels out of place compared to the reverence given toward Israelite ancestors and leadership throughout the Bible, but it makes sense given the larger Israelite political context. The average farmer, shepherd, merchant, mother, child, or family suffered a great deal thanks to decisions their leaders made. Daniel's justified resentment harkens back to truth about kingship laid out by Samuel in 1 Samuel 8: expect to suffer the consequences of choices made with minimal (if any) input from the commoner.

Daniel leans hard into appealing toward YHWH's compassion and forgiveness by admitting full responsibility on his people's behalf. Daniel does not try to sidestep culpability, claiming in verses 9–10 that "we have rebelled against [YHWH]" by ignoring his voice and rejecting his law. He makes no excuses for the situation and choices that led to it. Yet in verse 11, Daniel argues that "all Israel transgressed your law and turned aside from you," a statement the flies in the face of historical evidence, the realities of political failures, and Daniel's own words in verse 8. Daniel blames everyone and claims the exile is an act of divine punishment. On the surface this theological position appears sound: God and Israel made a covenant, Israel violated that covenant, so the protection God offers through the covenant becomes null. And yet, if leaders and their advisors make decisions affecting everyone, can we say that Israel in total violated the covenant? Does a nation's leadership reflect the entirety of its populace? Or do they reflect their own wants and choices?

Verse 12 lays out an even more peculiar understanding of the text's social and political moment, as Daniel again places blame upon the people and their rulers. He even decries them for "bringing a great evil upon us, one that had never been done under all the heavens." How then can Daniel speak for everyone in verse 13 when he claims that "we did not seek favor before YHWH our god"? Did he patrol each Israelite household, inspecting every square inch and ensuring that the tenants follow Moses' law without error? We know from a historical standpoint that Israel split and ultimately fell thanks to political maneuverings, so what Daniel does here is an attempt at interpreting and understanding the existential "why" of Israel's demise. Verses 14–15 are Daniel's explicit answer to this question: YHWH brought the destruction and ruin upon Israel because "we have sinned and we have been wicked."

What Daniel says next in verse 16 is telling. Instead of seeking God's mercy and a return to a more peaceful and stable covenant relationship, Daniel asks God to "turn your face and wrath from your city, Jerusalem." Christian interpreters read Daniel's request as a direct call for God to bestow forgiveness and benevolence. This is true, as highlighted by Daniel asking his god to "shine your face upon your desolate sanctuary" in verse 17. However, read together, verses 16–17 become the cries of an abused and battered people, reminiscent of Weems' groundbreaking work on biblical prophets.[16] Weems' argument is simple but deeply profound: biblical prophets use highly sexualized metaphors "to arouse in their audiences the kinds of emotions that would help underscore their messages of doom—emotions of disgust, contempt, terror, and shame."[17] Such imagery combines "to both fascinate and repel audiences."[18] Through this lens, Daniel's Israel is the victim of domestic abuse. Daniel 9 justifies horrors wrought upon Israel and its people through language of sin, iniquity, and personal negligence. One would hope, then, that at verse 16 Daniel is effectively trying to break up with God, terminating the toxic relationship between Israel and this deity. However, verse 17 shows Daniel stands stuck in the relationship that, according to his theological worldview, brought death and destruction upon thousands on account of the choices made by people in positions of power.

Daniel pours on the collective communal blame at verses 18–19 as he seeks forgiveness by asking God to see and hear what has become of Israel and grant them mercy. This act of prayer is a logical move for Daniel, given his religious background. It makes sense Daniel would beseech his god for peace and that the destructive horrors of war cease. But this act of asking raises a theological quandary of sorts: Why exactly is Daniel asking? According to the theological inclinations of Christian interpreters,

God stands in control of history. If this is the case, why would Daniel ask? Because if God is sovereign, asking the deity for anything is a fruitless, futile, and cruel gesture. Daniel's appeal appears quite genuine, which implies he asks because he believes his words might change things and improve Israel's situation. Changing the deity's mind has considerable biblical precedence. In Exodus 32:14, God changes God's mind about punishing the people over the golden calf. God forgives Moses and the people at Numbers 14:20, "just as you have asked." From a purely textual perspective, God can and does make decisions based on human prayers.

Through this lens, Daniel's prayer takes on a very different quality. He is no longer praying for forgiveness; he is asking God to stop the pain and suffering God placed upon Israel. Daniel attributes the nation's fate to God, and this prayer is Daniel's chance to say "enough is enough." Praying here is an act of defiance for Daniel, as he witnesses the calamities of Israel and tells God that the message is received; now it is time for God to forgive. Things have gotten so bad for Daniel and his people that he asks God just to look and listen, and the evidence speaks for itself. Daniel even admits in verse 19 that his people are worthy of forgiveness out of God's mercy and not their own piety or righteousness. Daniel openly confesses his sins and the sins of his people in verse 20, as if to ask, "What more do you want from me and from us? Have we not suffered enough?"

Despite Daniel's bold effort, God does not respond. Yes, the man Gabriel appears again in verse 21, but one would think based on Daniel's words and previous biblical appearances of the divine that his deity would make a grandiose appearance from a whirlwind or burning bush. That does not happen, as Daniel again talks with Gabriel and not God. Verse 21 references the vision of Daniel 8, but here in chapter 9 the text does not say Gabriel appears in a vision. He arrives in front of Daniel "during the time of the evening sacrifice" to bring "insightful understanding." Gabriel says "a word went out" in verse 23, which is why he stands before Daniel. Christian interpreters see Gabriel as a divine emissary here, but, like chapter 8, Daniel 9 is unclear as to who sent Gabriel. Gabriel speaks of love as he invites Daniel to "consider the word and understand the vision," which is peculiar because chapter 9 contains no vision.

What, then, is Gabriel there to do? He tells us at verse 24 by unpacking the "seventy weeks" decreed for Daniel's people and Jerusalem. Gabriel comes to unpack the prophecy of Jeremiah 25:11–12 mentioned in verse 2. Jeremiah's prophecy describes the coming Babylonian conquest at chapter 25, in which YHWH tells Jeremiah that "the whole land will become a ruin and a waste," with Israel and its allies serving the Babylonian king "for seventy years." Here again we return to dates and timelines as scholars consult Jeremiah's "seventy years" for assorted purposes. For example, biblical historians make Jeremiah 25 paradigmatic evidence for laying out an Israelite historical event timeline culminating in the return and restoration of Israel.[19] But, as one would expect given the wildly different historical conclusions rendered thus far from Daniel, the results and conclusions from Jeremiah are just as divergent. This makes Daniel 9's Jeremiah reference even more interesting, especially as Gabriel changes the specific chronology from Jeremiah's "seventy years" to "seventy weeks." Ambiguity around Gabriel's language prompts some readers to combine years and weeks into an otherwise unknown "seventy weeks of years," while still others lay a presumptuous anti-Semitic supersessionist replacement theology on this prophecy.[20] Both approaches are fundamentally off base and lack textual support. Jesus is not in Daniel 9, and the text is explicit and clear that Gabriel discusses seventy weeks, not weeks of years or some other elaborate chronological metaphor.

Jeremiah 25's prophecy itself is inexact. It states that "these nations will serve the king of Babylon for seventy years" without further specifics regarding this king's identity. Daniel 9 complicates the matter further in again using Darius the Mede as a timestamp. Since Darius the Mede did not exist, this leaves us without historical answers.[21] But perhaps that is the point. Apocalyptic literature is, by design, flexible historically and interpretively. Works in that genre can be applied across geographic space and time with considerable ease (hence the vastly different interpretations and conclusions yielded). And yet, the more complicated that readers make their interpretation, the less sense Daniel 9 makes. Further, following the Christian trend of making the final eight verses the chapter's exegetical focus undercuts the preceding prayer.

Taking a simple and concise approach to consider these seventy weeks and what they can mean offers an uncomplicated reading. In a biblical context, seven represents completeness. For example, in Genesis, God creates across the span of six days and rests on the seventh, establishing precedence and justification for the Sabbath coming on a seven-day cycle. The deity confirms this Sabbath rhythm in Exodus 20 through consecrating the seventh day. Leviticus 25 builds upon this idea, making every seventh year a Sabbath year in which "you should not sow your field or prune your vineyard" (Lev 25:4). Every seventh seven-year period will be a "jubilee" year in which all debts are settled, and the land can fully recover from previous harvests. The more complete something can be from a biblical perspective, the better. The number seven represents this idea.

Thus, Gabriel's "seventy weeks" is a clever and not-so-subtle wordplay on the number seven. A week has seven days in it, and Gabriel says everything Daniel witnesses will come to fruition after seventy periods of seven days. The number seventy is a play on seven, with seventy being divisible by seven ten times. Gabriel's words toy with the audience here, essentially saying that "all this will come to fruition when the completion of the complete is complete." Everything Daniel sees and Jeremiah foretold will happen when it happens, not a moment before or after. Anyone claiming otherwise projects themselves and their needlessly complicated timetable onto an otherwise straightforward illustration.

Christians buy into "apocalyptic panic" early and often. The internet is laden with conspiracy theories about how and when this world will end. We often use texts like Daniel 9 to justify otherwise unfounded paranoia, creating self-reinforcing feedback loops that spark and then confirm our apocalyptic dread. I guarantee that, one hundred years from now, conspiracy-focused Christians will have a fresh batch of theories backed up by their particular (and peculiar) Daniel 9 readings. But such work is yet another indication of interpreter projection. Gabriel does say atonement and eternal righteousness await at the seventy weeks' conclusion. But verses 24–27 carry even fewer specifics than Jeremiah 25, making any fixed timeline from Daniel 9 into an exercise in futility.

Let us consider verse 25 as an example. Verse 25 mentions "an anointed ruler" whose arrival inaugurates the temple's reconstruction. Identifying this "anointed one" is the source of much consternation and debate among scholars. Early Christian interpreters followed their established messianic path, making this unnamed ruler "Christ our Lord and Redeemer."[22] Calvin, Mede, Willet, Mayer, Bullinger, and other Protestant Reformers follow suit: the only possible person this "ruler" can be is Jesus. Jesus does not appear in Daniel 9. "Jesus" or "Christ" are absent. Daniel 9 does not reveal who this person is; it merely says this person's arrival ushers in Jerusalem and its sanctuary's restoration. Making this person Jesus is shocking in its unapologetic anti-Semitism. Contemporary Christian readers either stand oblivious or fail to care about such an obvious problem. According to such lenses, Daniel 9 is important because it foretells Jesus' arrival.[23] Approaches that are not anti-Semitic gravitate toward reading this ruler as an inexact high priest or the high priest Onias III.[24] Some lobby for it being Antiochus or Cyrus the Great, with still others presenting arguments for both options.[25]

Herein lies the power of this kind of text: Daniel 9 allows for all and none of the theoretical identities to be true. This unknown anointed ruler can be whatever the reader wants him to be, once again highlighting Daniel's capacity for being an interpreter's mirror. Scholars go to preposterous lengths to support their specific argument about who this person is, treating it as a sort of keystone to unlocking Daniel's prophetic code and, in turn, unlocking all of history itself. Radically different conclusions underline Daniel 9's narrative brilliance, as readers far too often decentralize the text to make themselves its focal point. Daniel 9 does not exist to bolster Christian messianic illusions, nor is its purpose to offer an accurate historical timeline. Daniel 9 exists to invite the reader into Daniel's world and to grapple with Daniel's trauma. Daniel unleashes a powerful and damning prayer, only to receive a vague, nondescript answer. And this answer does not come from God directly; it comes from Gabriel. The Hebrew in verses 24–27 is also quite muddled, with verse 27 varying considerably according to which translation one reads.[26]

This, then, is how chapter 9 ends: not with peace and resolution, but with further confusion atop looming destruction and desolation. Unlike chapter 8, we get no insight into Daniel's thoughts and reactions to Gabriel's words. Chapter 9 simply ends. The only hint of reprieve comes in verse 23 when Gabriel tells Daniel, "You are loved." But even that falls flat, considering the message came from another human being and not Daniel's god. Yet lacking a neat, clean ending solidifies Daniel 9's interpretive possibilities, making a measuring stick capable of uncovering predispositions and biases of the readers interpreting it. Daniel bares his soul in prayer and entreats the god of his people to show mercy and forgive. Gabriel's message, however cumbersome and indeterminate, speaks to Daniel's looming anxiety about the future of Jerusalem and its temple. Restoration will come to the city, but unknown forces will destroy the city and the sanctuary. Daniel begs for restoration, but the message of Daniel 9 is a humbling mixture of desperation and uncertainty, leaving us to wonder about what comes next.

9.3 So What?

In a note of striking narrative consistency, God still stands markedly absent in Daniel 9. Daniel spends the verses leading up to verse 21 praying and beseeching his god. One can hear the desperation in his voice as he cries out, confesses, and admits guilt on behalf of his people. He languishes with his words, crafting a tableau seeking forgiveness in which no one steps away innocent. It is a powerful testament to Daniel's faith in his god and his people. But what does this prayer get Daniel? How does God respond to this man laying his soul out on behalf of his people? By sending Gabriel. And that is it. No pillar of fire or cloud like with Moses in Exodus. No angel of God as with Hagar in Genesis. No whirlwind as with Job. Not a hint of the intimacy laid out in Genesis 3 when the deity discovers Eve and Adam ate from the wrong tree. Daniel's God stands silent. One could argue Gabriel speaks for God, but, if that is the case, why would God not speak for God's self? Further, why does the text not explicitly say that Gabriel came on God's behalf or that God sent the man? God's silence is disorienting. Like Daniel in his anguish, the text leaves us wondering: What lesson or theological insight are we to take from such absence?

God's silence here is a deeply profound theological statement. Christians often look for and want big, grandiose statements from God. We like to imagine ourselves in daily struggles as Moses, Hagar, Job, or some other biblical icon to whom God appears and speaks directly. Yet it seems our lived realities reflect the divine silence present throughout Daniel. We pray and seek guidance, with little to show for it, as one could make a compelling argument that what some Christians consider to be answers to prayers are nothing more than fortuitous coincidences. When a loved one is sick, where is this great and powerful God? When nations continually go to war over human political bickering, what prevents God from stepping in to stop it all? Does God not see humanity's great suffering? Does God not hear our cries of pain and anguish? What, then, does the silence of the deity in Daniel say about the human condition and our relationship to God?

Trite answers and solutions to these valid and important questions abound.[27] They reflect a myopic theology of prayer, one in desperate need of refinement. It is through divine silence that Daniel 9, then, becomes a platform for us to ask: What does prayer do? What is the point of prayer? And what do "answers" to prayer look like? Should we expect thunderous clouds and fiery towers, or something else? Daniel gets this "something else" in the man Gabriel, so what does that mean for us? Simply looking around offers an efficient and brutal assessment of the current state of prayer, and a most pressing example from an American context is the nation's epidemic of gun violence.

Each day, 106 Americans die from gun violence; and each day, 210 are shot and survive.[28] Firearms are the number-one cause of death among children and teens in the United States.[29] Gun violence is far less of an issue outside the United States thanks to stricter gun laws and restrictions. We Americans, however, trot out the vague, hackneyed "thoughts and prayers" response to all shootings. We use this "thoughts and prayers" response for almost everything we deem tragic, from hurricane damage to earthquakes to elementary schools and nightclubs getting littered with bullets. It seems a calamitous event cannot transpire without a celebrity or politician opting to make "thoughts and prayers" the only solution. This clearly is not working.[30]

Certain political and Christian leaders push back, claiming the solution lies in "putting prayer back in schools."[31] People supporting this view argue that more prayer will "restore" America and bring about a utopian peacetime:

> God is a vital concept in the American experience. We erase Him at our peril. It is not too late to restore this vital keystone to the basic political and social philosophy of our nation.[32]

Those with school-prayer zeal overlook the living reality of the nation to which they so desperately want to return. Slavery, legislated sexism, and other shocking discriminations are baked into the beliefs that founded America and within the men who penned the Constitution. Lobbying for this kind of prayer only allows us to bring back a dangerous and destructive way of life.

Which brings us back to the question: What does prayer do? Did Daniel's prayer in chapter 9 affect the history proceeding it? Cyrus the Great reestablished Jerusalem and the temple, only to have the Romans destroy everything again in 70 CE. Did God tell Daniel "no" and, in so doing, allow the deaths of thousands? What of the prayers made by those murdered in the Holocaust, or of soldiers fighting in unjust wars brought about by immoral and unethical leadership? If evidence for answered prayer is circumstantial, what then is prayer? Daniel 9 makes us ask this question, then gives us no answers.

Maybe this lack of answers is the point. What if, in a bold theological move, Daniel 9 lays out classic biblical tropes to tear them down to make us reconsider what we pray for and why we do it. If God said "yes" to every prayer, anarchy would reign across creation. Further, if the deity makes "yes" and "no" responses without justification (i.e., "God's will"), then that god ceases to be good and becomes a capricious and petty ruler. Prayer has become a tool we Christians use to deny our own finite humanity. We think when done properly, it allows us to transcend human limitations. But people who pray get sick and die. Countries prayed and labored over burn to the ground. Innocent voices cry out, only to get silence in return. Despite the untold collective millions of hours dedicated to prayer each week, suffering prevails.

A radical reconsideration of prayer is necessary. And the most perplexing thing about potential reconsideration is just how much actual reconsidering already exists. For example, James Cone asks his readers:

> Who can "pray" when all hell has broken loose and human existence is being trampled underfoot by evil forces? Prayer takes on new meaning. It has nothing to do with those Bible verses that rulers utter before eating their steaks, in order to remind themselves that they are religious and have not mistreated anybody. Who can thank God for food when we know that our brothers and sisters are starving as we dine like kings?[33]

Cone couches his understanding of prayer in Black Christian theology, arguing that white Christians use prayer "to reinforce the rightness of their destruction of blacks." For Cone,

> prayer is the spirit that is evident in all oppressed communities when they know that they have a job to do. It is the communication with the divine that makes them know that they have very little to lose in the fight against evil and a lot to gain.[34]

Black feminist theologian and AME Zion pastor Rev. Brandee Mimitzraiem goes further, arguing that Christians use prayer to "micromanage and order God around" and to "treat God like a servant," making prayer "a way to keep God on task and maintain human sovereignty."[35] We are not to reject prayer. What we need to reject are passively accepted notions of what prayer can be.

Praying is profoundly biblical and is essential to how God works throughout God's creation. It radically decenters us humans from our own predispositions, meant to compel us into finding where and how God lives and works among us. By inviting us to be part of God's active nature, prayer can show us what changes are needed, and what that change looks like in real time. Praying becomes a verb in every sense of the word and helps us reconstruct the core question in Daniel 9. Instead of asking, "What does Daniel pray?" we are now compelled to ask, "What does Daniel do with that prayer?" Instead of "What will you give me, O God?" prayer now becomes a chance to consider, "God, what do you want us to do?"

10
Daniel 10 Reconsidered

10.1 Translation

1 In the third year of Cyrus, king of Persia, a word was revealed to Daniel, who was named Belteshazzar; and the word was true; and a great conflict;[1] and he understood the word and he had understanding with the vision.

2 And in those days I, Daniel, had been mourning for three weeks.

3 I had eaten no rich food, and no meat and wine had entered into my mouth, and I had not anointed myself for the entirety of the three weeks.

4 And on the twenty-fourth day of the first month, I was by the great river, which is the Hiddaqel.[2]

5 And I lifted my eyes and I saw; and lo! A man clothed in linen and a waist girded in Uphaz gold.

6 And his body was like beryl, and his face an appearance of lightning, and his eyes like torches of fire, and his arms and legs like gleaming burnished bronze. And the sound of his words like the sound of the multitude.

7 And I saw, I, Daniel alone, the vision, and the men who were with me did not see the vision, but a great trembling fell upon them, and they fled to hide.

8 And I was left alone, and I saw this great vision, and there was no strength left in me. And my appearance turned to death, and I retained no strength.

9 Then I heard the sound of his words, and as I heard the sound of his words, I was made to fall asleep upon my face, and my face was to the ground.

10 And lo! A hand touched me, and it set me upon my knees and my hands.

11 And he said to me, "Daniel, beloved man, understand the words which I am saying to you. And stand yourself upright, for now I have been sent to you." And as he was speaking this word to me, I was standing, trembling.

12 And he said to me, "Do not fear, Daniel, for from the first day when you gave your heart to understand and to humble yourself before your god, your words have been heard and I have come because of your words.

13 And a prince of the kingdom of Persia stood opposite of me for twenty-one days, and lo! Michael, one of the chief princes, came to help me, and I was left there beside the kings of Persia.

14 I came for you to understand what will happen to your people in the latter days, for the vision of those days is still longer."

15 And when he was speaking these words to me, I set my face toward the ground and became silent.

16 And lo! One like a human being touched my lips, and I opened my mouth, and I spoke and I said to the one standing in front of me, "My lord, because of the vision pain comes upon me and I do not retain strength.

17 How is this servant of my lord able to talk this way with my lord? And I am now shaking; there is not strength in me to stand, and there is not breath left in me."

18 And again, the one with an appearance of a human touched me and strengthened me.

19 And he said, "Do not fear, beloved man; you are safe. Be strong and courageous!" And as he spoke with me, I became strong and said, "May my lord speak, for you have given me strength."

20 And he said, "Do you know why I have come to you? And now I must return to fight with a prince of Persia, and when I am going out, lo! A Yavan[3] prince will come.

21 But I will declare to you what is inscribed in a reliable book, and there is not one contending with me against these except Michael your prince."

10.2 Reading against the Grain

Daniel 10 begins like every other chapter: telling the reader who the ruling king is to date the chapter's narrative context. According to the text, a word is revealed to Daniel "in the third year of Cyrus, king of Persia." Verse 1 refers to Daniel as "Belteshazzar" for the first time since Daniel 5, possibly reaffirming Daniel's status as an Israelite working in a Persian court. This is the third time that Daniel mentions Cyrus, with the first two instances being 1:21 and 6:28. Situating Daniel 10 during Cyrus' third year seems at odds with chapter 1's claim of Daniel continuing his palace duties "until the first year of King Cyrus." Daniel 6 simply states that Daniel prospered under Cyrus, so no chronological conflict comes from that. But saying Daniel held his court position only until Cyrus' first year makes Daniel 10's "third year of King Cyrus" declaration worth considering.

If Daniel the book is correct, Daniel the person lived through the end of Jehoiakim's reign, survived Nebuchadnezzar's siege, thrived in Nebuchadnezzar's Babylonian court, was Belshazzar's advisor, prospered under Darius, and continues to bloom under Cyrus. This means Daniel was old enough to become one of Nebuchadnezzar's court advisors in or around 587 BCE, then lived until 536 BCE (which is the third year of Cyrus' reign). Psalm 90:10 claims that "the days of our life are seventy years, or perhaps eighty, if we are strong," making Daniel's lifespan feasible within a biblical context. However, stepping outside the Bible underscores the psalmist's outlook as an idealization.[4] Exceptionally high child mortality rates defined the ancient Levant, with archeological evidence complicating the already involved process of assessing ancient life expectancy.[5] Disease, flooding, food shortages caused by famine, war, and lack of widespread medical care made living into one's seventies or eighties highly unlikely. That said, the text makes no comment on Daniel's age, making him seemingly ageless and therefore a fitting emissary into this narrative world.

King Cyrus, otherwise known as Cyrus the Great, was the title given to Cyrus II of Persia. He was a real figure with considerable nonbiblical evidence to support his existence and reign as the founder of the Persian Achaemenid Empire. The Greek historian Herodotus writes at length about Cyrus and his ascent to power, and the archeological find known as the Cyrus Cylinder is a Babylonian account of Cyrus' 539 BCE Babylonian conquest.[6] Cyrus is famous for ending the Babylonian Israelite exile out of political pragmatism, a matter that the Bible takes to considerable ideological ends. Cyrus knew that one way to win over his recently conquered people was to appear magnanimous, which sheds light on why he ended the Babylonian captivity: the people were far more likely to express gratitude instead of animosity for granting them the chance to return home.

From a biblical standpoint, gratitude toward Cyrus is plentiful. Isaiah repeatedly sings Cyrus' praises, going as far as to call him God's anointed shepherd destined to rebuild Jerusalem.[7] Ezra presents Cyrus' decree to rebuild the temple as a direct response to their deity's command.[8] Ezra even has the Persian monarch speak the divine name at 1:2: "Thus says King Cyrus of Persia: YHWH, the God of heaven, has given me all the kingdoms of the earth, and he has charged me to build him a house at Jerusalem in Judah." Second Chronicles cements Cyrus' place in the Bible by claiming Cyrus' actions reflect God moving in and through him, calling his actions to be "in fulfillment of the word of the YHWH spoken by Jeremiah." In making Cyrus the monarch here, Daniel 10 brings the character's considerable biblical significance back to the reader's purview.

Cyrus is important outside biblical contexts as well. Cyrus conquered Asia Minor in 547 BCE and besieged Babylon in 539 BCE. The Cyrus Cylinder recalls Cyrus' Babylonian invasion, giving the monarch such titles as "the mighty king of Sumer and Akkad" and "the king of the four quarters of the world."[9] Written in Akkadian and incomplete, the cylinder features alleged firsthand remarks from Cyrus, though it is highly unlikely Cyrus penned or said these words. Cyrus calls himself "king of the world" who worships the deity Marduk while also striving for peace through labor relief and rebuilding temples and other sacred sites. Despite being overt Cyrus propaganda, the Cyrus Cylinder carries considerable importance for biblical depictions of the ruler, as it is evidence for Cyrus' existence and imperial success.

With this in mind, putting Daniel 10 in the third year of Cyrus' reign makes it a chapter about what happens when the "chosen one" has had some time to work, to lead, and to build. If, as Isaiah, Ezra, and the Chronicler believed, Cyrus comes to rebuild and repair, why are Daniel's first thoughts in verse 2 about mourning? Daniel speaks in the first person starting at verse 2, offering detailed accounts of his three-week mourning period. Daniel eats no rich food, meat, or wine to express his grief, which also may be a not-so-subtle call back to Daniel's self-imposed dietary restrictions in Daniel 1. Daniel says, "I had not anointed myself for the entirety of the three weeks," to share the depth and breadth of his mourning.[10] The text itself is unclear as to why Daniel mourns, creating space to argue that Daniel mourns what he previously witnessed in Daniel 9 or that his actions respond to what he is about to see in Daniel 10. Either way, Daniel's grief shows us that Cyrus' rule was not the national and religious panacea the prophets foretold. Daniel 10 makes Cyrus just another king, one among many in a lengthy line of rulers doomed to fail.

Verse 4 offers a specific month and date, separating Daniel 10 from preceding visions. The text is not clear as to which calendar it references with "on the twenty-fourth day of the first month," leading to a wide array of possible chronologies. This cannot be January 24, because the Gregorian calendar came into being over one thousand years after Daniel's composition. It is most likely a reference to the Hebrew religious calendar, making Daniel's fast unfold during Passover festivities, but even that position is speculative.[11] Daniel locates himself at "the great river" known in the Hebrew as the Hiddaqel and within larger historical context as the Tigris. The Tigris flows in modern-day Iraq and Turkey, thereby removing Daniel from Israel and Jerusalem by hundreds of miles. Daniel's location paired with the name that Daniel's colonizers gave him underscores a grim reality: despite Cyrus' claim to diversity and greater Israelite autonomy, the exile continues. Any hope of total Israelite restoration under Cyrus meets an abrupt halt now that Daniel still lives and sees visions far from home.

The vision here is—compared to a giant metal statue, four beasts emerging from the sea, and a warring goat and ram—quite tame. Daniel raises his eyes to see a man adorned in linen and "a waist girded in Uphaz gold." Jeremiah 10:9 discusses gold from Uphaz as well, making Daniel 10 and Jeremiah 10 the only biblical instances such a place receives mention. Daniel speaks of Uphaz gold with reverence, a sharp juxtaposition with Jeremiah's reference being within the context of shaming Israel for using gold from Uphaz to construct idols. Uphaz' exact location remains unknown, so it seems possible significance lies in using the gold's source as yet another call back to Jeremiah. In Daniel the gold's origins bear no weight on its status as either idolatrous or sacred.

Verse 6 describes this man in greater detail: a body like beryl, a face like lightning, eyes like fire torches, burnished bronze arms and legs, topped off with a voice "like the sound of the multitude." Despite such grandiose descriptions, this man is still just a man. He is described with the Hebrew אִישׁ, the common biblical Hebrew word for "man." His appearance, clothing, and voice make him remarkable, not his human ontology, but Christian readers use this description to make still more unsupported claims about this man being Jesus.[12] Readers supporting Jesus' presence in Daniel 10 may point to Revelation 1 and Jesus as he appears there. Such readings interpret Daniel through the book of Revelation, an academically and historically fallacious move, as Revelation came after Daniel. According to that chronological logic, Christians should interpret Revelation through the lens of Daniel. Making this man Jesus continues the anti-Semitic supersessionist streak plaguing Christian readings of Daniel, as, once again, Christian receptions make this text and its robust interpretive possibilities into a cliché. There is so much more to this man and the vision than Christian supersessionism presented as prophetic romanticizing. For example, the vision in Daniel 10 lasts only two verses. No extended, drawn-out sights here—just a simple, clean presentation of this unknown but remarkable man.

Daniel's vision echoes the prophet Ezekiel's own man dressed in linen. Ezekiel 9 presents the linen-man as a sort of errand runner, going through the city marking "the foreheads of those who sigh and groan over all the abominations that are committed in it" (Ezek 9:3). The deity speaks directly to this linen man, and he speaks back to the deity in Ezekiel 9:11, creating an intriguing dynamic between Ezekiel's human and his god. Their relationship continues as God instructs Ezekiel's linen man to spread "burning coals from the cherubim" across the city (Ezek 10:2). He even carries the fire of the cherubim in verse 7, making him a figure on par with divine messengers. But, like Daniel, Ezekiel's linen man is still a human being; Ezekiel never presents him as anything more than that.

Daniel's vision packs much into a brief space. Verse 6 describes five facets of the man, starting with his body like "beryl." Beryl is a crystal-like gemstone that appears biblically in Daniel, Exodus, and Ezekiel. Bible authors laud its beauty and preciousness, making it more than just a stone or trite descriptor. Beryl can be many colors, including a golden yellow, pink, deep green, or aquamarine. It seems, then, this description comes from a place of admiration and not fear as the man's face of lightning and eyes of fire leave a pronounced impression of light amid darkness. Contemporary readers may be quick to argue Daniel's use of lightning and fire emotes dread or terror, but in the ancient world lightning and fire were the only light sources beyond the sun and moon.

Light imagery evokes seeing and clarity, making the man's appearance pronounced and radiant. Such powerful light makes the burnished arms and legs shine, pulling Daniel's (and the reader's) eyes to examine the full figure. The man's voice "is like the sound of the multitude," an analogy conveying the volume and magnitude of what Daniel hears. "Multitude" (הָמוֹן) appears throughout the Bible, ranging from God describing Abraham's multitude of offspring to chaotic scores of people.[13] However, the only instance in which the Hebrew Bible employs "multitude" to describe sound is Ezekiel 23:42. Ezekiel's narrator, presented in the text as God, uses the phrase pejoratively to describe "the sound of a raucous multitude" surrounding an elaborately adorned woman. Ezekiel presents this woman as negatively sexual, which Daniel 10 does not do with this man. But describing human bodies aligns both Daniel 10 and Ezekiel 23, creating space to weigh the importance of admiring the physical form in this apocalyptic context.

Bodies play a vital role in Daniel. Nebuchadnezzar selects Daniel and his friends because they "are without any blemish and pleasing with appearance."[14] Sexuality is key as well, given that a person the text described as a eunuch plays a critical role in Daniel's success. Daniel and his friends fail without their bodies or the eunuch. One could argue bodies and sexuality are intrinsic to Daniel; to read it without embracing these human aspects is to deny what stands before us. To quote gender theorist and sociologist R. W. Connell, "Bodies cannot be considered a neutral medium. . . . Their materiality matters."[15] Contemporary human bodies hold places of considerable political, social, economic, and religious significance. American legislators win or lose elections based on what they make legal and illegal to do to and with human bodies. Entire American political parties define themselves based on stances regarding the human body and what bodies can do. People around the globe pay millions to alter their bodies, bringing themselves closer to culturally constructed beauty concepts. Many countries tell women what they can and cannot do with their bodies, including what to wear and the types of basic medical procedures to which they have access. Humans use other human bodies to sell everything, from food to fragrances and cars and houses. A body deemed culturally "good" or "ideal" frequently yields professional success and financial prosperity. Even the language we use to describe a body reflects physical paradigms, as we call someone unable to walk, to use both hands, to see, or to hear "handicapped" or "differently abled," as if such words as "normal" and "abled" carry any weight beyond their culturally constructed boundaries.

Daniel's descriptors bring predispositions about bodies to the fore. Artistic renderings of Daniel 10's man show him standing upright, usually with white skin, a trim build, a clean-shaven face, and a foreboding stare. Some give the man angel's wings, which does not make sense considering the text says nothing suggesting him as anything more than a man. But it makes sense for Christian artists to take indecent interpretive liberties, as "burnished bronze" arms and legs erroneously become Caucasian skin.

Christian interpreters make this man a blank slate of sorts upon which we interpreters project ourselves. Some make him Jesus, while others make him into a white savior angelic figure. But, to reiterate a previous point, according to the text, he is just a man.

What, then, justifies Daniel's response across the remaining verses? Verse 7 tells us other unidentified men stood with Daniel during this vision, but they did not see it. We do not know why Daniel alone sees the vision.[16] Despite not witnessing the vision, fear strikes them, causing them to hide after Daniel's vision, again raising the question: What provoked such fear? The men do not see the vision, but they may have heard the roaring multitude promoting terror and fright. This position lacks textual support as we do not hear from the men again. We do learn that Daniel experiences such fear that he loses all strength and his "appearance turned to death." The man's words make Daniel fall asleep on his face at verse 9, suggesting Daniel faints.

Despite Daniel's response, compared to other visions in Daniel, the linen man is tame and mild. We do not hear what the man says beyond Daniel's disturbed response. What makes Daniel so afraid? Possible answers lie in considering the heavy-handed role of sexuality and masculinity in Daniel 10 (and across all of Daniel, for that matter). Women are virtually nonexistent in Daniel's world. Their absence is striking. Only one woman speaks in this book: the queen at Daniel 5:10–13 who lobbies on Daniel's behalf before the king and his lords. But that is it. There are no other women in Daniel. And what makes examining how we Christians read and use Daniel even more disconcerting is the complete drought of considering women, sexuality, and gender across our readings. Gender and sexuality are essential elements for what it means to be human. To ignore that is to dehumanize both the characters in the text and the people who wrote it. Further, from a purely Christian perspective, without women, Christianity does not exist.[17] So this man and his striking appearance brings tensions of gender, sexuality, and humanity right to the forefront of how we read Daniel 10 and the Bible as a whole. To deny this is to deny the deeply human side of our sacred scriptures.

Chapter 10's answers continue the evasive and unclear trend Daniel 1–9 establishes. An unknown, unannounced human arrives, touching Daniel and helping him off the ground. Again, we see an emphasis on the human form, as verse 10 explicitly says "a hand" touches Daniel—not "something touched me" or "I was touched." It is a hand. We do not know to whom it belongs, despite interpretive efforts to make it Gabriel, Michael, or some other unnamed angelic figure. The speaker mentions Michael at verse 13, but nothing indicates the speaker is Michael. All we know about him comes from verse 12: he came to Daniel's aid because Daniel gave his heart and humility to his god. Our speaker never claims to come from or be sent by God. Someone sent the man, but the chapter offers no further details about the sending party.

Daniel's fear is palpable, as the speaker greets Daniel with a "Do not fear." But what the speaker says in the preceding verses does little to assuage fear or offer comfort by way of explanation. We get a reference to a Persian prince standing opposite our speaker for twenty-one days, followed by the mention of Michael's arrival and assistance. This seemingly unrelated story concludes with "and I was left there beside the kings of Persia," with no reference to Daniel's vision, nor does this speaker connect what he says to what Daniel witnesses. It is an overly confusing and muddling scene, highlighted by yet another instance of unclear and uncertain Hebrew. I render the phrase in question, "I was left there beside the kings of Persia."[18] English translations like the RSV, NRSV, NIV, and NLT rely on the Greek manuscript variants of Daniel 10 to yield something akin to "I left him there with the prince of the kingdom of Persia" (NRSV). Relying on the Hebrew or Greek yields the same interpretive conclusion: confusion.

Verse 12 sets up the speaker's vision analysis as we come to expect with Daniel: he tells Daniel not to fear, that his voice has been heard, and he stands ready to offer understanding. Yet verse 13 veers away from Daniel toward something akin to a personal anecdote about the speaker's whereabouts. This adds nothing to explain why Daniel sees a linen man adorned with gold, nor does it offer any sense of meaning. We get no specifics about the identity of this Persian prince, and the only discernable connection for this reference to twenty-one days is Daniel's three-week mourning period.

The reference to Michael at verse 13 prompts Christian interpreters to make further claims to Daniel 10 as part of a larger messianic prophecy. We associate this Michael with Revelation 12's archangel Michael, creating an amalgamated reading that sidesteps Daniel 10 to prop up unfounded claims about Daniel 10 foretelling the ultimate battle between Jesus and Satan.[19] Michael is a common biblical name with sixteen appearances. Jude and Revelation refer to an archangel named Michael, but in every other instance, including Daniel 10, Michael is just a man. Daniel 10 stresses this by calling him a "chief prince" and "prince" at verses 13 and 21, respectively. Daniel offers no information beyond that. This is likely an example of what I call "cultural separation," a common feature of apocalyptic literature. Vague aphorisms, perplexing idioms, and borderline coded language fill the Bible's apocalyptic books of Daniel and Revelation. They make little to no sense within our contemporary context, but readers during the books' original respective contexts likely would have understood. We contemporary people speak, think, and write in code so often that we fail to see what we are even doing.

For example, one aspect of learning English as a second language is the problem of idioms. American English speakers say things like "break a leg" when wishing someone good luck or "bite the bullet" when making a difficult decision or completing a tenuous task. Couched in West Texas vernacular, American president Lyndon B. Johnson encountered this communication gap in 1966 when discussing American's military support for the South Vietnamese war effort. He said he wanted "coonskins on the wall" in relation to the war, prompting mass confusion among South Vietnamese officials. To Johnson, this was a common way of saying, "Give me some proof that our efforts are working." To the South Vietnamese, the words meant nothing. Herein lies a possible solution to Michael's identity: perhaps contemporary readers are too far removed from the chapter's cultural, political, and social contexts to understand the reference. There are many references to an angelic figure named Michael outside Daniel, but, if that were the case here, Michael would have the descriptor of "angel"; in Daniel 10 he is just a chief human prince.[20] Labeling him as anything more than that in this context is mere speculation.

Verse 14 is important to understanding why the speaker is here. It is also significant in reading Daniel 10–12 as something closer to one literary piece as opposed to three disparate chapters. This man wants to help Daniel understand his people's fate, prompting Daniel's silent prostration. He then touches Daniel's lips in an act of intimate reassurance, which compels Daniel to explain his behavior: the vision is too painful, making him too weak to continue. He, like the reader, does not understand what he sees or how the man can address Daniel in this manner. The speaker touches Daniel again, further highlighting a particular level of intimacy between Daniel and this unknown man. Touching empowers Daniel and gives him strength, showing a profoundly human moment in an otherwise confusing set of circumstances.

One word sticks out from the speaker at verse 19: he calls Daniel "beloved" for the second time in this chapter. The Hebrew here is חֲמֻדוֹת, and it appears in this form only nine times throughout the Bible. Six of those nine instances are in Daniel, with the other three coming in Genesis

27, Ezra 8, and 2 Chronicles 20. The word conveys a sense of rare and significant value, so the speaker's word choice elevates Daniel beyond merely a vessel or emissary. Daniel is special to the speaker. His words and actions show it. He calls Daniel "beloved," soothes his anxieties, and calms his nerves through touch. Daniel is receptive to the man's words and actions, creating a remarkable relationship between two men. Given modern discourse about masculinity and what it means to be a "Christian man," the level of vulnerability and genuine sensitivity between this pair is admirable.[21]

We Christian readers give away our true motives behind this chapter's interpretive trends with verses 20–21: we make the speaker's words, "And now I must return to fight with a prince of Persia," into a statement proclaiming a celestial war between good and evil unfolding in the heavens. There is also an overt sense of determinism behind traditional accepted approaches to these final two verses. For example, S. Miller confidently claims:

> In this passage humanity is afforded a glimpse of the behind-the-scenes activity that took place in the Persian government. Cyrus released the Jews, but unknown to the Persian monarch angelic forces played a part in this decision. Satan and his demons had been bound so that the will of God would be accomplished.[22]

S. Miller's reading is conjecture to the highest degree, but his comments align with more Christian readings than they do not.[23] For example, Jerome refers to the political history of Greece and Rome in relation to Daniel and exclaims, "Truly marvelous are the secret counsels of God," while Mayer reads the final verses as a sort of furtive divine chess game for the fate of humanity.[24]

In addition to having no textual support, the "heavenly war" reading neglects Daniel's ongoing confusion and mystery. The speaker asks, "Do you know why I have come to you?" This question is an abrupt shift in narrative confidence, as the speaker goes from reassuring Daniel to inquiring about the very nature of his presence. Does he now seek reassurance from Daniel, perhaps wanting to hear that Daniel knows what is happening? Or is he genuinely asking? Perhaps he asks out of desperation since he follows up this question by telling Daniel that after he leaves another prince will arrive. The next prince hails from Yavan, otherwise known as Greece. It is unclear as to whether this statement should provide comfort or Daniel should heed it as a warning: despite the Persian prince's defeat, another will take his place.

Here, then, is the chapter's conclusion: no resolution. Daniel mourns at the beginning and receives comfort from our unknown, unnamed interpreter. They share moments of concern and consolation, only for the final verses to tell Daniel and us that the cycle will continue. Michael and the vision interpreter will fight the Persian and Yavan princes, but despite their efforts the political cycles of violence continue. One leader replaces another, with more violence and war sure to follow. To make matters more anxiety inducing for Daniel, the final verse shows just how dire the situation is: "There is not one contending with me against these except Michael your prince." Antagonistic forces reign, and these words fall flat when held against the backdrop of war and political maneuvering. Only two people fight on Daniel's behalf; should he expect victory and promise? Or should he expect defeat, and the speaker tells him these things to soften the blow?

Daniel 10 certainly raises more questions than it answers. Reading it in conjunction with Christian receptions only underlines the text's complexity without further clarity. We interpreters do our best to put an idealistic spin on the chapter, which denies the inherent uncertainty the vision brings upon Daniel. There is not a single "hallelujah" or exorbitant praise toward hope and renewal, regardless of what Christians project onto it. What we really have is a marked display of discomfort, especially when considering that once again God does not show up or speak. Daniel mourns and fasts, hoping to hear or see God working in the moment. Instead, he gets into a conversation with an elusive interpreter who complicates matters even further.

10.3 So What?

A major failure in American Christianity stems from our rejection of the physical body. Contemporary evangelical culture builds upon the notion that the human body is "fleeting" and "temporary," with the promise of an afterlife without bodies. We will be "free" from pain, suffering, and death. We will be separated from the very things that make us human. Daniel 10 jerks our attention toward the physical, as the mere sight of a human body makes Daniel so afraid that he passes out. It reminds us of how essential bodies are to human existence. And any Christian claiming this approach is too "current" and "contemporary" would change their tune when pressed about one major issue of Christian doctrine: Do you believe in bodily resurrection or not? Those responding with an assertive "yes" underline the hypocrisy around bodily importance. Resurrection doctrine and belief are inconsequential to working with Daniel, but within the context of Christianity it shows just how much Christian theology depends and builds upon physical, tangible bodies.

At the time of this writing, Americans wage significant political battles over human bodies. The two primary points of focus are abortion and transgender persons. American evangelical Christians made abortion a political lightning rod long before *Roe v. Wade* made it federally legal, but their efforts multiplied following the 2016 election of President Donald Trump. A key part of Trump's political platform was appointing Supreme Court judges who favored overturning *Roe v. Wade*. That is exactly what he did by appointing three judges whose opinions overturned the long-standing ruling in June 2022. Fallout from this ruling sent shockwaves across the country and around the world. Many states acted swiftly to enact twelve-week and six-week abortion bans, prompting considerable outcry among pro-choice voters. The rhetoric they employ focuses on bodily autonomy, with language like "my body, my choice," "bans off our bodies," and "everyBODY is sacred." Conversely, pro-life supporters claim the sanctity of life in utero, in which a new body according to their understanding of biology supersedes the pregnant person's body. Christians on both sides of the abortion debate have one thing in common: human bodies are important, essential, and foundational.

Politicians dragged transgender persons to the front of political and social discourse during the same period. Discussions of gender and sexuality permeate the nightly news and state senate halls, where politicians enact laws prohibiting where certain bodies can be, alongside how medical professionals can legally assist children and young people. Christians on the conservative end of the political spectrum point to "biblical support" for two genders, arguing that the physical genitalia a person has at birth is "God's will." Christians at the fundamentalist Protestant organization "Focus on the Family" lump abortion and transgender rights into one theopolitical issue, claiming it is a Christian "right to believe in two genders and preborn life."[25]

I use these examples to highlight Daniel's emphasis on the physical. Daniel 10 reminds us that bodies matter. Our bodies matter within and beyond Christian thought. The palpable fear Daniel experiences can reflect the anxieties we carry, and the confusion wrought by the chapter's content and syntax make working with chapter 10 more jarring. Unknown forces physically pull Daniel from place to place without warning and consent throughout the book, which takes a considerable toll on him. It is entirely possible that the other men around Daniel flee and hide because of how

Daniel reacts and behaves. They witness someone walking with them suddenly entering a physically shocking trance that makes him throw his body upon the ground. These men do not fear the power of God, as Christian interpreters speculate; they fear for their safety. Underplaying the raw vulnerability offered here only reinforces cultural standards of expendable physicality. The mere sight of the man clothed in linen is enough to shake Daniel to his core. His distress is so palpable that the unknown, unnamed speaker touches and soothes this broken man. What happens to Daniel in this chapter matters. It is insufficient to default and claim some form of divine historical determinism. If we are to take these words seriously, we would be wise to honor Daniel's fear.

Christians who use biblical passages like Daniel 10 to support clichéd theology with proverbial dictums like "trust in God!" and "God has a plan!" discount the bold theological possibilities here. Why does the Bible always have to produce some vague, immaterial precept in the face of continual violence and destruction? The interpreter tells Daniel another prince will replace the current one, and, based on Daniel's exilic experience, this will not be a peaceful or smooth transition. Daniel does not know what is going to happen. Confusion and a profound sense of disconnect fill chapter 10. But perhaps that is the point. Daniel 10 unveils the arrogance we bring to the Bible and tears it down. We contemporary Christians are so quick to find meaning in uncertainty that we settle for something easy and effective for our purposes at the moment. But here Daniel 10 sets an example on having the courage and humility to not understand.

There is great strength in admitting we do not have all the answers. We Christians gloss over that which contradicts our sense of God and self, completely avoiding the possibilities they hold. For example, S. Miller completely sidesteps the chapter's complex and indefinite Hebrew, saying at verse 13: "Regardless of the exact meaning of this last clause, the point of the verse is clear."[26] No, the point of this verse is not clear. Little about Daniel 10 is clear, and, when we acknowledge this, we see just how much the cycles and failings of our world match that of biblical Israel. The small nation tore itself apart and in so doing became a pawn in larger political games. Mass confusion reigned as Israelite citizens searched for answers and entreated their deity, only to have their worlds shattered. Israel and its people had to adapt or perish.

The glimmer of hope these words offer us stems from that adaptation. Instead of folding and dying, the Israelites endured. They authored their stories, beliefs, laws, and practices, ensuring that their identities and histories would continue long after their deaths. They believed in each other and God, despite the ongoing rise and fall of imperial forces. The comfort Daniel experiences and shares with this man can be a model for how we comfort each other. Verse 14 says, "I came for you to understand what will happen to your people in the latter days, for the vision of those days is still longer." It seems the interpreter tells Daniel that the men of war will still come, as they always have. Daniel knows this, as shown by the pain and fear he experiences.

Christians want to make Daniel easy and digestible. Chapter 10 reminds us that this book is anything but easy. It is difficult and confusing, building us up for a grand reveal only to have those hopes dashed. But it is in having those hopes dashes that a new path of interpretation opens. Verse 21 ends things on a seemingly dour note: only the speaker and Michael fight against antagonistic forces. But reconsidering this verse as a call to action radically reshapes how we read what precedes and proceeds. What stops Daniel from stepping up and joining the fight? Is he like the men who surrounded him and fled in terror? Or is he something more?

American Christians often carry a misplaced sense of persecution. For example, despite every president in the nation's history being openly Christian, American Christians claim Barack Obama's healthcare plan attacked businesses like Hobby Lobby or nonprofits like Little Sisters of the Poor for making them pay the cost to cover contraceptives.[27] What makes this example even more outlandish is that both Hobby Lobby and Little Sisters of the Poor won their Supreme Court cases on the grounds of religious freedom. At the time of this writing, of the nine U.S. Supreme Court justices, only one is not Christian.[28] More senators and members of Congress are openly Christian than not, yet many, many Christians claim their voices get "silenced." Christians hold an overwhelming political majority in the United States.

Fear that we Christians manufacture for ourselves is misguided.[29] Daniel's fear is not. Daniel knows what happens when people turn on each other. He knows the horrors of war. What, then, is Daniel to do? How should he respond? What, then, are Christians to do with the constantly shifting political tides? How are we to act when our very bodies are at stake? How are we to be when one "prince" replaces another? Daniel 10 does not answer these questions; it only raises them. And that just may be the point.

11
Daniel 11 Reconsidered

11.1 Translation

1 And I, in the first year of Darius the Mede, stood to be strong and strengthen him.

2 "And now I will declare truth to you. Lo! Again, three kings standing in Persia. And the fourth will be richer than them all. And when he is strong through his riches, he will stir up the entire kingdom of Yavan.[1]

3 And a strong king will stand, and will rule many dominions, and he will do as he pleases.

4 And as he arose, his kingdom shall be broken and be divided to the four winds of the heavens. And it will not be for his descendants, and it will not be a dominion according to how he ruled. For his kingdom will be uprooted and will go to other from among these.

5 And the king of the south will grow strong, and from his princes will be one stronger than him that will rule a dominion greater than his dominion.

6 And after some years they will form an alliance, and the daughter of the king of the north will come to the king of the south to make an agreement, and she will not retain her powerful strength, and his offspring will not stand; she will be given up, she and her attendants and her child and her supporter in this time.

7 And a branch of her roots will rise up in his place, and he will go to the army and will enter into the fortress of the kingdom of the north and will act against them, and he will prevail.

8 And even their gods with their statues with their vessels of previous silver and gold, he will carry into captivity in Egypt, for years he will stand away from the king of the north.

[9] And he will come into the kingdom of the king of the north, but he will return to his land.

[10] And his sons will provoke war and will gather a multitude of many forces, which will keep coming and overflow and cross over, and will carry the war until his fortress.

[11] And the king of the south will be enraged, and he will go out and fight against him, the king of the north, and he will raise a great multitude, and the multitude shall be given over to his hand.

[12] And when the multitude is carried off, his heart will be inflated, and he will overthrow tens of thousands, but he will not prevail.

[13] And the king of the north will return and will raise a multitude larger than the first, and after some years he will come with a great army and many supplies.

[14] And in those times many will stand against the king of the south, and the sons of violence from you people will lift themselves for vision fulfillment, and they will fall.

[15] And the king of the north will come, and he will set up siege-works and will take a well-fortified city, and the forces of the north will not stand, even his best troops; and there will be no strength to take a stand.

[16] And he, the one who comes against him, will do as he pleases, and there will be no one standing against him, and he will stand in the beautiful land and will destroy it by his hand.

[17] And he will set his face to come with authority of all his kingdom, and upright ones with him, and he will act, and a daughter of the women will be given to him in marriage to destroy it. And it will not succeed, and it will not be his.

[18] And he will set his face to the coastlands and will capture many; then a commander will put an end to his insolence, except he will turn his insolence back on him.

[19] And he will set his face toward the fortresses of his land, and he will stumble and fall and not be found.

[20] And one will arise in his place, an exactor oppressing the glorious kingdom; and within a few days he will be broken, and not in anger or in war.

[21] And a despicable person will rise in his place, and the splendor of the kingdom will not be given to him. And he will come without warning and obtain the kingdom with flatteries.

22 And armies will be swept away from before him, and they will be broken, and the leader of the covenant as well.

23 And from alliances made with him, he will act deceitfully and will go up and be strong with a small nation.

24 With ease he will come to the province's richest ones, and he will do what his fathers and fathers' fathers never did, and scattering plunder and spoils and goods for them. And he will devise plans against fortresses for a time.

25 And he will stir up his strength and his heart against the king of the south with a great army, and the king of the south will wage war with a much greater and stronger army, and he will not stand, for there will be plots planned against him.

26 And the ones eating from the royal portion will break him, and his army will be swept away, and many will fall defiled.

27 And the two kings, their minds toward evil, will speak a lie upon a table; and he will not succeed, for there is still an end to the appointed time.

28 And he shall return to his lands with great wealth, and his heart will be against the holy covenant. And he will work and return to his land.

29 At the appointed time he will return and will come to the south, and this time will not be like the last time.

30 And the ships of Kittim[2] will come for him, and he will be disheartened and retreat, and he will be engaged against the holy covenant, and he will work, and he will return, and he will pay attention to those who forsook the holy covenant.

31 Forces sent from him will take up position in and profane the holy fortress and remove the regular offering and will set up the abomination that desolates.

32 And those who violate the covenant: he will seduce them with deceptive flattery. And a people who know its god will be strong and take action.

33 And the wise among the people will bring understanding to many, and they will fall by the sword and flame with days of captivity and plunder.

34 And in their stumbling, they will receive little help, and many will join them by way of deceptive flattery.

[35] And from the wise ones will come stumbling, for their refinement and purification and to be made white, until the time of the end for there is still an appointed time.

[36] For the king will do as he pleases, and he will exalt himself and magnify himself over any god, and against the god of gods he will speak wonderfully. And he will prosper until the indignation is complete, for what is decreed will be done.

[37] And he will not pay attention to the gods of his fathers, or to the one desired by women or to any god; he will not pay attention because he magnified himself against all others.

[38] And he will pay honor to the god of fortresses; and to the god which his fathers did not know he will honor with gold and silver and precious stones and costly gifts.

[39] And he will deal with a strong fortress in company with a foreign god; whoever acknowledges him he will make more honorable, and he will appoint them as rulers over many, then he shall divide the land for a price.

[40] At the end of the time the king of the south will gore him, and the king of the north will come upon him like a great whirlwind, with chariots and horsemen and many ships; and he will come into the lands and cross over like a flood.

[41] And he will come into the beautiful land, and many will stumble, and these Edomites and Moabites will escape his hand, along with many sons of Ammon.

[42] And he will send out his hand across the land, and the land of Mitzrayim will not be able to escape.

[43] And he will rule the hidden treasures of gold and silver, and all the treasures of Mitzrayim, and the Lubbites and the Kushites will be in his train.

[44] And reports from the east and the north will terrify him, and he will send out great fury to bring great wrath and destruction.

[45] Then he will plant palatial tents between the sea toward the beautiful, holy mountain; and he will come to his end, for there is no one to help him."

11.2 Reading against the Grain

At forty-five verses, Daniel 11 is the book's second-longest chapter. Daniel 11's length gives way to fierce theological, historical, and apologetic debates in Christianity. There is much to unpack around what Christian readers have done to Daniel 11 before engaging the text itself, but the truth of the matter is Daniel 11 is a simple and straightforward chapter. It shows a world defined by political manipulation, machination, and misuse of power. Its directness gets muddled in misplaced efforts to ground Daniel 11 in one historical timeline that, when pressed with actual historical evidence, falls apart. That said, my reading of Daniel 11 here explicitly pushes back against overly confusing and biased readings that, despite their differences, always make the person(s) reading the text its central focus. What if we dared to say that Daniel 11 focuses on someone other than the "mythical" us? What if we decentered ourselves from this chapter and sought something more from it than hackneyed historical conviction? What if we approached it with the courage of reading beyond a Christian-centric worldview and instead saw it as a meditation on the human condition, the much larger world, and theological insights that may bear fruit?

Self-serving confusion with Daniel 11 starts early and often. J. Collins addresses the text's inherent complexity by noting its muddled sense of history alongside "the quality of Hebrew . . . is exceptionally poor."[3] Early Christian receptions present the chapter as picking up where chapter 10 left off, with Daniel 11 being an expansion on the vision and discussion between Daniel and Michael. This first verse is fraught with translation difficulty, as Christian interpreters wrestle with an inconsistency between Hebrew and Greek manuscripts.[4] The Masoretic Hebrew, which I use for the translation offered here, reads, "And I, in the first year of Darius the Mede."[5] The OG reads, "In the first year of King Cyrus," perhaps to bring Daniel 11:1 into agreement with 10:1.[6] Christian interpreter Theodoret uses the Greek rendering as his primary reading for verse 1, a choice that radically changes how chapter 11 reads. This decision is particularly noteworthy, as Theodoret builds the rest of his translation and commentary on the Hebrew and not the Greek. Jerome relies on the Masoretic Hebrew and, in so doing, splits Christian interpretive streams.

Theodoret's position quickly becomes minoritized as Wigand, Melanchthon, Calvin, and Willet rely on the Hebrew. But Theodoret's handpicked exception shows how desperately Christian readers want to connect Daniel 11 with Daniel 10. The ways in which contemporary interpreters force chapters 10 and 11 together are indicative of much larger interpretive trends. For example, Sprinkle argues 11:1 is a narrative flashback "to the beginning of the 'first year of' Persian rule."[7] Nothing in Daniel 11 suggests or supports this flashback theory. Such a move is inconsistent with the narrative chronology established in chapters 7–10. Going further and making claims at a textual critical level, Hartman and Di Lella argue that the "Darius the Mede" portion is a later interpolation, which Collins refutes with evidence from the Dead Sea Scrolls.[8] All this effort is to avoid simply considering the possibility that chapter 10 and chapter 11 may be read separately and not as a single entity.

The text offers additional evidence to read against this interpretive grain of seeing chapter 11 as a continuation of Daniel 10. Such evidence warrants reading Daniel 11 in conjunction with Daniel 10 while keeping vigilant in knowing this is its own chapter with its own messages. In addition to the shift from Cyrus to Darius the Mede, we also do not know who is speaking at verse 1 and throughout the chapter. The speaker in verses 1 and 2 describes himself or herself as "I" without further detail. Reception streams gloss over or supplant this unidentified speaker with assumptions built upon the determination to make Daniel 10–12 one apocalyptic literary unit. Many argue that chapter 11 actually begins at verse 2, with verse 1 being a holdover from Daniel 10.[9] Again, this approach is nothing more than a theory that lacks textual or manuscript evidence.[10] Daniel 10 ends at verse 21, and Daniel 11 begins at verse 1. No names appear in Daniel 11: no Michael, no Daniel, and no Gabriel. Thus, if Daniel 11 was merely a continuation of Daniel 10, Michael's name would surely appear. In addition, Daniel 11 does not mention the linen man of Daniel 10, nor does it point back or establish larger, more obvious connections to the preceding chapter.

Addressing and deconstructing Daniel 11:1 and the relationship between chapters 10 and 11 is essential for interpretive reconsideration. We must address them to move past them, because chapter 11 brings themes of political chaos, global intrigue, destiny and fate, economic class, and military might back to the fore. This chapter is complex and layered with metaphors that readers may read quickly, or they may get bogged down and become lost in apocalyptic fulfillment minutiae. Daniel 11 is a text grounded in stark, painful realities of war. It connects with so many readers because of how closely the abstract history laid out in its verses aligns with the histories so many live and will live. The vision we read about is remarkable in its unremarkability as it describes every major military conflict brought about by misguided, selfish rulers. Self-appointed rulers vie for power, trapping and exploiting untold thousands forced to do their bidding. When a ruler falls, another takes their place. The cycle continues.

Mainline Christian interpreters construct a timeline that aligns neatly with Daniel 11, much like we do with Daniel 2 and Daniel 7. The general outline, which is quite complicated, is like this: four Persian kings will reign and rule, with the fourth being wealthy and powerful. The fourth uses that wealth and power to arrogantly attack Greece in 480 BCE. Greece defeats Persia, and Alexander the Great takes control. Alexander then dies, and his kingdom is divided between his four top generals in 323 BCE. The "southern kingdom" is Egypt, ruled by Ptolemy I. Seleucus I rules the "northern kingdom." Later, to form an alliance, Ptolemy II arranges a marriage between his daughter, Berenice, and the current northern king, Antiochus II. Ptolemy II's daughter dies, replaced by Antiochus II's wife Laodice. Berenice's brother, Ptolemy III, takes power and invades Syria, the northern kingdom, and makes Seleucus II his subject king. Seleucus II retaliates and attacks the south. There is then a time jump as Seleucus III and Antiochus III now reign, respectively. Ptolemy IV attacks Antiochus III, prompting Antiochus III to later respond and overthrow Antiochus V. Antiochus III tries an alliance himself, sending his daughter to marry Ptolemy V. This plan backfires, as Antiochus III is later killed and his son Seleucus IV becomes king. This paves the way for Seleucus IV's son, Antiochus Epiphanes, to rule. Antiochus Epiphanes attacks Egypt, drawing the ire of Rome. His attempts to reengage Rome led to his attacking Jerusalem, resulting in the more heavily religious events that conclude Daniel 11.

This historical overview laid upon Daniel 11 is as confusing as it is factually problematic. Thirteen Persian kings ruled between the fall of Babylon in 539 BCE and Alexander the Great's rise in 331 BCE.[11] Thus, it is incorrect to take Daniel 11:2's claim of only four kings standing between Babylon's fall and Alexander's rise literally. Where, then, do scholars using the incorrect timeline get this argument? It comes from Jerome's *Commentary on Daniel*, meaning their positions stand upon an argument conceived and written in the fourth and fifth centuries CE. So not only do we Christians supporting this timeline deny other historical evidence, but we openly accept the historical reconstruction of one man from over fifteen hundred years ago. This makes less sense when compared against the varied specifics readers overlay upon Daniel 11, making these hypothetical timelines even more confusing. For example, at verse 17, Jerome and Jewish commentators Pseudo-Saadia, Ibn Ezra, and Rashi read, "And he will set his face to come with authority of all his kingdom," as referring to Ptolemy's kingdom, while Calvin argues it is the Seleucids.[12] How can one scripture allusion mean two historical things simultaneously? The answer is simple: all of chapter 11 is designed to mirror a given reader's historical circumstances. It fits multiple timelines because multiple historical timelines have so much in common. Such is the way of apocalyptic literature set against political and social backdrops defined by war.

The text itself lets the reader know in verse 1 that the "history" shown in Daniel 11 is not history as it was; it is a historiographic reconstruction. The first marker that Daniel 11 is more than just a straightforward historical retelling is, once again, an opening reference to a person that did not exist: Darius the Mede. Darius appears in chapters 5, 6, 9, and here to reorient the reader to what will unfold, as Darius is a signpost indicating that we should not take what we are about to read literally and rigidly. Darius is a caricature of kings. He occupies the space Daniel needs him to occupy and keeps the narrative moving. We do a considerable disservice to the biblical authors in arguing they would not indulge in such hypotheticals; their brilliance is evident with every word on the page. Just as Samuel warned the Israelite people about the consequences of their zeal for a king, the wars and destruction kings wrought again finds Daniel.

Evangelical Christian approaches to Daniel 11 mark it as prophecy over apocalyptic to make it fulfilled in the life, death, resurrection, and eventual second coming of Jesus.[13] Herein lies why we Christian interpreters, evangelicals in particular, are persistent in our understanding of both Daniel's historicity and the historical accuracy of prophecy in general: all prophecy, according to Christian interpretive paradigms, culminates with Jesus' second coming. This approach severely undercuts the value prophecy has in and of itself, much less the highly anti-Semitic supersessionism inherent to it. But Daniel is not just a prophecy; it is an apocalyptic text, meaning that it carries prophetic elements that also point toward a larger, unknown future.

Limiting prophetical fulfillment to its historical accuracy is shortsighted and myopic. Yet evangelical Christians do so with borderline callous bravado that ignores the valuable theological differences in reconsidering the role of prophecy in a biblical context and the church at large. For example, evangelical Christians make prophetic historical accuracy a theological apologetic "either/or." Either someone believes that prophets accurately predicted history (therefore God exists, and therefore we must worship this God), or the prophets' predictions are inaccurate (therefore God does not exist, making Christianity a sham).[14] This dichotomy is, in a word, false.

As stated throughout this book, biblical apocalyptic texts are inherently flexible. They carry profound textual polyvalence to create a continued and persistent relevance, transcending time, geography, and history.

Daniel 11 can match up with specific historical events, but its value does not stop there. Daniel offers more than mere historical reassurance. And the pathway to broader understanding lies right in front of us. There is a method of understanding ancient prophecy of all kinds that helps us reconsider the kind of apocalyptic prophetic work Daniel 11 presents. This method is called *ex eventu* prophecy.

Ex eventu is a shorthand way of discussing *vaticinia ex eventu*, which is Latin for "a prediction from the event." *Ex eventu* prophecy fits Daniel 11 well and helps the chapter make sense. The reason it "predicts" future events with considerable accuracy is because it was written after the events in question. It recalls historical events and reframes them as prophecy. This means Daniel was written after the events it "foretells," which accounts for its accuracy. Lester Grabbe lists this as one possible approach to studying Daniel, and he is openly indebted to J. Collins' work with Daniel as *ex eventu*.[15] J. Collins directly reads Daniel 11 as an *ex eventu* prophecy meant to "'predict' the ongoing rise and fall of kings and kingdoms" that comprise human historical landscapes.[16] It is possible Daniel 11 ends with an attempted prediction of future events at verse 45, but even that is up for debate.[17] This reading is indebted to Grabbe and J. Collins for their forthright academic honesty and for the jumping-off point their work provides. I want to go a step further and engage the theological possibilities that reading Daniel 11 as *ex eventu* offers. J. Collins' rationale about "why" Daniel 11 is *ex eventu* reverts to the traditional theological notion of divine sovereignty: "that history is predetermined and has nearly run its course."[18]

Biblical and ancient Near Eastern scholars are more than comfortable reading nonbiblical texts as *ex eventu* prophecies, and some, like J. Collins, present it as a widespread biblical phenomenon.[19] But wrestling with *ex eventu* and what it means for the theological branches of biblical studies persists. The question then becomes, why do Christians avoid this conclusion? What makes us so hesitant not only to consider this as a viable interpretive option but to truly engage with the theological possibilities such an approach can offer?

This question brings us back to the text and Darius the Mede. Starting with Darius the Mede demarcates these words as historiography, not history. What unfolds in Daniel 11 is a highly idealized reconstruction of the Greco-Roman history surrounding Israel after the exile. Our unknown, unnamed narrator stands in strength to support "him." The identity of this "him," like the rest of Daniel 11, divides scholars. Some, like Theodoret, Isho'dad, and Ephrem, say it is the angel Gabriel. Still others suggest it may be Daniel or Michael.[20] The text is unclear and disregards possible hesitations or questions this lack of clarity may raise as it jumps directly into a declaration at verse 2.

The speaker says, "I will declare truth to you." The Hebrew word for "truth" is אֱמֶת, and it appears over one hundred times across the Hebrew Bible. It carries no inherent ethical, theological, prophetic, or spiritual weight. The word simply means that which is true and not false. Yet such simplicity does not stop Christian authors from making something out of nothing, like when Sprinkle ties this אֱמֶת to the reliability about "God's revelation about the future."[21] In the context of the book's larger Daniel corpus, the speaker's reassurance is meant to ground Daniel in a level of certainty. Daniel is right to question what he sees and hears, as his journey to this point has put his life on the line multiple times. So, in short, Daniel is about to learn something he can trust.

What Daniel hears in these verses carries a harsh truth: more destruction is coming. Persia's rule does not end the tumult brought upon Israel and its neighbors. It is just the beginning. These battles and power struggles will bring Daniel, his people, and the world great distress. On top of this, his deity's marked absence continues. When the speaker declares that Persia will prosper to the point of attacking Greece, Daniel knows the depth of the Persian king's stupidity. The first Persian invasion of Greece occurred in 492 BCE, lasting until a decisive Greek victory in 490 BCE. It was a foolish endeavor at its conception and in its action only confirmed just how ill-advised the tactic was. Greece was a formidable military and economic power, so Daniel hearing that the Persians, the supposed "saviors" of Israel, would crumble at the hands of the Greeks shocks him.

Set against the backdrop of pro-Cyrus and pro-Persian Israelite prophecy, the apocalyptic narrative reshapes Israel's sense of history. Isaiah sings Cyrus' praises at Isaiah 45:1, describing Cyrus as the LORD's "anointed . . . whose right hand I have grasped to subdue nations before him and strip kings of their robes." It is worth noting here that "anointed" comes from the Hebrew משה. This holds significance as משה, transliterated as *mšh*, is where Christians get the word "messiah," meaning "anointed one." Cyrus even speaks in Ezra 1 and claims, "YHWH God of heaven has given me all the kingdoms of the earth." Second Chronicles 36 frames Cyrus as "fulfillment of the word of YHWH spoken by Jeremiah." The Bible frequently says God stirs up and empowers Cyrus, making Cyrus a divine instrument. Thus, within the context of Israelite prophecy, Cyrus is a messianic figure. However, according to Daniel 11, his leadership and actions are fruitless, as those who follow him will lead Persia and, in turn, Israel down paths of destruction. Cyrus is now a failed messiah.

Daniel 11, then, becomes a radial critique of what came before it regarding Cyrus, or any supposed "messiah" world leader. Cyrus' overwhelmingly positive presentation up to this point highlights just how quickly people in desperate situations align themselves with someone making grand promises. Despite his promises and calls to rebuild, Daniel 11 shows that Cyrus' empire crumbles in less than a verse, replaced by an unnamed Greek king who himself will fail.

Daniel 11:4 is a not-so-subtle nod to Alexander the Great and his kingdom's failure following his death. History shows that dividing Alexander's kingdom among his four top generals was a mistake, as that sowed seeds of discontent, which led to power struggles, backdoor political dealings, and ultimately the destruction of what Alexander built. This is what kings do, and Daniel 11 brings the harsh realities of a monarchy system full circle. The "strong king" at verses 3–4 "will rule many dominions" and "do as he pleases," making Israel just another cog in the imperial wheel. More kings will rise, raising and ruling more dominions greater than those coming before. Royal families like the "branch of her roots" at verse 7 will use armies to wage war among the south and the north, which, when couched within the "four winds" reference of verse 4 creates an image of war's totality. South and north here could be references to specific places with specific kings, but the image also works in the sense of north and south being two points on a map, going to war and wrecking havoc on everything in between.

The cyclical nature of these verses is as shocking as it is mundane: one king arises and brings his army against another king, only to fall. Some will stand against another king, like with verse 13 and the northern king's raised multitude "with a great army and many supplies." But those efforts do nothing to change their fate. Men and women in power do not learn from their ancestors and the past therein, as they keep amassing more only to have their eventual destruction all the more decisive. Daniel 11 reiterates three times that each king "will do as he pleases," making everything and everyone else in between expendable. Alliances and covenants will be made and praised, only to fall. They will loot, plunder, and, according to verse 24, scatter those goods among "the province's richest ones." Ships will be sent, armies will be made even bigger, fortresses will be sieged, and the cycle will continue.

Christian readers make much of this "holy covenant" referenced at verse 28 and verse 30, leading to arguably the most hotly contested image in Daniel 11: the "abomination that desolates." Understanding the "holy covenant" and "abomination that desolates" shows the depths of imperial power. In the traditional Daniel 11 timeline, these two images highlight Antiochus Epiphanes' destruction and looting of the Israelite temple for gold to fund his larger war effort. In the more general sense, it highlights how the powerful never stop, as not even the boundaries of the sacred quell their lusts for power. The "abomination that desolates" gets traction in Christian circles because a similar Greek phrase appears as part of Jesus' teachings in Matthew 24:15 and Mark 13:14.[22] It appears twice in Daniel: here at 11:31 and again at 12:11.[23] Scholars generally understand the king in these verses to be Antiochus Epiphanes, perhaps in an effort to reinforce the more rigid understandings of Daniel 11's historical timeline. Still more theories lobby for Antiochus Epiphanes setting a statue of Zeus in the Israelite temple, but this theory builds upon reading 2 Maccabees 6:2 on top of Daniel.[24] Other approaches dig into a possible wordplay with the language itself, arguing the Hebrew could be a sophisticated linguistic dalliance disguising the Phoenician god *Ba'al šāmên*, meaning "lord of heaven."[25] But if either the Zeus or *Ba'al* option were the case, why not be more direct? Daniel 11 is not shy about using specific names for specific places when necessary, and to suggest that a cryptic message lies hidden in the text brings this discussion closer to conspiratorial thinking than it does actual textual engagement.

Once again, unnecessary interpretive complexity overruns the narrative's simplicity. A more direct resolution arises after stripping away the interpretive baggage placed upon it: ruling powers will desecrate a sacred site. Nothing is off limits to them. Political idealists need not hold fast to their beliefs, as invading forces think nothing of places and things deemed "holy" by the people being invaded. This presents a radical shift in Israelite thinking: God is not going to swoop in and stop this "abomination that desolates." It will happen, as the "holy fortress" once held so dear is now just another conduit for imperial power, making the Israelite religion a pawn in a much larger game of conquest.

The king at verses 36–39 presents a striking image. This unnamed figure holds himself "over any god, and against the god of gods he will speak wonderfully." Catastrophe has reached its logical conclusion: a king sees himself as a god, not just a divine instrument. "Wonderfully" here denotes a sense of self-aggrandized power and awe, which the king flaunts in the face of the people he rules and their gods. This king's behavior brings Daniel full circle, as Nebuchadnezzar in Daniel's early chapters sees himself as a god among humans. Daniel 11's king takes things further, declaring himself a deity.

Yet, as shown at verse 40, this king's fate is the same as those who came before. The north and the south besiege and destroy his kingdom. He will flee to an unknown "beautiful land" (v. 41), but he will try to further extend his rule. Edom, Moab, and some Ammonites will escape, but the Lubbites, Kushites, and Egyptians, here known as Mitzrayim, will suffer his looting and pillaging. But despite his best efforts, and despite his self-glorification, verse 45 tells us, "He will come to his end, for there is no one to help him." This, then, is how the chapter ends—not with a grand divine display of power, but with a faint whimper of another failed king's destruction. The power and might of these nameless, faceless rulers fall to ruin under the zeal for imperial rule. Each king cancels out the next, with each collapse being another sign of what comes next.

And yet, despite the gloom and doom surrounding the events in Daniel 11, one cannot but think back to Daniel 1 and the inherent tension that Daniel's social, economic, and political status holds. Daniel 1 makes it explicit and clear the king selected Daniel because of his good looks, academic prowess, and royal lineage. Daniel does not represent the Israelite commoner; he represents those in power whose choices led to Israel's downfall. Silenced Israelite voices scream at us as we read Daniel's rise to Babylonian success. What happens in Daniel 11 tears down the structures that Daniel benefits from, rendering his influence and access useless. It is entirely possible, then, that certain early readers would celebrate the destruction of imperialist powers. Grand plans laid out to conquer and control the world are now moot, not by God's hand but by the very people who build and benefit from those systems. Are we to feel sympathy for what is lost? Or are we to celebrate the end of these regimes and the horrors they bring? Reading Daniel 11 through these questions underlines the chapter's keen neutrality. One could argue Daniel 11 uses a certain sense of irony to show its readers a simple but stark truth: everything these empires made for themselves will come crumbling down, and it will be their fault. Whether it should instill fear or cultivate hope is the reader's decision.

11.3 So What?

Far too often, Christian biblical studies and theology fall into self-imposed traps. We read texts like Daniel 11 to reinforce what we believe.

Our self-imposed paradigms make Daniel 11 a chapter about historical fulfillment because we want it to be a chapter about historical fulfillment. This makes us guilty of weaving confirmation biases into our textual work, our theology, and our much broader Christian worldview. But how we read Daniel 11, or any sacred text for that matter, is a matter of choice. We chose to make Daniel a book about one thing and one thing only. We construct boundaries according to what we believe, to use our theology to interpret and shape the text, instead of using the text to shape our theology. Evangelical Christians read Daniel 11 as a road map pointing toward Jesus' eventual second coming and, in so doing, undercut Jewish perspectives and approaches. Similarly, so-called "liberal" and "progressive" Christian readers see it as confirming their belief in a sovereign deity, one that oversees and controls all history. Even still other Christians avoid reading Daniel 11 altogether, thereby creating space for extant readings to become unquestioned norms. Daniel 11 is so much more than any of these options.

Evangelical Christian approaches to history and prophecy focus on apologetics. The general position is this: without total historical accuracy, Daniel 11 is useless because it does not confirm Jesus' triumphant return. Not only that, but "God offers successful prophecies as evidence that people can use to know that he alone is the true and living God."[26] According to this logic, only if everything that happens in Daniel 11 occurs as it says it will occur does Christianity justify its existence. Such second-coming focused readings are the origins of opposition to Daniel 11 as *ex eventu* prophecy. Language of "trusting prophecy" equaling "trusting God" permeates evangelical biblical hermeneutics. Such language hides a distressing truth: in claiming that prophecies in Daniel and throughout the Bible culminate in Jesus, evangelicals perpetuate unapologetic supersessionist anti-Semitism.

This is inherently immoral, unethical, and unchristian. Arguing that Jesus fulfills Israelite prophecy eliminates Judaism and replaces it with Christianity. It also perpetuates the destructive myths of "Jews killed Jesus" and "Jews rejected Jesus; therefore, God rejects Jews." Many Christians, like Pope John Paul II, openly repudiate supersessionist replacement theology. Despite such prominent opposition, anti-Semitism thrives thanks to Christian supersessionist theology. It was a foundational backbone to the Nazi war machine's political ideology,[27] and contemporary Christians use it to justify political support for the current nation of Israel.[28] Supersessionism is a marker of disrespect and unfounded Christian superiority.

Saying Jesus "fulfills" Judaism only destroys it because such Christian "fulfillment" is a thinly veiled claim toward Christian supremacy.

Similarly, other Christian voices opposing such an evangelical approach stand mired themselves. Claiming Daniel 11's deity is sovereign over history is difficult, if not impossible, to argue thanks to the deity's textual absence. God does not speak in chapter 11. God actively does nothing in chapter 11. God is not in chapter 11. Despite this, we Christian readers plug our sense of God into the text as it fits us, which is its own type of destructive reading. What happens when something challenges that understanding of God? Are we to abandon our faith completely, or do we ignore pain and suffering by doubling down on explaining history for our benefit? Such is the trap we set for ourselves instead of wrestling with this question: is God even in Daniel 11?

It is not an option to ignore Daniel 11 or rest on painless resolutions. We must read these texts because voices silenced therein cry out to us, and voices of those silenced by destructive readings entreat us to listen. Daniel 11 is an overtly political text in which imperial powers use religion for personal gain. The Jerusalem temple and its sacred instruments get paraded around and manipulated to reinforce kings whose power and might will ultimately fall. Christians quick to say that such wanton human frailty reinforces God's control over history ignore what we so callously call "collateral damage." Daniel 11 emphasizes the fleeting nature of human empires, but at what cost? The deity's shocking absence becomes even more pronounced when read against this backdrop of people and places we never know. Daniel 11 then becomes just as much about what (and who) is not on the page as it does what is written.

And yet, despite what Daniel 11 lacks, a deep and profound sense of hope reverberates from its pages. Making God not culpable for imperial destruction liberates us from blindly accepting that everything that happens in history is "part of God's plan." God, like us, sees these events happening beyond our control and stands with us. It is as if Daniel 11 shows us that God does not have to step in and overthrow corrupt governments; they will do that to themselves. Further, seeing such wanton destruction and political impropriety shows us what happens when God is not involved. Daniel 11 then becomes a way for us to consider if the world is truly as God wants it or if it is how we want it. Destruction brought on by human decisions defines the chapter; how different might this history have been had people turned to each other and to God?

Here then lies a challenging theological tension: Are we modern Christians sitting idle and letting us tear each other to pieces? Or are we stepping in? Are we passive, or are we active? The fatalism in Daniel 11 shows us what will happen if we stay passive. Instead of praising God for holding sovereign control over history, what if we hear and listen to what the chapter says: if no one steps in, this is what history will look like, and it is just going to keep happening. Daniel 11 then becomes a chapter about faith and hope, but not in the traditional sense. It is about the faith we have in each other and in God, and the hope that we carry in knowing we are with God in pushing against violent tides of history. To read Daniel 11 and say God approves is to discount the thousands who died and millions who suffered so that one leader could attempt (and ultimately fail) to expand an empire doomed to fall. Daniel 11 is now a challenge to stand up and push back, to say the cycles of history are not set in stone. They can be changed. And if Daniel 11 then becomes about changing history to move away from bloodshed and death toward life and strength, is that not the essence of apocalyptic thought?

12

Daniel 12 Reconsidered

12.1 Translation

1 “And at that time, Michael, the great prince, the one standing over the sons of your people, will arise, and there will be a time of distress the likes of which has not been since the nation came to be. And in that time your people will be delivered, each that is found written in the book.

2 And many sleeping in the land of dust will awaken, these to eternal life, and these to shame, to eternal contempt.

3 And the wise ones shall shine like the brightness of the sky, and those causing many to be just, like the stars forever and ever.

4 And you, Daniel, conceal the words and seal the book until the end time; many will go to and fro, and knowledge shall greatly increase.”

5 And I looked, I, Daniel, and lo! Two others were standing. One here toward the bank of the stream, and one here toward the bank of the stream.[1]

6 And he said to the man clothed in linen, who was up the waters of the stream, “When will the wonders end?”

7 And I heard the man clothed in linen, who was up the waters of the stream; he raised his right and left hand to the heavens, and he swore by the life of the eternal one, “for a time, times, and a half, to be complete when the hand of the holy people is shattered, all of these will be accomplished.”

8 And I heard and I did not understand, and I said, “My lord, what is the outcome of these?”

9 And he said, “Go, Daniel, for the words of the end time are closed and sealed.

[10] Many shall be purified and made white and cleansed. And the wicked will do wickedly, and all the wicked will not understand; the ones doing wisely will understand.

[11] And the regular will be turned aside, and the abomination which desolates will be set up one thousand two hundred and ninety days.

[12] Blessed are the ones waiting and who will touch one thousand three hundred thirty-five days.

[13] And you go to the end, and rest and rise for your allotment at the end of days."

12.2 Reading against the Grain

This concluding chapter comes in at only thirteen verses, making it Daniel's shortest chapter. Its brevity is quickly overshadowed in Christian circles, as readers focus efforts on verse 2 to foretell the total bodily resurrection that will occur upon Jesus' second coming. And Christian receptions use verse 1 to buttress Christian-centric readings, using the Michael character as a fulcrum to pivot toward messianic prophetic fulfillment. In so doing, these readings fall into the same supersessionist replacement theology tied to Daniel 1–11.

Michael indeed makes another appearance and inaugurates this final chapter as "the great prince, the one standing over the sons of your people." Christians make Michael into an angel or archangel despite verse 1 describing him as just "the great prince." But, at this point, we know that Christian readings self-reinforce one another despite a pronounced lack of supporting evidence. Fifth-century CE Christians Cassiodorus and Pseudo-Dionysius claim Michael is an angel based on their theological convictions with no textual evidence from Daniel supporting their claims. Oecolampadius, Diodati, and Wigand take a peculiar turn by going even further to claim Michael is the Son of God. They each cite Daniel 10 as evidence, but these claims of Michael being anything other than a political leader are simply avenues toward inserting Jesus where he is not. According to the text, Michael is a political leader, hence calling him a "prince" and saying he stands "over the sons of your people."

Arguing Michael is the Son of God is also foundational to Jehovah's Witness belief and doctrine. Witnesses believe Jesus is just another iteration of the archangel Michael and include Daniel among other biblical citations like Jude 9, 1 Thessalonians 4, John 1, and much of Revelation for support. Witnesses go as far as to say Michael taking on the name Jesus follows the biblical trend of people having more than one name.[2] What makes the Witness perspective so interesting when read against these early Christian claims for Michael as "the Son of God" is how contemporary Christians openly rebuke it.[3]

Verse 1 also presents a brief but distressing description of the future. It ends with assurance of Daniel's people being delivered from the coming calamity, but terse words preceding that assurance give us pause. The narrator dispenses with pleasantries and renounces elaborate metaphors in favor of fearfully awestruck language: "There will be a time of distress the likes of which has not been since the nation came to be." Gone is any mention of animals or mythic beings foretelling looming disasters. No metaphor seems appropriate for the speaker, so the speaker tells the reader, "If you thought what happened already is bad, it does not even compare to what will happen." Reference to "the nation" points to biblical Israel and is a not-so-subtle dig at biblical authors bemoaning the gloom and doom of the exile. Daniel 12 wants us to know what is coming far surpasses the exile. This is not to say the Israelite exile was overblown and exaggerated; the opposite is the case. Saying that what comes next surpasses the distress level "which has not been since the nation came to be" acknowledges the horrors of the exile while also offering a point of comparison.

Historicity around this "time of distress" divides scholars. Like other historical events read into Daniel, readers typically choose methods allowing them to craft an apt historical timeline, but said chronologies work only within the confines of that method's assumptions and desired conclusion. Critical, historical scholars read it as predicting Antiochus IV's rule or the Maccabean revolt; others read it as more *ex eventu* prophecy about Antiochus IV in addition to the Maccabean revolt.[4] Some attempt to find a "middle way" that creates space for an Antiochus-oriented view alongside an eschatological end.[5] Still others draw a much harder apocalyptic line, arguing that "the proper time period is that of the great tribulation when the antichrist will be active . . . the great tribulation preceding the second coming of Christ."[6] Difficulty in articulating specifics around this very general "time of distress" goes back to early Christians, with Hippolytus saying it is a more generalized persecution directed toward Christians.[7] Wigand follows a similar generalized path, while Calvin reads verse 1 as proclaiming "God to be in general the guardian of his church."[8]

The vague ambiguity of verse 1 and this unknown, unnamed "time of distress" is the apocalyptic genre as its best. It is vague and ambiguous on purpose. Sparse details are not keys to secret knowledge that unlock history, nor is it a narrative hole waiting for Christian theology to fill. Verse 1 is intentionally nondescript to prevent the reader from getting bogged down in further unknowable specifics. The narrator wants readers to know more struggles will come, perhaps to ward off fallacious prognosticators exclaiming, "The end is nigh!" Verse 1 also makes clear that deliverance after this time will come, but not yet. We modern Christians use Daniel 12 to mire ourselves in end-times predictions. Contemporary political and military strife fills news outlets, creating space for fictitious connections between Daniel 12 and the current moment. Daniel 12:1 cuts through all of that to say this thing will happen, and all the distress will come to an end, but not yet. If Daniel's compilers wanted additional information making this "time of distress" a specific event, they would have included it. They did not. Claiming to see "beyond" the text and into divine history via overly complicated theories only leads to false predictions and misguided pretension.

Language of deliverance in verse 1 draws interpretive attention as well, as the narrator says each person "found written in the book" will be delivered. This may be a reference to the "reliable" from Daniel 10:21, but the Hebrew here is nondescript. Verse 1 simply presents it as "in the book."[9] Sacred "books" containing names of the righteous and the unrighteous is a common biblical motif.[10] Particularly striking here is the use of passive verbal constructions, like with "your people *will be delivered*, each that *is found* written in the book."[11] The narrator does not say who will do the delivering or who wrote what in the book, or tell us who exactly is doing the finding. There is ample space to project God into these passive verbs, which Christian readers do. Underneath this language and imagery lies a compelling question: What metric is used to determine the difference between what verse 2 describes as those worthy of "eternal life" and those worthy of "shame, to eternal contempt"? Since Daniel 12 sits against the backdrop of Israelite religion, arguing that the difference is belief in Jesus of Nazareth is erroneous and anti-Jewish.[12] True to its apocalyptic ideals, Daniel 12 does not tell us the difference. It just simply says it will happen.

As with all of Daniel, there lies a simple and elegant solution to what exactly the speaker means in verse 2 with "And many sleeping in the land of dust will awaken." It is a callback to Ezekiel 37's valley filled with bones and to Isaiah 26:19: "Your dead shall live, their corpses shall rise. O dwellers in the dust, awake and sing for joy!" Ezekiel 37 and Isaiah 26 use elaborate metaphors to describe what Israel's rebirth and renewal will be like, and Daniel 12 puts an apocalyptic spin on that imagery. Nothing is secret or hidden about the message; it refers to Israel awakening and being reborn. It is not talking about the Christian concept of resurrection, or any Christian concept for that matter.

For Christians to take this explicitly Israelite image and make it Christian is, once again, supersessionist replacement theology rearing its head. The thing that is so damning about the Christian penchant to make everything about us is how brazenly unapologetic it is. For example, Sprinkle wraps up his discussion of 12:1–2 by saying, "Those who trust in the resurrected Christ will themselves be resurrected, and he will preside over the final judgement on the Father's behalf."[13] First, Daniel 12 does not mention Jesus. Second, verse 2 uses "sleeping" and "awaken," not "resurrection." "Sleeping" comes from the Hebrew root ישן, which quite literally means "to sleep." Similarly, "awaken" is קיץ, meaning "to wake up from sleeping." Sleeping language is likely a metaphor for death, but to make this death specific to Christians is a misstep.[14] The concept of resurrection that Christians project onto Daniel 12 can vary wildly as well, with some Christians using it to justify objections to bodily cremation.[15] Still others understand it as a more metaphorical, spiritual resurrection.[16]

All this Christian speculation misses the mark. Daniel 12 is talking about the reconstruction and renewal of Israel as prayed over and prophesied in Isaiah, Jeremiah, and Ezekiel. Decentering the Christian worldview in this way radically reorients what Daniel 12 is saying and doing. Reading verse 2 as foreshadowing a final Christian resurrection is dangerous in its prejudices and faulty in its textual support. Instead of defaulting to end-times focused paradigms, Christians now can find what apocalyptic texts like Daniel 12 may mean for us outside such old, antiquated foregone conclusions about antichrists and Christian persecutions. That said, Daniel 12 does not stop at verse 2. The remaining eleven verses finish Daniel with honest apocalyptic suspicion-laden confidence. Like contemporary readers, the people that wrote and compiled Daniel had no clue when everything presented in its pages would end. They just knew that it would.

Verse 3 gives us the only hints as to what differentiates between eternal life and eternal shame, but it first adds a wrinkle by referring to "the wise ones" that "shall shine like the brightness of the sky." It is unclear whether these wise ones refer to those receiving eternal life or if they represent another category in verse 1's book. Verse 3 also mentions "those causing many to be just," adding a possible fourth category. These shall "shine like the brightness of the sky . . . like the stars forever and ever." Stars and celestial bodies are common metaphors across the Bible, including the very prominent discussion between God and Abram in Genesis 15. One could argue these stars calls back to Genesis 15, which would make for a nice connection to the biblical portrayal of Israel's origins alongside its future rebirth. Numerous biblical examples underscore the metaphor's use and purpose, so to take it as a literal prescription of people becoming stars in the afterlife lacks textual merit.[17] Israel will become what God promised to Abram, which is a bold political statement given the nation's original rise and destruction. Israel's future is not behind them; it sits before them like the stars in the sky.

Our narrator speaks directly to Daniel at verse 4, offering a command about his immediate next steps. The speaker instructs him to "conceal the words and seal the book until the end time," which is the opposite of what one expects Daniel may want to do with this dire and important news. However, this secrecy is consistent with Daniel itself, as Gabriel tells Daniel to "seal the vision because it is in reference to many days" at Daniel 8:26.[18] Neither chapter 12 or 8 tells us why Daniel should seal and conceal the book. Further, verse 4 is unclear as to what this "book" is; it could be the book of Daniel itself, the vision Daniel has just witnessed, or the book mentioned in verse 1. Here again we may have another apocalyptic intracultural reference with this book, meaning that any specifics about verse 4's book are mere speculation.

Verse 4 brings scholarly speculation about when this "end time" will occur back to the fore. This is where evangelical readers construct or hypothesize about timelines by pointing back to Daniel 7:25 and "a time, two times, and a half a time" or the "seventy weeks" in Daniel 9. Daniel 12 withholds particulars and just tells us, "Many will go to and fro, and knowledge shall greatly increase." This general language fits all of history: many people come and go, and knowledge as we know it continues increasing. The narrator is telling Daniel that life will continue as normal without major signs or harbingers because the end will happen when it happens; do not waste time stressing about anything more than that.

A widely accepted scholarly theory speculates that verses 5–13 are a separate textual unit from verses 1–4.[19] The theory claims Daniel's instructions in 12:4 are the "end" of the vision begun in chapter 10, but, despite interesting potential, manuscript evidence in Hebrew and Greek support Daniel 12 as one self-contained unit. Thus, to read Daniel 12:1–4 and 5–13 separately undercuts what the chapter can do in its entirety. Nothing about verse 5 stands out as odd or inconsistent with Daniel, as the book uses the conjunction "and" to keep stories and visions moving. Further,

Daniel uses the exclamation "lo!" in the middle of chapters, so it does not operate as a demarcation point between one section and another.[20]

There is another narrative shift at verse 5, with Daniel returning to his spot as narrator and seer. What we get in verses 5–13 is explicitly Daniel's perspective. He sees two others, each standing "toward the bank of the stream." The vision has not ended, as verse 6 hosts the return of "the man clothed in linen." What happens in verses 5–6 connects directly with verse 4, as Daniel hears one of the men asking the returned linen man from Daniel 10, "When will the wonders end?" The text here expertly employs a subtle but clear metaphor to highlight how the linen man knows more about the given situation: it situates him further up the stream than the two men and Daniel. Verse 5 is unclear as to what or who exactly these "others" are, but the default Christian paradigm reads them as angelic figures.

They could be angels, but the text does not say who or what they are; mindful of that, it is just as possible they are two other men standing with Daniel. Perhaps their presence is another bridge between Daniel and biblical prophets, meaning the "two others" symbolize Israelite prophets preceding Daniel. Such a show of good faith simultaneously affirms their warnings alongside Daniel's vision while also affirming Daniel's humanity. Daniel is a deeply human figure, with flaws and limitations hindering how he understands what he sees. Despite this humanity, he can still carry the message. Further, Daniel has come all this way based on Nebuchadnezzar selecting him back in chapter 1. For him to stand beside others paying witness to such a vision shows the power humans can have.

The linen man answers in verse 7 by first dramatically raising both hands high and swearing "by the life of the eternal one," an oblique reference to God; one wonders why the linen man does not refer to the deity by its name or by the more general "Elohim." If we have learned anything about Daniel up to this point, it is that the book favors cryptic ambiguity over straightforward responses. Despite the move to answer, the linen man's response retains Daniel's trademark inconclusiveness: "For a time, times, and a half, to be complete when the hand of the holy people is shattered, all of these will be accomplished." On the surface, this seems like a retread of Daniel 7:25, but looking closer shows a small difference:

> Daniel 7:25: for a time, times, and a half a time
>
> Daniel 12:7: for a time, times, and a half

This discrepancy between "half a time" and "a half" is not the only place Daniel 12 diverges from Daniel 7's time language. Daniel 7 uses "time" against the backdrop of the little horn's reign, and Daniel 12 says this "time" will "be complete when the hand of the holy people is shattered." Thus, Daniel 7 uses it to demarcate how long the little horn reigns, but Daniel 12 uses "times" to tell the unnamed speaker that things will not be complete until the aforementioned hand shattering.

It is unclear what the "hand of the holy people" imagery conveys, but within the context of Daniel a metaphorical possibility exists. Daniel 1:2 uses the Hebrew word for "hand" as a euphemism for Nebuchadnezzar's military power, and Daniel 9:15 uses "hand" to describe God's liberation of Israel from Egyptian captivity.[21] It appears throughout the Bible, often used in reference to YHWH and Elohim's strength and power.[22] One may think this language implies how future Israelite success hinges upon the nation's ability to overcome its colonizing enemies militarily. Herein lies the brilliance of apocalyptic literature: military might is doomed to fail, so trying to defeat it with more military violence only perpetuates the cycle. Each of Daniel's chapters presents kings whose power stems from their ability to wield a formidable military. Each of those kings and the kingdoms built for them falls. Daniel 7–11 features elaborate metaphors that emphasize the futility of human military strength, as armies just get bigger and stronger to match their opponent. The future of Israel will not stand upon military victories. Only after the "hand" of the holy people shatters will "all of these . . . be accomplished."

Daniel's response in verse 8 supports this inversion of expectations: "And I heard and I did not understand." He addresses the speaker directly, even using the title of "my lord" before seeking more specifics about the outcome. Here Daniel plays the consummate reader surrogate and says what many of us may be thinking: How can victory come from something shattered? Biblical prophets lobbied for and celebrated Cyrus as their messianic figure, only for history to show that he and his empire were just more cogs in the turning imperialism wheel. The speaker's answer tells him and us that the military "hand" will not be the expected vehicle for rebirth. Daniel's uncertainty is only natural given his upbringing in times of perpetual war. It is not an indictment of Daniel's character or ability to understand what he hears; it is just how Daniel sees the world.

The speaker's response in verse 9 effectively rebuffs Daniel's uncertainty. He tells Daniel to "Go" because "the words of the end time are closed and sealed." Verses 10–11 paired with verse 12's "one thousand three hundred thirty-five days" draws considerable interpretive attention given the numbers and potential timelines 1,290 and 1,335 days can yield. But Christians often misunderstand the line "Many shall be purified and made white and cleansed." For example, Duguid erroneously equates the shattered hand and purification metaphor to suffering, saying the coming destruction is "God's consistent pattern of working in this world, moving through suffering to glory."[23] He continues: "In God's wisdom the way in which we are cured of our brokenness is precisely through fiery trials."[24] Beyond having no textual merit, such readings reflect considerable naïve idealism based in a place of considerable privilege. Destruction wrought by this kind of "suffering is God's will" theology far outweighs any benefit while also reinforcing the military and violence that Daniel 7–12 works so hard to combat. Channeling Isaiah 2, only when swords are beaten into plowshares and spears into pruning hooks will nations stop lifting swords against each other, casting war and knowledge of war aside.

It is quite peculiar to read timelines constructed according to the 1,290 days of verse 11 and 1,335 days of verse 12. Seventh-day Adventists traditionally take the "days as years" approach and connect it to what they call "the 2300-prophecy of Daniel 8:14."[25] Hippolytus, Theodoret, and Jerome tie the 1,290 days to the antichrist, with Jerome being direct in saying it is "the time when the antichrist shall obtain possession of the world and forbid the worship of God."[26] Modern evangelicals take up this strain and tie the numbered days to an apocalyptic "tribulation period of the last days."[27] Still others create a labyrinthian timeline bringing all the Daniel numbers together with the "time, times, a and half a time" reference, creating something that is as myopic as it is incomprehensible.[28] Each of these readings and many others commit an egregious, Western European–centric misstep when they ascribe the calendar understanding of one year equaling 365 days. The modern Western calendar did not go into effect until 1582 CE, over one thousand years after Daniel's setting and composition. Reading Daniel's timeline as "our" timeline makes modern Christianity's understanding of time the center of God's creation, a move rife with hazardous self-centeredness.

What, then, do the numbered days in Daniel 12 mean? Aside from faulty chronological measurement, Christian readings build these timelines from our understanding of "the abomination which desolates." As discussed in previous chapters, this image is a mystery. There are numerous possibilities for what it can be, with each one showing more about the reader's particular background or interpretative agenda than the actual text itself. The bottom line is Christians pinning a specific event to "the abomination which desolates" stand tied to Jesus-centric readings, making their event the first domino to fall in a line that ends with Jesus' return. Any theory about "abomination which desolates" is just that: a theory.

A more important piece of this puzzle comes from acknowledging Daniel 12 is not about the end of the world. It is about the restoration of Israel. To stretch the chapter's point and purpose to encapsulate creation in its entirety is to ignore Daniel's narrative context as well as Daniel's persistent focus on Israel. The timeline is inconsequential, as shown by the wordplay of verse 7 and "time, times, and a half." Verse 10 builds upon this playful rhetoric by saying that a lot of people will do wise things and a lot of people will do wicked things; the wise will understand, while the wicked will continue to be wicked. The speaker tells Daniel at verse 11 "the regular will be turned aside," phrasing that connects back to verse 1 and the "time of distress the likes of which has not been since the nation came to be." This is another bold accusation on readers that claim to unlock or unravel Daniel's secrets. First, nothing in the chapter is secret. It is a shockingly straightforward chapter. Second, what makes it straightforward is the speaker's continued language of extreme and dire situations. He explicitly tells Daniel the end will be unlike anything anyone has ever seen. Nothing can or will compare to it. Therefore, the speaker wants Daniel (and, by virtue of Daniel's status as our surrogate, us) to settle on what he knows: the wicked and the just will receive requisite judgments. Those "causing many to be just" will shine and bask in eternal life; the rest will bear eternal shame and contempt. Daniel's instructions then become to act and live justly and cause many to become just.

The speaker's words at verses 9 and 13 support this claim, as he tells Daniel simply to "go." He answered Daniel's questions, and whether Daniel does not like or fully understand the answer is irrelevant. Daniel's next step is to go, rest, and rise for his allotment, because "the words of the end time are closed and sealed." It is not for Daniel to know when this will happen; all he needs to know is that it will happen and that the just will be dealt with justly, and the wicked wickedly. The end is certain. What Daniel does between now and then is up to him.

12.3 So What?

General approaches to apocalyptic literature are, in a word, selfish. We readers ground ourselves as the text's center, creating apocalyptic universes revolving around us. We construct elaborate schedules that make us the victors, cementing our self-created pedestals. Many, many people, including early Christians like Paul and the Gospel writers, believed the world would end in their lifetimes. It did not. Countless contemporary Christians do the same, and yet the sun still rises. Daniel 12 desperately pulls us past selfish worldviews and entreats us to consider a world where this mythical "we" is not the center. Daniel repeatedly asks when what he sees will end, and what the outcome will be, only to be told to go and live.

A surface reading of Daniel's instructions to go and live makes him, and in turn humanity, seem powerless. This is not true. Verse 3 tells us that "the wise ones" will shine like stars in the sky because they lived "causing many to be just." The wise share their wisdom and help guide others down the just path, knowing that it leads to a righteous judgement. The wicked focus only on themselves, facing eternal shame and contempt. Christian readers hastily tie this image to Revelation 20:15 and the "lake of fire," but there is a considerable difference between a lake of fire and shame and eternal contempt. This false equivalency is as destructive theologically as it is textually disingenuous. Daniel never once mentions the Christian concept of "hell."[29] Further, Daniel never mentions the Christian idea of heaven, either. To say "eternal life" is eternity in heaven is a considerable theological leap that disregards Daniel 12's actual content. Daniel does not ask about an afterlife, nor does the outcome presented in Daniel 7–11 intimate that the goal is something otherworldly. Daniel 12:2 talks about "many sleeping in the land of dust" awakening to eternal life, suggesting that people who were once dead will live again. Nowhere in Daniel does this suggest that "awakening" means something metaphorical in the sense of a soul moving on to heaven. Like the valley of dry bones in Ezekiel, it is a metaphor for the restoration of Israel.

Making Daniel 12 about deciding who goes to heaven or hell also seriously undercuts political ramifications spread across the chapter. There remains a profound and humble courage in knowing human governments and the horrors they spread across the planet will end. We do not know when that will happen, but, if there is a lesson from history as Daniel reconstructs it, it is that human might will fall. We know this because it always has. The mighty Roman Empire now lies in ruins, as do the once seemingly invincible armies of Babylon and Persia. More apocalyptic-minded Christians welcome and in some cases pray for the mythic "end" to arrive, but we often ground our prayers in a dire assumption that needs questioning and critiquing: we assume our names are in this "book" from verse 1. Daniel 12 takes on an entirely different orientation if we read it not as the ones getting eternal life but instead as those awakening to shame and eternal contempt.

Another theological trend laid upon Daniel 12 comes from Christians interpreting suffering as a tool God uses to refine and sharpen God's people. This kind of Christian theology is rooted in glorifying the violence and suffering Jesus endured during the crucifixion. For example, Duguid says so outright:

> If Christ could endure the agonies of the cross for the sake of joy that was set before him, so also we should ensure the far lesser agonies that we face with our eyes firmly fixed on heaven's great joys. When we read heaven's distant shore, it will all have been worth it.[30]

Duguid is not alone with this perspective.[31] Reading Daniel 12 as an endorsement for God approving of and using human suffering to achieve God's plan is a grave misstep. Daniel 12 does present suffering as a reality and consequence of war, but it never blesses suffering as something God wishes upon people. To return to a theme presented throughout Christian readings of Daniel, this pro-suffering theological worldview is rooted in a very particular understanding of divine sovereignty. Daniel 12 opposes such blind allegiance, as twice the speaker tells Daniel to "go" and decide whether he will be one who causes people to be just or if he will be among the wicked.

Wickedness saturates Daniel's world, so much so that Daniel cannot imagine a world without it. Like Daniel, we often feel powerless to change anything. But Daniel 12 dares us to be different. It dares us to consider a different world without violence and the military as denoting strength. His military worldview highlights just how much of a product of his environment Daniel is; he cannot escape it even if he tried. The same goes for current systems that violate, oppress, and dehumanize—they hide in plain sight. For example, Angela Davis argues in *Are Prisons Obsolete?* that the American prison industrial complex thrives on human suffering and dehumanization of those that society deems "criminal." Davis calls out language used to describe incarcerated persons, like using "felons" and "ex-con" to describe someone to separate "us" from "them." Davis dares her readers to envision a world without prisons, a world where, as her book title suggests, prisons are obsolete. Davis receives considerable push back and criticism for her views, specifically pertaining to questions of, "Where would society put felons and criminals?" Pushing back, Davis wants humanity to picture a world without crime and the social inequities leading to it. She argues the solutions are multifaceted:

> Rather, positing decarceration as our overarching strategy, we would try to envision a continuum of alternatives to imprisonment—demilitarization of schools, revitalization of education at all levels, a health system that provides free physical and mental care to all, and a justice system based on reparation and reconciliation rather than retribution and vengeance.[32]

Some critics may read Davis as idealistic and/or naïve, but doing so only highlights how deeply ingrained these systems are to American Christians. Daniel's response to the shattered hand shows the deep ties he has to military power and control, which the speaker uses to underline his need to break those bonds. If the answer Daniel seeks is more military and war, then that is all he will get. Only by seeking something else will the violence cycles be broken.

The same goes for us. Our world is our world. We feel like we cannot change anything, to the point of some Christians crafting entire theologies to justify doing nothing. But the reality is the exact opposite. We can change things. We can stop cycles of violence and war, creating a world not run by ruthless monarchs with an insatiable lust for power. Daniel walks away from his visions being told the end is set and sealed. These visions and their interpretations render null any attempt to give an exact date or cause. But Daniel has his life, and he can live knowing that he can be part of the solution or part of the problem. Like Daniel, we have a choice. We can choose to do nothing and wait, despite knowing we may face eternal shame and contempt. Or we can be wise, just, and led by God in daring to dream of something different.

Conclusion

What's Next?

I wrote this book to actively push against the grain of Christian approaches to Daniel. I reiterate those motives here to be explicit and clear about my intention. I know some of what I argue and claim will draw ire and adverse zeal. Good. I welcome the push back, because it is in pushing against how we have been told to read the Bible that we can finally start to read it for ourselves. For far too long, Christians have grown comfortable. We are too comfortable in keeping the Bible safely within the confines of constructed traditions. We are too comfortable regurgitating one or two interpretations ad nauseam. Instead of actually preaching or teaching the Bible, we resort to trite sayings or shallow explanations. Or worse, we lose ourselves in overly complex and self-serving arguments disconnected from the books so many fought so hard for so long to pass down. We do our ancestors a considerable disservice by not wrestling with the text and what it can mean. We sell short the possibilities of God by letting books like Daniel lay silent only to be read, studied, and preached by a select few.

The point of this book is straightforward: reconsider how Christians read Daniel in light of accepted and entrenched interpretations. In reconsidering Daniel, we open the door to reconsider theological issues like prayer, destiny, divine intervention, the role of humans in God's working in the world, and the very nature of God. We uncover how economics, gender, politics, history, ethnicity, and religion intersect across Daniel's twelve chapters. We also uncover the ways in which interpreters restrain Daniel by reusing antiquated readings to the point of deifying long-dead readers. We treat Jerome, Tertullian, Calvin, Luther, and so many others as gods themselves, never daring to consider the possibility those men could be wrong. We neglect how their social, political, economic, and cultural environments affected and shaped their work, only to allow their histories to become our own.

For example, Luther was a shockingly anti-Semitic man. His hatred of Jewish people is palpable across his work, including but not limited to his anti-Semitic treatise *On the Jews and Their Lies*. It is a horrible book filled with Luther's overt prejudices and hatred, but, despite such hate, Protestants put Luther's life and work on par with the life of Jesus and scripture itself. One only needs to read Christian commentaries on Daniel to see the widespread use and acceptance of such damning anti-Semitism. Evangelical Christians in particular make Daniel into a Jesus-centered manifesto that completely disregards the overt textual and historical evidence saying otherwise. Instead of reading Daniel as a bold and demanding apocalyptic text, we make it into just another proof-text for own misguided Christian agendas.

Luther is not the only Reformer we use as a catalyst. As early as 1634 CE, Puritans in America used Calvin's concept of total depravity to dehumanize Black people for the purposes of enslavement.[1] Calvin's theology becomes a gold standard of sorts when working with Daniel, as Christians take God's continued silence and absence as evidence for the deity's invisible but total control over history. As nice as this sounds on paper, it completely disregards human choices that cause the suffering, poverty, war, famine, and death that define our world. We use Daniel's silent deity to justify an apparent lack of God's working in the world, only to set ourselves up to completely miss what God may be calling us toward. What we call "divine sovereignty" becomes another excuse to stand idle.

This does not even begin to consider how Christians engage the politics laid out in Daniel. Some take an approach like that of Augustine's *City of God*, in which we say Daniel highlights God's eternal truths over and against humanity's innate wickedness. But through the lens I present here, Daniel himself does nothing but support and entrench the political systems around him. Far from being anti-imperialist, Daniel gets promoted as kings pour glory and praise upon him for appeasing their sensitivities in light of dream-visions that quite literally predict their downfall. On top of this, Christians celebrate Daniel as an ideal worker bee, doing his part to hold up the government only to neglect how that very government oppresses Daniel's people.

Reconsidering Daniel liberates its apocalyptic focus, making us ask challenging questions of the text and even harder questions about ourselves. For example, why do we make children's "Bibles" that remove major pieces of Daniel's stories in chapters 1 through 6? Is it because we think children are incapable of critical theological thought? If so, we are dooming the future of the Christian church to abject failure. Is it because we cannot manage those ideas ourselves, or simply do not want to read and consider the theological implications of a story like chapter 6 that ends with innocent men, women, and children eaten alive? If that is the case, then we have condemned ourselves to similar fates as Christianity becomes a religion of blissful idealisms.

The deconstruction applied in this book shows how we Christians continually make the text about us and our wants. Like Protestant Reformers claiming that the fourth beast in Daniel 7 is the Catholic antichrist, only to have Catholic supporters retort in saying Protestants are the real fourth beasts, we cannot see that the only reason Daniel lines up perfectly with our sense of history is because we make it so. Daniel, and the Bible in general, can be molded and shaped however we like. But instead of seeing this as an opportunity to liberate and recover Christianity from the clutches of manipulative power, far too often we Christians wield our scriptures like tools designed for bitter hatred, political expediency, and ineffective passivity.

That is why scholars consider deconstruction a taboo in biblical studies and Christianity: it decenters unquestioned power through daring to read the Bible anew. Like Phyllis Trible's powerfully simple take on Genesis 2–3 that pushes against sexist readings of the Eve and Adam narrative by asking, "What if Eve is the culmination of creation, not merely the last thing created?" reading familiar narratives with fresh eyes can change everything we think we know about Christianity.[2] Deconstruction makes us focus on texts themselves and not interpreters. It shines a light on the borderline idolatrous approach Christians take toward using church fathers and Protestant Reformers as the final say on biblical interpretation. Deconstruction does not destroy a text; it liberates it.

When we read the Bible, the future of biblical studies, theology, homiletics, ethics, and how we understand history is quite literally in our hands. Biblical scholar Herbert Marbury uses an example in his book *Pillars of Cloud and Fire* that articulates my position well. Marbury tells us of Ukawsaw Gronniosaw, a formerly enslaved person whose writings are widely considered to be some of the first published by an African in Britain. Gronniosaw's most famous work is his autobiography, *A Narrative of the Most Remarkable Particulars in the Life of James Albert Ukawsaw Gronniosaw, an African Prince, as Related by Himself.* Marbury describes Gronniosaw's eager excitement to get his hands on the book he saw a Dutch ship's captain talking to and hearing from. Marbury describes Gronniosaw's thoughts:

> Since the book had spoken to the captain, then why not him? As soon as he was alone, he approached the volume, lifted it to his ear, and listened, but the book gave him no response. Finally, Gronniosaw read the disappointing silence and spoke for the book: he knew that it, like everything else in the new world, despised him because he was Black.[3]

The book in question is the Bible, and Gronniosaw's realization uncovers the cold, hard truth: people use the Bible to justify whatever they want.

For example, would-be fitness profiteers use Daniel 1 to make outrageous claims about so-called Daniel diets. One such example is called "The Ultimate Daniel Fast," and it includes lists of "Foods to Eat" and "Foods to Avoid."[4] Approved foods include whole grains, beans and legumes, nuts and seeds, vegetables, fruit, oils, and an ambiguous "other." Things listed under "other" are unleavened bread, soy products, and "all herbs, spices, and seasonings . . . including salt and pepper."[5] The people responsible for this diet plan claim their insights come directly from Daniel itself, with a focus on Daniel 1 and 10. However, nowhere in all twelve of Daniel's chapters does Daniel eat soy, nuts, legumes, or anything other than vegetables and water while also avoiding rich food, meat, and wine. This fast is completely fabricated, but the testimonies listed online praise it for bringing people closer to God. What is most shocking (but honestly not surprising) is how "The Ultimate Daniel Fast" is but one of hundreds of variations on this idea, including one published in the popular magazine *Good Housekeeping*.[6] This "Daniel diet" example opens the door to recall much more dire cases mentioned throughout this book, like Manifest Destiny, enslavement, colonization, racism, and systemic sexism. All these things had (and in some cases still have) unwavering support from Christians who claimed their beliefs have biblical support.

Contemporary Christians would be wise to heed and understand Gronniosaw's personal revelation. We may not actively commit something as egregious as genocide or condone government-mandated discrimination based on race or gender, but, when we fail to question long-standing ideas around prayer, divine sovereignty, and political power, we deny the very things that make Daniel sacred. Imagine if we reconsidered each of these things. How different might they become, and, in turn, how might we Christians change the world we built for ourselves?

Let us first consider prayer. Prayer is a fickle thing. On the one hand, we Christians like the idea of talking to God and relating our sorrows, concerns, and struggles. All branches of Christianity put considerable emphasis on prayer, but few really consider the logical inconsistencies in how we pray. Daniel prays multiple times across the book's twelve chapters. In some instances, Daniel gets what he prays for; in others, Daniel gets answers that disturb and terrify him. Prayer in Daniel is extremely complicated, and in this complexity Daniel invites us to reconsider our respective theologies of prayer. Do we pray openly and honestly, being receptive to whatever kind of answer or resolution it brings? Are we prepared for our prayers to seemingly go unanswered? Is our faith strong enough to handle what God may tell or want from us? Or do we pray hoping that we get what we want, and nothing else? Further, are we prepared to learn that prayer on its own is not enough? Daniel prays and prays and prays but does nothing to change or influence his surroundings. Yet he is still surprised and upset over how the empires for which he works will end; what does he expect? Should we be like Daniel and do nothing, or should we instead see Daniel as an example of what not to do? Because if God treated prayer like we treat prayer, none of us would like the outcome.

Which brings us to the theological precept I have pressed the most throughout this book, divine sovereignty. When I began research on Daniel's reception histories and interpretation streams, I expected more theologically conservative voices to emphasize their understandings of God's historical preeminence and dominion. I did not expect such an approach to appear unquestioned in every commentary I consulted. I lean hard into and against interpreters who use Daniel to build their theological understandings of history atop divine sovereignty, because doing otherwise only further deifies the concept. There is a certain comfort in believing God controls anything and everything across history, but there is also a deep and profound sense of dread.

Daniel itself displays a sense of cultural dissonance and uncertainty toward divine sovereignty, as outlined and dissected by Amy Merrill Willis in *Dissonance and the Drama of Divine Sovereignty in the Book of Daniel*. Willis focuses her work on Daniel 2 and 7–12, but the trail Willis blazes also works with all of Daniel: to claim Daniel presents a comfortable and unwavering approach to theological determinism misunderstands the depth, breadth, and multiplicity of how God interacts with Daniel's sense of history.[7] Daniel and his friends do the best they can with what they have before them. They may not do much more than survive amid their circumstances, but in the most literal sense that is enough because the book's very survival means that we still discuss, consider, and wrestle with it.

But is Daniel's survival enough? Should we be asking more of him and ourselves? Daniel itself is highly critical of governments and the people aligning with them. The ongoing message of Daniel 7–12 is that all human governments will fall thanks to decisions we make for ourselves. Similarly, Daniel 1–6 shows the desperation that imperialist powers put upon us, forcing us to sacrifice who we are down to our very names. The first six chapters also read considerably different when we realize one of the things slave traders and masters did in the United States was force enslaved persons from the African continent to change their names and reject their histories. It is in seeing how Daniel allows himself to become an imperialist pawn that these issues of prayer, divine sovereignty, and political power coalesce into the most daring and damning of apocalyptic questions: Whose side are we on?

Daniel makes it clear what side God is on, and what is truly remarkable about Daniel is how it seemingly stands at odds with itself. As noted in chapter 1, one of the first things we learn is that God gave Israel and Jerusalem into Nebuchadnezzar's hand. Or so the authors of Daniel 1 want us to believe, as Daniel 1–6 highlight how inept those governments are, while 7–12 show the complete and utter destruction coming their way. Those who wrote Daniel make a daring and courageous decision to keep theological ideas that oppose each other in the same book. We Christians should be grateful for such apparent incongruity, as the world in which we live reflects a striking disharmony. On one hand, humans can love one another with such power that said love makes pain into joy, hatred into respect, and despair into hope. On the other, humans construct differences around race, gender, economic class, age, and a myriad of other factors to craft the most horrible distinction between "us" and "them."

This, finally, brings us back to a word I use throughout this book: sacred. Christians often take the word "sacred" to mean "unquestionable" or "unwavering," meaning that we do not question the Bible. In doing so, we limit both sacred texts and sacred power. Christians can read and know these old readings, but they and the people who wrote them are not God. They are not scripture. Scripture is scripture, and scripture is a path that we each walk. How we choose to walk that path is up to us. Daniel presents us with choices: Do we align with power, given we know how that power will ultimately fall before God's justice? Or do we see Daniel as a template for what happens when passivity is the norm? Daniel does not give us an answer. How we decide where we stand is between us and God. What could be more sacred than a book that shows and dares us to do just that?

Notes

Introduction

1 Nebraska Wesleyan University in Lincoln, Nebraska.

2 Frederic Baumgartner, *Longing for the End* (New York: Palgrave, 1999), 167–70.

3 WADB 7:722, 744.

4 George Aichele and the Bible and Culture Collective. *The Postmodern Bible* (New Haven: Yale University Press, 1995), 120.

5 Annalisa Azzoni, "Betraying the Text: Creation Narratives in Their and Our Context," in *Focusing Biblical Studies: The Crucial Nature of the Persian and Hellenistic Period; Essays in Honor of Douglas A. Knight*, ed. Jon Berquist and Alice Hunt (New York: T&T Clark International, 2012), 83–91.

6 Jehoiakim reigned from 609 to 598 BCE. See John Collins, *Introduction to the Hebrew Bible* (Minneapolis: Fortress, 2004), 258.

7 Louis Hartman and Alexander A. Di Lella, *The Book of Daniel* (Garden City, N.Y.: Doubleday, 1977), 128.

8 I used "Levant" here and not "ancient Near East" for two reasons. First, claiming something is "ancient" tends to make people discredit or see it as "lesser than" compared to our contemporary contexts. Second, "Near East" reflects a highly Western worldview, as the people who lived during these eras would not have been "east" of themselves. Thus, "Levant" is a much more balanced descriptor.

9 Many scholars, including Carol Newsom, John Collins, C. L. Seow, and John Goldingay, engage issues of dating at a much deeper (and objectively dependable) level. I rely on them heavily for my approach. See their works referenced in this chapter for extensive and valuable discussions regarding specifics around the book of Daniel's origins and composition.

10 W. Sibley Towner, *Daniel* (Louisville: Westminster John Knox, 1984), 44.

11 Towner, *Daniel*, 44.

12 Daniel Smith-Christopher, *Daniel* (Nashville: Abingdon, 1996), 76.

13 Smith-Christopher, *Daniel*, 77.

14 C. L. Seow, *Daniel* (Louisville: Westminster John Knox, 2003), 14.

15 Seow, *Daniel*, 22.

16 Seow, *Daniel*, 22. Seow's book lacks citation regarding which Calvin work he consults, but divine sovereignty is indeed a prominent theme throughout Calvin's Daniel commentaries. See John Calvin, *Commentaries on the Book of the Prophet Daniel*, trans. Jean Calvin and Thomas Myers (Grand Rapids: Eerdmans, 1948).

17 Carol Newsom's commentary also presents Daniel's deity as an ever-present and unquestioned sovereign entity. See Newsom, *Daniel* (Louisville: Westminster John Knox, 2014).

18 John Goldingay, *Daniel* (Grand Rapids: Zondervan Academic: 2019), 583.

19 Goldingay, *Daniel*, 438.

20 Goldingay, *Daniel*, 566.

21 Hartman and Di Lella, *Daniel*, 280.

22 Adela Yarbro Collins, "The Influence of Daniel on the New Testament," in *Daniel*, by John Collins (Minneapolis: Fortress, 1993), 90–123.

23 J. Collins, *Daniel*, 268. John Collins does this throughout his commentary, including in his explanation of Dan 7:9 (p. 301), Dan 7:18 (p. 318), and the OG addition of Susanna (pp. 433–34, 437).

24 Stephen R. Miller, *The New American Commentary: Daniel* (Nashville: Broadman & Holman, 1994), 34–36.

25 S. Miller, *Daniel*, 35.

26 Tremper Longman III, *The NIV Application Commentary: Daniel* (Grand Rapids: Zondervan, 2002), 27.

27 Justin Martyr, *Dialogue with Trypho* (orig. 2nd century CE), trans. Thomas Falls (Washington, D.C.: Catholic University of America Press, 2003), 118. Also, unless otherwise noted, the Greek version consulted is Jacques Paul Migne, *Patrologiae Cursus Completus* (Alexandria, Va.: Patrologia Latina Database, 1996).

28 Irenaeus, *Adversus haereses* (orig. 180 CE) (Cambridge: Typis Academicis, 1857), 5.26.2.

29 The version consulted for the *Scholia* is A. Mai, *Script. Vet. Collectio Nova*, I.iii, 29–56. Quotations from the *Commentary on Daniel* are from the Greek version found in Hippolytus, *Kommentar zu Daniel*, trans. Georg Nathanael Bonwetsch (Berlin: Akadamie Verlag, 2000); and Hippolytus, *Commentaire sur Daniel* (orig. 211 CE), vol. 14, trans. Maurice Lefevre, intro. by Gustave Bardy (Paris: Editions du Cerf, 1947).

30 Cyril of Jerusalem, from the heading of "Catechetical Lecture 15." All citations from Cyril's Catechetical Lecture 15 are from Edwin Hamilton Gifford, *From Nicene and Post-Nicene Fathers*, Second Series, vol. 7, ed. Philip Schaff and Henry Wace (Buffalo, N.Y.: Christian Literature Publishing, 1894.)

31 Jerome, *JCD* (orig. 407 CE); Theodoret of Cyrus, *Commentary on Daniel*, trans. Robert Hill (Boston: Brill, 2006).

32 For a rich introductory overview of literary and biblical studies, see David J. A. Clines, *On the Way to the Postmodern: Old Testament Essays 1967–1998*, vol. 1 (United Kingdom: Sheffield Academic Press, 1998).

33 Danna Nolan Fewell, *The Children of Israel: Reading the Bible for the Sake of Our Children* (Nashville: Abingdon, 2003), 117.

34 Anathea Portier-Young, *Apocalypse against Empire: Theologies of Resistance in Early Judaism* (Grand Rapids: Eerdmans, 2011), 223.

1 Daniel 1 Reconsidered

1 D. J. Wiseman, *Nebuchadnezzar and Babylon* (New York: Oxford University Press, 1985).

2 A. K. Grayson, *Assyrian and Babylonian Chronicles* TCS 5 (Locust Valley, N.Y., 1975), 102.

3 Robert Allen Warrior, "Canaanites, Cowboys, and Indians," in *Native and Christian: Indigenous Voices on Religious Identity in the United States and Canada*, ed. James Treat (New York: Routledge, 1996), 100.

4 Renita Weems, *Battered Love: Marriage, Sex, and Violence in the Hebrew Prophets* (Minneapolis: Fortress, 1995).

5 The Hebrew for "handsome" here is טוֹב.

6 H. Vanstiphout describes literate individuals as a "class of literates" that "will be closely connected and eventually identical with cult personnel and the priesthood." *CANE*, volume 4, 2188.

7 J. Collins, *Daniel*, 136. Collins defaults to James Montgomery's Daniel commentary, especially pp. 119–21. Montgomery focuses on discussing historicity around language used in the text, the identity of the group labeled "Chaldeans," and the type of education the foursome received.

8 Newsom, *Daniel*, 42.

9 Seow, *Daniel*, 24.

10 Diodorus Siculus, *The Library of History*, vol. 2, trans. C. H. Oldfather, Loeb Classical Library (Cambridge, Mass.: Harvard University Press, 2004), 2.29.2–3.

11 רַב סָרִיסָיו

12 Academic discourse around סָרִיס remains fraught with cultural biases and assumptions about assumptions. For example, "Eunuchs in the Bible" by F. P. Retief, J. F. G. Cilliers, and S. P. J. K. Riekert presents assumptions and conjecture as fact, thereby reinforcing the narrative of sometimes it means a person whose genitals have been altered, and sometimes it means chief official. For example, the

authors say, "It is unlikely that [Potiphar] was a eunuch," "Genesis 37:36 and 39:1 probably refer to the office of courtier or captain of the palace guard," and "there is no reason to assume that Pharaoh's cupbearer and baker were necessarily eunuchs either." Their arguments rest on nothing more than variations in English translations, thereby creating a self-reinforcing interpretive loop. "Eunuchs in the Bible," *Acta Theologica Supplementum* 26.2 (2006): 251.

13 Many, many options are available. Examples include Fiona Wesley, *Bible for Kids: A Collection of Bible Stories for Children* (2014); David Cook, *The Action Bible* (Colorado Springs: David C. Cook, 2010); Sally Tagholm et al., *Children's Bible Stories* (New York: DK Publishing, 2013); VBS Curriculum, *Knights of the North Castle* (Nashville: Cokesbury, 2020). One notable exception is *The Children's Bible*, retold by Anne de Graaf (Copenhagen, Denmark: Scandinavia Publishing House / Casscom Media, 2017). De Graaf's retelling makes a point to say Shadrach, Meshach, and Abednego are the characters' Babylonian names.

14 John Day. "The Daniel of Ugarit and Ezekiel and the Hero of the Book of Daniel," *Vetus Testamentum* 30, no. 2 (1980): 174–84. Academic discourse around this subject is vast, with all signs pointing toward the biblical Daniel's roots reaching back to the Ugaritic Dan'el character. What is more fascinating for interpretation is that use of Dan'el in Ugarit is so fluid that it implies an extant knowledge on behalf of the Ugaritic writers. Thus, it is highly likely that the nonbiblical writers pulled from extant sources as well, making Daniel a character with rich and diverse literary and culture histories.

15 Goldingay, *Daniel*, 19; Smith-Christopher, *Daniel*, 44; Charles Swindoll, *Daniel, Volume 1: God's Man for the Moment* (Texas: IFL Publishing House, 2008), 17–18.

16 Seow, *Daniel*, 26; Klaus Koch, *Daniel: Biblischer Kommentar; No. 1–6* (Germany: Neukirchener Verlag des Erziehungsvereins, 1986), 64–65; Goldingay, *Daniel*, 18.

17 Many biblical characters drink wine without reproach from God, including Noah and his family. Lev 10 forbids drinking wine but only when ending the tent of meeting (10:9). Num 6 instructs Nazirites to not drink wine and strong drink, but this does not apply to average Israelites, nor are Daniel and his friends Nazirites. God instructs Moses to offer wine with sacrifices, meaning that God likes wine. Wine appears in Deuteronomy, Joshua, Judges, 1 Samuel, the prophets, Job, Psalms, Proverbs, and Ecclesiastes and throughout the Hebrew Bible. The continued consumption and discussion of wine points to one thing: the beverage does not break

Israelite purity laws. In similar fashion, "portion of the king" is merely a descriptor of food that comes from the king, meaning that unless Ashpenaz has a secret food stash not shared in Dan 1, Daniel and his friends still eat food from the king.

18 Seow writes, "The narrator never loses sight of the theological focus implicitly laid out at the beginning. The test immediately goes on to show that God made Daniel's decision work." *Daniel*, 27.

19 Billy Graham, "The Rise of the Antichrist," *Hour of Decision*, September 16, 1972, https://billygraham.org/audio/the-rise-of-the-antichrist/.

20 Swindoll, *Daniel*, 1.

21 See sermons and devotionals by Wayne Barder, Dave Roper, Chip Dean, Greg Breazeale, and John Piper.

2 Daniel 2 Reconsidered

1 Chul-hyun Bae, "Aramaic as a Lingua Franca during the Persian Empire (538–333 B.C.E.)," *Journal of Universal Language* 5, no. 1 (2004):1–20.

2 Seow, *Daniel*, 37; Newsom, *Daniel*, 66.

3 Johannes Meinhold, *Die Composition des Buches Daniel* (Greifswald, Germany: Julius Abel, 1884); Gustav Hölscher, "Die Entstehung des Buches Daniel," *Theologische Studien Kritiken* 92 (1919): 113–38; J. Collins, *Daniel*, 29; Towner, *Daniel*, 5–6; Goldingay, *Daniel*, 322–24 (2019); Newsom, *Daniel*, 6–12.

4 Jerome, *JCD* 32; CCL 75A: 794.

5 Jerome, *JCD* 40.

6 Martin Luther, *WADB* 11, 2:4–6; Giovanni Diodati, *Pious Annotations upon the Holy Bible* (British Museum, 1651), 2:40; John Calvin, *CTS* 24:162–63 (*CO* 18:589–90).

7 Hans Brosamer disseminated a pro-Catholic, anti–Martin Luther woodcut that depicts Luther as the fourth beast of Daniel 7, which is a clear response to Luther's anti-Catholic interpretations.

8 Justin Martyr, *Dialogue with Trypho*, 48–50. Also, unless otherwise noted the Greek version consulted is Migne, *Patrologiae*, cols. 539–64.

9 Jerome, *JCD* 40.

10 Theodoret, *Commentary on Daniel*, 53.

11 P. Schaff et al., eds., *A Select Library of the Nicene and Post-Nicene Fathers of the Christian Church* (Buffalo, N.Y.: Christian Literature, 1887–1894; repr., Grand Rapids: Eerdmans, 1952–1956; repr., Peabody, Mass.: Hendrickson, 1994), 7:467.

12 To name a few: James Hamilton and D. A. Carson, *With the Clouds of Heaven: The Book of Daniel in Biblical Theology* (Illinois: IVP Academic, 2014); Andrew Steinmann, *Daniel* (Missouri: Concordia, 2008); Sinclair B. Ferguson and Lloyd John Ogilvie, *Daniel* (Tennessee: Thomas Nelson, 1988); Iain M. Duguid, *Daniel* (New Jersey: P & R Publishing, 2008); Dale Ralph Davis, *The Message of Daniel* (Illinois: IVP Academic, 2013).

13 John Collins, *The Apocalyptic Vision of the Book of Daniel* (Scholars Press for Harvard Semitic Museum, 1977), 43–44.

14 Jerome, *JCD* 1.

15 Hippolytus, *Scholia on Daniel* 2.5.

16 Johann Wigand, *Brief Exposition of the Prophet Daniel* (Explication Brevis, 1571), 43–44.

17 Tisa Wenger, *Religious Freedom: The Contested History of an American Ideal* (North Carolina: University of North Carolina Press, 2017).

18 Charles C. Mann, *1491: New Revelations of the Americas before Columbus* (New York: Vintage Books, 2005).

19 Mark Knoll, *A History of Christianity in the United States and Canada* (Michigan: Eerdmans, 1992), 38–39.

20 Howard Zinn, *A People's History of the United States* (New York: Harper Perennial, 2015), 14.

21 Roxanne Dunbar-Ortiz, *An Indigenous Peoples' History of the United States* (Massachusetts: Beacon, 2014), 73.

22 Jayson Casper, "The Wartime Prayers of Ukraine's Evangelicals," *Christianity Today*, March 11, 2022, https://www.christianitytoday.com/ct/2022/march-web-only/ukraine-prayer-bible-help-evangelical-christians-russia-war.html.

23 Casper, "Wartime Prayers."

24 Timothy Bella, "Pat Robertson Says Putin Was 'Compelled by God' to Invade Ukraine to Fulfill Armageddon Prophecy," *Washington Post*, March 1, 2022, https://www.washingtonpost.com/world/2022/03/01/pat-robertson-putin-god-russia-ukraine/.

25 Chris Moody, "How US Right-Wing Views Putin amid Russian War on Ukraine," *Al Jazeera*, March 4, 2022, https://www.aljazeera.com/news/2022/3/4/how-us-right-wing-views-putin-amid-russian-attack-on-ukraine.

3 Daniel 3 Reconsidered

1 LXX uses εἰκόνα, meaning "image."

2 Herodotus, *Herodotus*, ed. A. D Godley and W. Heinemann (London: William Heinemann Ltd, 1920), 1:183–84.

3 Henry Thompson, "Dura," in *ABD*, 2:240–41.

4 Hippolytus, *Scholia on Daniel* 3.47; *ANF* 5:188.
5 Isho'dad of Merv, *Commentary on Daniel* 3.22; CSCO 328:106.
6 Irenaeus, *Against Heresies* 4.20.11.
7 Hippolytus, *Scholia on Daniel* 2.92(25).
8 Jerome, *JCD* 43–44.
9 Jarl Fossum, "Son of God," in *ABD*, 6:128–36.
10 Terry Lindvall, *God Mocks: A History of Religious Satire from the Hebrew Prophets to Stephen Colbert* (New York: New York University Press, 2015), 5–15
11 Dennis G. Jones, *Read with Me Bible: An NIV Story Bible for Children* (Grand Rapids: Zondervan, 1993), 227.

4 Daniel 4 Reconsidered

1 Goldingay's translation renders this as "lookout" (עִיר) instead of "watcher." This interpretive move demystifies the entity, as making it anything more than a divine emissary (as is common in apocalyptic literature) is disingenuous. Goldingay, *Daniel*, 245–48.
2 The above translation and following discussion rely on the Aramaic chapter demarcation.
3 If readers would like to contest this, do so by all means! They will quickly find, however, more dead ends and dodges than actual critical inquiry and engagement into the issue.
4 Theodoret, *Commentary on Daniel*, 103–5.
5 Calvin, *Commentaries on Daniel*, in *CTS* 24:243–44 (*CO* 18:647–48).
6 See Duguid, *Daniel*; D. Davis, *Message of Daniel*; Sinclair Ferguson, *The Preacher's Commentary: Daniel* (Nashville: Thomas Nelson, 2002).
7 J. Collins, *Daniel*, 222.
8 J. Collins, *Daniel*, 222; Seow, *Daniel*, 66–67; Newsom, *Daniel*, 136.
9 Goldingay, *Daniel*, 245.
10 Prov 3:18, 11:30, 13:12, 15:4; 2 Esd 2:12, 8:52; 4 Macc 18:16; Rev 22:2, 14, and 19.
11 Erik Hornung, "Ancient Egyptian Religious Iconography," in *CANE*, volume 3, 1715–16.
12 Portier-Young, *Apocalypse against Empire*, 223–79. See also Danna Nolan Fewell, *Circle of Sovereignty: Plotting Politics in the Book of Daniel* (Nashville: Abingdon, 1991). Fewell's entire argument builds upon the ideas of Daniel being an anti-Babylonian voice.
13 Ephrem, *Commentary on Daniel* 4.19; *ESOO* 2:208.
14 Jerome, *JCD* 50.

15 Theodoret, *Commentary on Daniel*, 119; Seow, *Daniel*, 69–72; Smith-Christopher, *Daniel*, 73–74. Paul House, *Daniel* (IVP Academic, 2018), 96; S. Miller, *Daniel*, 132–36.

16 J. Collins, *Daniel*, 226; Duguid, *Daniel*.

17 Theodoret, *Commentary on Daniel*, 131.

18 Ephrem, *ESOO* 2:210.

19 Calvin, *CTS* 24:298–99 (*CO* 18:686–88).

20 Magedah Shabo, *Techniques of Propaganda and Persuasion* (Prestwick House, 2008), 7.

21 Jason Stanley, *How Propaganda Works* (New Jersey: Princeton University Press, 2015), 41.

22 Examples of propaganda appear throughout *A Companion to Ancient Egyptian Art* (ed. Melinda K. Hartwig [Chichester, U.K.: Wiley Blackwell, 2015]). Multiple authors mention the use of propaganda throughout Egypt and across multiple dynasties.

23 Ronald Leprohon, "Ideology and Propaganda," in Hartwig, *Companion*, 312.

24 Jonathan Z. Smith, "'Narratives into Problems': The College Introductory Course and the Study of Religion," *JAAR* 56 (1988): 733.

25 Katheryn Pfisterer Darr, "Ezekiel," in *The New Interpreter's Bible Commentary*, volume 6, 1156.

26 Darr, "Ezekiel," 114.

27 Seow, *Daniel*, 73.

28 John Owens, "Daniel," in *The Broadman Bible Commentary: Volume 6* (Tennessee: Broadman Press, 1971), 404.

29 Smith-Christopher, *Daniel*, 76.

30 Olivia Olander, "Trump: 'God Made the Decision' Overturning Roe," *POLITICO*, June 24, 2022, https://www.politico.com/news/2022/06/24/trump-to-fox-god-made-the-decision-overturning-roe-00042284.

31 Robert Jeffress, "Pastor Robert Jeffress: Biden Is President-Elect—How Should Christians Respond?" *Fox News*, November 7, 2020, https://www.foxnews.com/opinion/biden-elected-christians-response-robert-jeffress.

32 Gregory A. Smith, "About a Third in U.S. See God's Hand in Presidential Elections, but Fewer Say God Picks Winners Based on Policies," Pew Research Center, March 12, 2020, https://www.pewresearch.org/fact-tank/2020/03/12/about-a-third-in-u-s-see-gods-hand-in-presidential-elections-but-fewer-say-god-picks-winners-based-on-policies/.

33 Daniel Burke, "Rick Perry Says Trump (and Obama) Were 'Ordained by God' to Be President," *CNN*, November 25, 2019, https://www

.cnn.com/2019/11/25/politics/rick-perry-donald-trump-god/index.html.

34 Dave Miller, "Did God Choose Barack Obama as President?" *SBC Voices*, November 8, 2012, https://sbcvoices.com/did-god-choose-barack-obama-as-president/.

35 Stephen Mansfield, *The Faith of George W. Bush* (New York: Tarcher-Perigee, 2003), 108.

36 Mansfield, *Faith*, 109.

37 "Costs of the 20-Year War on Terror: $8 Trillion and 900,000 Deaths," Brown University, September 29, 2023, https://www.brown.edu/news/2021-09-01/costsofwar.

38 Darr, "Ezekiel," 1156.

5 Daniel 5 Reconsidered

1 This translation sticks with the Aramaic's verse numbering.

2 J. Collins, *Daniel*, 243.

3 Jerome, *JCD* 5.2.

4 John Calvin, *Commentaries on the Book of the Prophet Daniel*, trans. Jean Calvin and Thomas Myers (Grand Rapids: Eerdmans, 1948), 1:361.

5 Theodoret, *Commentary on Daniel*, 133. Philippus Melanchthon, *Commentaire de Philippe Melanchthon sur le livre des révélations du prophète Daniel: Item les explications de Martin Luther sur le mesme prophète adjoutées à la fin, le tout nouvellement traduict. [Précédé de l'Argument du livre des révélations du prophète Daniel, par Jean Calvin]* (Geneva: J. Crespin, 1555), 90.

6 Seow, *Daniel*, 76–78; Goldingay, *Daniel*, 285–87; Towner, *Daniel*, 70–72; Smith-Christopher, *Daniel*, 80; J. Collins, *Daniel*, 243.

7 Roy Swim's claim that the king is holding a "Profane Orgy" is incorrect and baseless, and lacks supporting textual evidence (though it could be emblematic of what Christians project onto the book of Daniel in its entirety). See "Daniel," in *Beacon Bible Commentary*, vol. 4 (Kansas City: Beacon Hill Press, 1966), 560.

8 Literally, "fingers of a man's hand."

9 Duguid, *Daniel*, 88.

10 Jones, *Read with Me Bible*, 232–33. The trend in *Read with Me Bible* continues to be the norm and not the exception. See also Sally Tagholm et al.'s *Children's Bible Stories: Share the Greatest Stories Ever Told* (London, England: DK Publishing, 2021), 159.

11 Tagholm et al., *Children's Bible Stories*, 159.

12 *CANE*, volume 4, 2188.

13 J. Collins, *Daniel*, 250.

14 Towner, *Daniel*, 75; Goldingay, *Daniel*, 291.

15 Seow, *Daniel*, 82.
16 J. Collins, *Daniel*, 250–52.
17 J. Collins, *Daniel*, 253; Newsom, *Daniel*, 175. Newsom is particularly noteworthy. She claims that "the inscription that Daniel reads and interprets does have the quality of a riddle," based solely on the "variety of interpretive decisions" possible. But her argument builds upon the theoretically unpointed Aramaic originals and not the extant text itself.
18 Swindoll, *Daniel*, 70; Jerome, *Commentary on Daniel*, 5:30–31.
19 Towner, *Daniel*, 70.
20 Goldingay, *Daniel*, 281.
21 Theodoret, *Commentary on Daniel*, 151–53.
22 Xenophon, *Cyropaedia* 7.5.24–30, trans. Walter Miller (New York: Macmillan, 1918).
23 Swindoll, *Daniel*, 74.
24 Towner, *Daniel*, 76.
25 Seow, *Daniel*, 84.
26 Luther, *WADB* 11, 2:8–10.
27 Johann Gerhard, *Postilla: An Explanation of the Sunday and Most Important Festival Gospels for the Whole Year*, vol. 1, *Sermons for the Church from Advent through Pentecost* (Center for the Study of Lutheran Orthodoxy, 2003), 21.
28 Theodoret, *Commentary on Daniel*, 151.
29 Eccl 8:11–13: "Because sentence against an evil deed is not executed speedily, the human heart is fully set to do evil. Though sinners do evil a hundred times and prolong their lives, yet I know that it will be well with those who fear God, because they stand in fear before him, but it will not be well with the wicked, neither will they prolong their days like a shadow, because they do not stand in fear before God."
30 Ruth Graham, "Southern Baptists to Release List of Ministers Accused of Sexual Abuse," *New York Times*, May 24, 2022, https://www.nytimes.com/2022/05/24/us/southern-baptist-sexual-abuse.html.
31 Bob Smietana, "When Abuse Victims Are Adults, They're Often Treated as 'Sinners,' Threats to Churches," *Word and Way*, July 8, 2022, https://wordandway.org/2022/07/06/when-abuse-victims-are-adults-theyre-often-treated-as-sinners-threats-to-churches/.
32 Smietana, "Abuse Victims."

6 Daniel 6 Reconsidered

1 This translation starts with 6:1 according to the Aramaic, not according to the discrepancy between 5:31 and 6:1 customarily done in English translations.

2 The Aramaic here is הַרְגִּשׁוּ from the root רגשׁ, meaning "to throng." A synonym of "to throng" is "to crowd."

3 Towner, *Daniel*, 78.

4 Towner, *Daniel*, 78.

5 Theodoret, *Commentary on Daniel*, 159.

6 "Darius the Mede," in *ABD*. Hartman and Di Lella, *Daniel*, 35–36.

7 Hartman and Di Lella, *Daniel*, 191.

8 S. Miller, *Daniel*, 171–76.

9 Thought that does not stop people from assuming divine intervention. See Goldingay, *Daniel*, 314.

10 S. Miller, *Daniel*, 179.

11 Portier-Young, *Apocalypse against Empire*, 261.

12 It is possible translators allowed the Greek version of Daniel to influence their work, but, if that is the case, why stop there? Why not just rely on OG Daniel entirely?

13 See J. Collins, *Daniel*, 267, n. 49.

14 Miller erroneously calls them "bloodthirsty," as there is no textual support for such a claim (see S. Miller, *Daniel*, 159).

15 John Mayer, *Commentary upon All the Prophets*, 536.

16 Goldingay, *Daniel*, 320–21.

17 S. Miller, *Daniel*, 185; Duguid, *Daniel*, 106.

18 D. Davis, *Message of Daniel*, 111.

19 S. Miller, *Daniel*, 186.

20 Goldingay, *Daniel*, 321.

21 Portier-Young, *Apocalypse against Empire*, 223. Unapologetic support for Darius' conflicted feelings defines Portier-Young's sentiment about Daniel: "No book of the Hebrew Bible so plainly engages and opposes the project of empire as Daniel." Portier-Young supports her claim further by citing Danna Nolan Fewell's *The Children of Israel*: "The book of Daniel may be the Bible's foremost book of resistance against political domination."

22 Newsom, *Daniel*, 198.

23 Jerome, *JCD* 67.

24 Ephrem, *ESOO* 2:213.

25 Towner, *Daniel*, 84. It should also be noted that Towner takes the opportunity to offer an unrequested bit of his Christology: "The fundamental difference in the two accounts emerges just here, of course; Jesus really did die and was raised, whereas for Daniel an angel shut the lions' mouths and when he emerged from the den 'no kind of hurt was found upon him, because he had trusted in his God.'" Duguid takes a similar approach, going as far as to title a section "The Lions' Den and the Way of the Cross."

26 Hartman and Di Lella, *Daniel*, 200.

27 Goldingay, *Daniel*, 322.
28 Towner, *Daniel*, 84.
29 Theodoret, *Commentary on Daniel*, 167.
30 Seow, Tanner, Newsom, Owens, Towner, and many others overlook this narrative gaffe.
31 OG and θ Daniel mention nothing about moving the stone, and the critical apparatus in the *BHS* confirms consistency across different manuscripts and various sources.
32 Seow argues that chapter 6 highlights "that Darius is not above the law that he has made." Seow, *Daniel*, 92.
33 Chrysostom, *On the Epistle to the Hebrews*, homily 27.4
34 Cyril of Jerusalem, *Catechetical Lectures* 5.4.
35 See Towner, Goldingay, Smith-Christopher, Tanner, Swindoll, Seow, Owens, S. Miller, Duguid, and many, many others.
36 V. Gilbert Beers, *The Early Reader's Bible* (Grand Rapids: Zondervan, 2001), 273.
37 *The Action Bible* (Colorado Springs: David C. Cook, 2010).
38 Joe Sprinkle, *Daniel* (Washington: Lexham Press, 2021), 162–63.
39 J. Paul Tanner, *Daniel* (Washington: Lexham Press, 2021), 390.
40 Seow, *Daniel*, 95; Smith-Christopher, *Daniel*, 93.
41 Jerome, *JCD* 6.25–27.
42 Duguid, *Daniel*,
43 Heinrich Bullinger, *Daniel Sapientissimus Dei Propheta* (Zurich: C. Froschouerus, 1576), 59.
44 Ephrem, *ESOO* 2:213.
45 "The point is not that God will surely deliver but that God can when God wills. In this case, God does and does so marvelously" (Seow, *Daniel*, 94). "God allows his people to endure times of trial, though he is present with them and other works to save his people" (Sprinkle, *Daniel*, 165). "Whatever the risk we may face, however, we can be sure that the Lord is going to be faithful to us" (Tanner, *Daniel*, 394). "God prevails and vindicates his servant Daniel against insuperable odds. The story offers a foretaste of the coming victory of God over all foes, even death itself" (Towner, *Daniel*, 88).
46 "Pat Robertson Says Haiti Paying for 'Pact to the Devil,'" *CNN*, January 13, 2010, http://www.cnn.com/2010/US/01/13/haiti.pat.robertson/index.html. Robertson also claimed the 2005 landfall of Hurricane Katrina was God punishing America because of abortion.
47 John O'Sullivan, "Annexation," *Democratic Review* 17 (July–August, 1845): 5.
48 Alexander Koch, Chris Brierley, Mark M. Maslin, and Simon L. Lewis, "Earth System Impacts of the European Arrival and Great Dying in the Americas after 1492," *Quaternary Science Reviews* 207 (2019): 13–36.

49 United Nations, "Slave Trade," accessed October 29, 2023, https://www.un.org/en/observances/decade-people-african-descent/slave-trade.

50 Hugh Thomas, *The Slave Trade: The Story of the Atlantic Slave Trade, 1440–1870* (New York: Simon & Schuster, 1997). See also Rachel L. Swarns, "My Research into the History of Catholic Slaveholding Transformed My Understanding of My Church," *New York Times*, March 16, 2021, https://www.nytimes.com/2021/03/16/us/catholic-church-enslavement.html.

7 Daniel 7 Reconsidered

1 בִּשְׁנַת חֲדָה ("In the first year"). Witnesses read, "in the first year," except for θ, which has ἔτει τρίτῳ, "third year." The latter is probably secondary, for it anticipates 8:1 and harmonizes with it.

2 מֶלֶךְ בָּבֶל ("King of Babylon"). θ reads, βασιλέως Χαλδαίων, "king of the Chaldeans"; and OG reads, "reign over the country of Babylonia." Vg and Peshitta corroborate the Hebrew/Aramaic, but θ echoes τῶν Χαλδαίων in 5:30 with χαλδαιων.

3 חֵלֶם חֲזָה וְחֶזְוֵי רֵאשֵׁהּ ("this dream and visions of his head"). OG lacks "dream," meaning OG has the Daniel character experiencing only a ὅραμα ("vision"). θ concurs with the Aramaic, as Daniel has a "dream and visions of his head" (ἐνύπνιον εἶδεν καὶ αἱ ὁράσεις τῆς κεφαλῆς αὐτοῦ). Vg follows OG with only the singular dream without a vision. Peshitta reads: "Daniel dreamed a dream; there were visions in his head." Goldingay notes that this "double description of the dream vision is characteristic of Daniel style." See Goldingay, *Daniel*, 334.

4 θ follows the Hebrew and Aramaic, saying, "And he wrote down the dream," while OG says he "wrote down the vision that he saw" (τότε Δανιηλ τὸ ὅραμα ὃ εἶδεν, ἔγραψεν).

5 הֳקִימַת is a peculiar form, as it is the only Hophal form in Daniel.

6 OG, θ, and Peshitta are expansive with the inclusion of "beast."

7 The Aramaic has שָׁלְטָן, which is reflected in all the Vrss, except OG, which has γλῶσσα ("tongue/language"), as if reading לשן. The latter is probably an error for שלטן (so J. Collins, *Daniel*, 274).

8 One witness to θ and Hippolytus include "and its claws were of bronze," which Collins attributes to intentional or accidental scribal commingling of 7:7 with 7:19 (see J. Collins, *Daniel*, 274).

9 The Vrss corroborate the Aramaic, except for OG, which offers an interesting variant: καὶ βουλαὶ πολλαὶ ἐν τοῖς κέρασιν αὐτοῦ (lit. "and there were many counsels in its horns").

10 The form סִלְקַת is anomalous—as if combining סִלְקַת (peal perfect 3 fs) and סָלְקָה (peal participle fs), The perfect 3 fs form (so a few

MSS), attested in 7:20, is probably correct, though the Masoretes may have been influenced by the participle (though plural) form in 7:3 (so Goldingay, *Daniel*). OG and θ appear to corroborate the perfect 3 fs.

11 OG appears to have a shorter reading: καὶ τοὺς κύκλῳ ("And as for the rest"), which is the *lectio brevior* that is possibly original; see Gustav Jahn, *Das Buch Daniel nach der Septuaginta hergestellt, übersetzt und kritisch erklärt* (Leipzig: Eduard Pfeiffer, 1904), 70.1.

12 The Aramaic has the singular, but OG, θ, and Vg have plural neuter, perhaps in anticipation of the plural form מִלַּיָּא.

13 θ attempts to make the attendant's response parallel to the narrator's inquiry, reading: εἶπέν μοι τὴν ἀκρίβειαν ("and he told me the truth"); the Peshitta reads as θ: "and he spoke truthfully to me."

14 Vg describes both the teeth and the nails as iron (*comedebat*), perhaps to harmonize with 7:7 and its lack of reference to bronze.

15 OG expands what the beast devours, reading: κατεσθίοντες πάντας κυκλόθεν. θ is closer to the Aramaic with the participle ἐσθίον.

16 The form and pointing of this verb are problematic. Aramaic points the verb passively but neglects the *yod* between the second and third root consonants. OG, θ, Peshitta, and Vg each offer active verbal forms, perhaps using the Aramaic root without its pointing. LaCocque, based on the work of H. Ewald, suggests the pointing and root discrepancy can be attributed to a haplography error. See André LaCocque, *The Book of Daniel* (Oregon: Wipf and Stock, 2015). This translation renders it as an action done by the Ancient of Days based on the preceding manuscript evidence and it possibly being a stative verb.

17 Some versions attempt to make the creature more grandiose, as θ has "surpass" (ὑπερέξει) and Vg has "will be greater than" (*quod majus erit omnibus regnis*). The Peshitta's rendering is similar to Vg with "will be preeminent over."

18 OG has "earth" (γῆν), which may be a dittography error from blurring the proceeding line with the one in question. Or, read in conjunction with the latter portion of the verse, OG may have switched "earth" with "it," as OG reads, ἀναστατώσει αὐτὴν. Use of ἀναστατώσει, "agitate," here further differentiates OG from Aramaic.

19 OG reads: τὰ δέκα κέρατα τῆς βασιλείας ("the ten horns of the kingdom"); θ: καί τα δέκα κέρατα αὐτοῦ ("and his ten horns"); and Vg: *decem ipsius regni* ("ten horns of that kingdom").

20 OG (καὶ αὐτὸς διοίσει κακοῖς ὑπὲρ) and θ (ὃς ὑπεροίσει κακοῖς παντας τους ἔμπροσθεν) have variations on "will surpass in evil,"

likely a move to remain consistent with OG and θ 7:23. Vg has "greater" (*potentior*), as does the Peshitta.

21 OG reads, καὶ παραδοθήσεται πάντα εἰς τὰς χεῖρας αὐτο ("and all shall be given into his hands"). θ retains the singular, as does Vg (*et tradentur in manu ejus*). This translation retains "hand" to echo the many instances in which references to power and control, both human and divine, are referred to as being in someone/something's "hand."

22 4QDan[a] and the Peshitta lack the conjunction, but many witnesses attest it. However, this translation eliminates it from the translation for stylistic purposes and its minimal impact on translation.

23 θ omits "people of," likely a continuation of issues from 7:18 and קַדִּישֵׁי. The Aramaic places a disjunctive accent under לְעַם, which suggests the Masoretes understand it as an appositive, making the entire phrase read: "to the people, the righteous ones of the Most High." This translation glosses the grammar while retaining the meaning.

24 John Collins, *The Apocalyptic Imagination*, 3rd ed. (Michigan: Eerdmans, 2016), 1–52.

25 Karl Marti, *Das Buch Daniel*, HKAT 18 (Tübingen: Mohr, 1901).

26 Read Duguid, Miller, Towner, and Goldingay's respective commentaries, the sections on Daniel 7, to see how their work clashes with others like J. Collins, Seow, Smith-Christopher, and Newsom.

27 J. F. Borghouts, "Witchcraft, Magic, and Divination in Ancient Egypt," in *CANE*, volume 3, 1783. See also S. A. L. Butler, *Mesopotamian Conceptions of Dreams and Dream Rituals* (Münster: Ugarit-Verlag, 1998).

28 F. Stolz, "Sea," in *DDD*, 737–42.

29 Scholars once viewed Hermann Gunkel's 1895 work *Schöpfund und Chaos* as seminal in the realm of biblical studies and ancient Near Eastern literature, as he argues Gen 1, Rev 12, and Dan 7 incorporate ideas and images from Babylonian creation narratives. Gunkel, the Christian son and grandson of Lutheran pastors, taught biblical studies and theology in Germany. However, his work is deeply troubling as it is shockingly anti-Semitic. Thus, I lend his positions no credence. Further, Gunkel takes the comparison too far by intimating that the similarities between these narratives convey possible intentionality on the biblical authors' part, meaning they willingly readapted stories for Genesis, Daniel, and Revelation. This position is unprovable as it ventures beyond theorizing into broad speculation.

30 Read any of their works cited in this book, and this trend becomes abundantly clear.

31 Verse 4: "its wings were plucked off (simple passive of מרת), it was lifted up (simple passive of נטל) from the ground and was made to stand (simple passive of קול) upon its feet like a human, and the mind of a man was given to it (simple passive of יהב)." Similarly, the bear in v. 5 is "raised up" on its side and gets instructed by a disembodied voice. The leopard in v. 6 "was given" dominion.

32 Amy C. Merrill Willis argues that the verbiage "renders the divine grammatically invisible as the doer of the action and thus somewhat elusive as an agent within human history." *Dissonance and the Drama of Divine Sovereignty in the Book of Daniel* (London: T&T Clark, 2010), 70–71.

33 See Sprinkle, Tanner, Seow, Owens, Miller, Swim, and Montgomery (among others). Goldingay presents the paradigm but couches his support by calling language around the animals and their descriptions "allusive" (*Daniel*, 358–59). Towner also decries putting "too much emphasis" on this "animal/history correlation, for one is hard pressed to find any corresponding link for the three remaining beasts" (*Daniel*, 93).

34 Tanner claims "the sea merely depicts the chaotic scene from which these Gentile nations arise" (*Daniel*, 407). See also Sprinkle, *Daniel*, 172; Chrysostom, *Commentary on Daniel*; Theodoret, *Commentary on Daniel*; Hippolytus, *Scholia on Daniel*; Diodati, *Pious Annotations*.

35 Common English Bible, the Complete Jewish Bible, God's Word Translation, New Living Translation, and New Revised Standard Version.

36 For a summary of the arguments, see Bob Becking, "Ancient of Days," in *DDD*, 44–45.

37 Smith-Christopher, *Daniel*, 104; Helge S. Kvanvig, *Roots of Apocalyptic: The Mesopotamian Background of the Enoch Figure and of the Son of Man* (Neukirchener Verlag, 1988), 445.

38 For a definitive assessment of scholarly discussions around the phrase and its possible etymology, see J. Collins, *Daniel*, 304–10.

39 And if they do use OG Daniel, they do not make their decision known, nor do they remain consistent in choosing to rely on OG Daniel and not the Aramaic throughout the rest of their translations.

40 See Babylonian Talmud Gittin 4a (50), 11QtgJob 32.2, P Gn15:9, P Lv1:5, P 1S6:10, P Esth8:10, BT BQ 80b(19).

41 Tanner, *Daniel*, 444.

42 Eugene Peterson, *Reversed Thunder: The Revelation of John and the Praying Imagination* (San Francisco: Harper & Row, 1988), 30. Note here Peterson falsely equivocates Daniel and Revelation as one text.

See also Duguid, *Daniel*; D. Davis, *Message of Daniel*; Ferguson, "Daniel," in *Preacher's Commentary*; and more than could possibly be listed here.

43 Hippolytus, *On the Antichrist*; Cyril of Jerusalem, *Catechetical Lectures*.

44 Pick any Christian reader cited thus far to see just how quickly their readings align themselves with the redeemed.

45 Tanner, *Daniel*, 414.

46 Theodoret of Cyrus, *Commentary on Daniel*, 185.

47 Tertullian, *Against Marcion* 4.10.

48 Cyril of Jerusalem, *Catechetical Lectures* 15.15.

49 Duguid, *Daniel*, 113.

8 Daniel 8 Reconsidered

1 The Hebrew here is בַּ֣עַל הַקְּרָנַ֔יִם, which when translated literally is "lord of horns" or "master of horns" (see Waltke and O'Connor, 9.5.3b, 13.6a, and 22.5a). This phrase appears only at Dan 8:6 and 8:20, and none of the translations or authors consulted for this book acknowledge the בַּ֣עַל in both verses. Translations offer "two horns" as הַקְּרָנַ֔יִם is in the dual, but there is no mention of the preceding בַּ֣עַל. My translation incorporates it to remain true to the text as it appears in the *BHS*, the most commonly and widely accepted scholarly rendering of the Hebrew. I also consulted the θ, OG, and Vulgate. Each lacks the Greek equivalent of בַּ֣עַל. There are also no textual variants in either verse in the *BHS*. The only instance in which בַּ֣עַל הַקְּרָנַ֔יִם is rendered as "having two horns" is in Benjamin Davidson, *The Analytical Hebrew and Chaldee Lexicon* (Grand Rapids: Zondervan, 1993), 102, though this is likely a result of the English translation stream around the verse that begins at the KJV. I render it as "lord of horns" because בַּ֣עַל is in the singular construct form.

2 The Hebrew at v. 11 lends itself to considerable interpretive variance. For example, Goldingay reads, "He grew big to within reach of the leader of the army; by him the daily offering was removed, and his sacred place and an army were overthrown." J. Collins translates it as, "He grew great even up to the prince of the host, from whom the daily offering was taken away and whose sanctuary place was cast down." Here are others: KJV ("Yea, he magnified himself even to the prince of the host, and by him the daily sacrifice was taken away, and the place of his sanctuary was cast down"); NRSV ("Even against the prince of the host it acted arrogantly; it took the regular burnt offering away from him and overthrew the place of his sanctuary"); NIV ("It set itself up to be as great as the commander of the

army of the LORD; it took away the daily sacrifice from the LORD, and his sanctuary was thrown down").

3 See Calvin, Luther, Tanner, et al.

4 *CANE*, volume 2, 1014–15.

5 Theodoret, *Commentary on Daniel*, 205; Ephrem, *Commentary on Daniel* 8.3.

6 A key example that became paradigmatic is Jerome's take on the ram's identity: "He calls Darius, Cyrus's uncle, a ram. He reigned over the Medes after his father, Astyages. And the one horn, which was higher than the other and growing still larger, signified Cyrus, who succeeded his maternal grandfather, Astyages, and reigned over the Medes and Persians along with his uncle, Darius, whom the Greeks called Cyaxeres." Jerome, *JCD* 84. Nothing in Daniel 8 supports Jerome's claim, yet he makes it with peculiar certainty.

7 OG Daniel includes the east here, possibly to round out the four cardinal directions. My translation relies on the MT since *lectio brevior*; OG Daniel here appears to be an editorial gloss.

8 Scott Noegel, "On the Wings of the Winds: Towards an Understanding of Winged *Mischwesen* in the Ancient Near East," *Kaskal* 14 (2017): 15–54.

9 Sprinkle, *Daniel*, 211; Tanner, *Daniel*, 490. Still others, like Towner (*Daniel*, 121), skip it in favor of readings straddling the line between metaphor and literal (LaCocque, *Daniel*, 161–62).

10 Ephrem, *Commentary on Daniel* 8.9.

11 Antiochus' proponents cite Porphyry's critique of Daniel, which is where much of the scholarly consensus originates.

12 Arthur J. Ferch, "The Book of Daniel and the 'Maccabean Thesis,'" *Andrews University Seminary Studies* 21, no. 2 (1983): 129–41. What makes this article interesting within the context of this book is that Ferch constructs an anti–Maccabean Thesis argument to claim Daniel was written during the sixth century BCE amid Babylonian exile and not the widely accepted theory of its composition during the second century BCE. Despite a radically different goal, Ferch's work supports my point quite nicely.

13 The Hebrew is הַפֶּשַׁע שֹׁמֵם.

14 Newsom, *Daniel*, 267; Goldingay, *Daniel*, 424; LaCocque, *Daniel*; see also Ephrem and Isho'dad.

15 W. Miller employs something called the "day-year principle," which is a tool employed by Seventh-day Adventists and Jehovah's Witnesses to justify their already specious math. Supporters of the theory argue it goes all the way back to fourth-century rabbinical teachings, but such an approach falls flat with the Hebrew itself. There is an entirely different word for "year," which is not employed in Daniel.

16 Luther, *WADB* 11, 2:16–18.

17 Goldingay argues that the word describing Gabriel, גֶּבֶר, denotes some kind of "macho" hypermasculine figuring, thereby elevating him to some kind of celestial status (see *Daniel*, 427). But this argument is self-defeating, as גֶּבֶר appears throughout the Hebrew Bible in reference to human men.

18 Uriah Smith, *The Prophecies of Daniel and the Revelation* (Battle Creek, Mich.: Review and Herald), 1904.

19 Most English Bibles disregarded "not his power" and instead use the Greek in OG and θ Daniel for their translation, as OG and θ Daniel lack this phrase.

20 J. Collins, *Daniel*, 336.

21 Smith-Christopher, *Daniel*, 117; Newsom, *Daniel*, 271; Tanner, *Daniel*; Sprinkle, *Daniel*; Goldingay, *Daniel*, 425 (who pretends to be Daniel in explaining what Dan 8 means, which is an odd choice given Goldingay wrote his commentary as a man in the twentieth century and not a Jewish person nearly two thousand years ago).

22 Liz Mineo, "Racial Wealth Gap May Be a Key to Other Inequities," *Harvard Gazette*, June 17, 2021, https://news.harvard.edu/gazette/story/2021/06/racial-wealth-gap-may-be-a-key-to-other-inequities/.

23 World Population Review, "Incarceration Rates by Country 2023," accessed October 30, 2023, https://worldpopulationreview.com/country-rankings/incarceration-rates-by-country.

24 Kevin Murphy, "Kansas Lawmaker Suggests Immigrants Be Shot like Hogs," *Reuters*, March 25, 2011, https://www.reuters.com/article/us-immigration-kansas/kansas-lawmaker-suggests-immigrants-be-shot-like-hogs-idUSTRE72O71H20110325.

25 Julian Borger, "Fleeing a Hell the US Helped Create: Why Central Americans Journey North," *Guardian*, December 19, 2018, https://www.theguardian.com/us-news/2018/dec/19/central-america-migrants-us-foreign-policy.

26 Acts 22 presents Paul as a Roman citizen, and the freedom of movement he has across the Roman Empire as he wrote his letters reflects a level of access off-limits to noncitizens during the first-century CE Roman world.

9 Daniel 9 Reconsidered

1 A considerable majority of English translations, including but not limited to NASB, NRSV, RSV, ASV, ESV, KJV, NKJV, render this word "prince." The Hebrew here, נָגִיד, can mean "prince," but its primary meaning is "leader." It likely comes from the verbal root

נגד, "to be conspicuous" or "to be in front." This makes נָגִיד a verbal noun, with the proposed literal translation in BDB being "one in front."

2 The meaning of the Hebrew here is quite uncertain. This translation takes a more literal approach to עַל כְּנַף, which literally means "upon a wing."

3 "Darius the Mede," in *ABD*. Hartman and Di Lella, *Daniel*, 35–36.

4 J. Collins labels his section in chapter 9 as "Seventy Weeks of Years," a move that overlooks the seventeen verses in which Daniel prays directly to God (*Daniel*, 344). Seow engages the prayer more than Collins but still devotes considerable space to engaging the chapter's numerology (*Daniel*, 134–51). Newsom makes it simply another apocalypse, like chapters 7 and 8 before it (*Daniel*, 287).

5 Irenaeus, *Against Heresies* 5.25.5; Augustine, *On the Trinity* 3.10.

6 Melanchthon, *Commentaire de Philippe Melanchthon*.

7 Wigand, *Brief Exposition*, 292–93.

8 Megan Bishop Moore and Brad E. Kelle, *Biblical History and Israel's Past: The Changing Study of the Bible and History* (Grand Rapids: Eerdmans, 2011), 334–35.

9 Stuart Irvine, *Isaiah, Ahaz, and the Syro-Ephraimitic Crisis*, SBLDS 123 (Atlanta: Scholars Press, 1990). See also 2 Kgs 15:37, 16:5–9; Isa 7:1–9; 2 Chr 27:1–9, 28:1–27.

10 Henri Cazelles, "Syro-Ephraimite War," in *ABD*, 6:282.

11 2 Kgs 24:10–16 and the Babylonian Nebuchadnezzar Chronicle corroborate these events.

12 Biblical and archaeological evidence confirm the siege and destruction. See Israel Finkelstein and Neil Asher Silberman, *The Bible Unearthed: Archaeology's New Vision of Ancient Israel and the Origin of Its Sacred Texts* (New York: Touchstone, 2001), 307.

13 Mark Smith, *The Origins of Biblical Monotheism: Israel's Polytheistic Background and the Ugaritic Texts* (Oxford University Press, 2003).

14 Moore and Kelle, *Biblical History*, 357.

15 See chapter 7, "The Exilic or Neo-Babylonian Period," in Moore and Kelle, *Biblical History*.

16 Weems, *Battered Love*.

17 Weems, *Battered Love*, 2.

18 Weems, *Battered Love*, 2.

19 Peter Craigie, Page Kelley, and Joel Drinkard, *Jeremiah 1–25* (Dallas: Word Books, 1991), 366; C. F. Whitley, "The Seventy Years Desolation: A Rejoinder," *Vetus Testamentum* 7 (1957): 416–18; Patrick Miller, "Jeremiah," in *The New Interpreter's Bible Commentary* (Nashville: Abingdon, 1994), 761–62; Avigdor Orr, "The Seventy Years of Babylon," *Vetus Testamentum* 6, no. 3 (1956): 304–6.

20 Tanner, *Daniel*, 543: "The most fundamental issue to this passage is the question of whether or not this is a messianic prophecy fulfilled in Jesus Christ."

21 "Darius the Mede," in *ABD*. Hartman and Di Lella, *Daniel*, 35–36.

22 Joseph Mede, *Daniels Weekes: An Interpretation of Part of the Prophecy of Daniel* (London, 1643), 11. Mede likely follows precedent established by Basil of Seleucia, Theodoret, Tertullian, Primasius, and Ephrem the Syrian, each of whom makes their reading into a heavy-handed Christology. See Basil of Seleucia, *Homily* 38.1; Theodoret, *Commentary on Daniel*, 245; Tertullian, *An Answer to the Jews* 8; Primasius, *Commentary on the Apocalypse* 3.11; Ephrem, *Commentary on Daniel* 9.27.

23 Tanner, *Daniel*, 596; Sprinkle, *Daniel*, 267.

24 Newsom, *Daniel*, 306; J. Collins, *Daniel*, 355.

25 Seow, *Daniel*, 150; Towner, *Daniel*, 143; Hartman and Di Lella, *Daniel*, 250–51; Owens, "Daniel," 440.

26 NIV: "A covenant will be put into effect with many people for one 'week.' In the middle of the 'week' sacrifices and offerings will come to an end. In one part of the temple a hated thing that destroys will be set up. It will remain until the LORD brings the end he has ordered."

RSV: "And he shall make a strong covenant with many for one week; and for half of the week he shall cause sacrifice and offering to cease; and upon the wing of abominations shall come one who makes desolate, until the decreed end is poured out on the desolator."

NRSV: "He shall make a strong covenant with many for one week, and for half of the week he shall make sacrifice and offering cease; and in their place shall be an abomination that desolates, until the decreed end is poured out upon the desolator."

KJV: "And he shall confirm the covenant with many for one week: and in the midst of the week he shall cause the sacrifice and the oblation to cease, and for the overspreading of abominations he shall make it desolate, even until the consummation, and that determined shall be poured upon the desolate."

27 "The righteousness of God, thus, reflects God's will to do what is right for humanity, whatever the cost may be (compare Rom. 3:21–26)." Seow, *Daniel*, 143.

28 Team ENOUGH, "Gun Violence Statistics," accessed October 30, 2023, https://www.teamenough.org/gun-violence-statistics.

29 Matt McGough, Krutika Amin, Nirmita Panchal, and Cynthia Cox, "Child and Teen Firearm Mortality in the U.S. and Peer Countries," KFF, July 18, 2023, https://www.kff.org/global-health-policy/

issue-brief/child-and-teen-firearm-mortality-in-the-u-s-and-peer-countries/.

30 Ed Rendell, "No More 'Thoughts and Prayers'—Pass the Gun Laws America Needs," *Hill*, March 28, 2023, https://thehill.com/opinion/criminal-justice/3922561-no-more-thoughts-and-prayers-pass-the-gun-laws-america-needs/.

31 David Marcus, "It's Time to Bring Back Prayer in Public Schools," *Federalist*, June 4, 2021, https://thefederalist.com/2021/06/04/its-time-to-bring-back-prayer-in-public-schools/.

32 Marcus, "It's Time."

33 James Cone, *A Black Theology of Liberation: Fortieth Anniversary Edition* (New York: Orbis Books, 2011), 123.

34 Cone, *Black Theology*, 123.

35 Brandee Mimitzraiem, interview with author, November 25, 2022.

10 Daniel 10 Reconsidered

1 To say the Hebrew here is opaque is an understatement. In Hebrew it reads as וְצָבָ֣א גָד֔וֹל, which I keep literal with "and a great conflict." The NRSV renders it as "and it concerned a great conflict," making the phrase connect with the word Daniel receives. But "it concerned" does not appear in the text. There is not textual variant in Hebrew, and OG and θ add words to resolve the interpretive issue. OG says, "and the multitude was strong" (καὶ τὸ πλῆθος τὸ ἰσχυρὸν), while θ reads as "and great power and wisdom was given to [Daniel]" (καὶ δύναμις μεγάλη καὶ σύνεσις ἐδόθη αὐτῷ ἐν τῇ ὀπτασίᾳ). Scholarly engagement highlights the phrase's grammatical incongruity. Newsom wrestles with the Hebrew and states plainly, "The phrase . . . could refer to the content of the revelation. . . . [It] could be a contrast term . . . and refer to the difficulty of the revelation and the hard labor required to understand it." But Newsom does not offer further resolution beyond the text's possibility, a move that I follow here. Though awkward to read, this literal translation creates space for interpretation and discussion: What does the text mean here? What are the possibilities? What can be gleaned about Daniel, and perhaps the nature of scripture itself, from this considering the realities of working with the Bible in Hebrew? Newsom, *Daniel*, 325.

2 Commonly rendered as "the Tigris."

3 Typically rendered "Greek."

4 P. Zerafa, "The Old Testament Life Span," *Angelicum* 65, no. 1 (1988): 99–116.

5 Joachim Bretschneide, "Life and Death in Nabada," *Scientific American*, January 1, 2005, https://www.scientificamerican.com/article/life-and-death-in-nabada/. See also Leonard Curchin, "Old Age in

Sumer: Life Expectancy and Social Status of the Elderly," *Florilegium* 2 (1980): 61–70.

6 Heleen Sancisi-Weerdenburg, "Darius I and the Persian Empire," in *CANE*, volume 2, 1039–40.

7 Isa 44:28, 48:1.

8 Ezra 6:14.

9 British Museum, "Object: The Cyrus Cylinder," accessed October 30, 2023, https://www.britishmuseum.org/collection/object/W_1880-0617-1941.

10 Three weeks of mourning is quite long, as the only other instance of three mourning weeks in a biblical context is 2 Esd 6:35.

11 J. Collins, *Daniel*, 373.

12 See Jerome, Hippolytus, Ammonius of Alexandria, John Mayer, and Andrew Willet (among many others, both contemporary and past).

13 Gen 17:4; 1 Sam 14:16.

14 Dan 1:4 (my translation).

15 R. W. Connell, *Masculinities* (California: University of California Press, 2005), 58.

16 The text itself says nothing on the matter, yet Hippolytus makes the baseless claim of "they were not worthy" (see *Commentary on Daniel* 4.38.3). Theodoret theorizes they "heard a great voice" prompting their hiding (see *Commentary on Daniel* 10.7). Ammonius calls them "unbelievers" who "do not know Christ," which has less textual support than Hippolytus' position (see *Fragments on Daniel* 10.8).

17 The first people to witness Jesus' resurrection were women. Paul addresses multiple women by name in his letters, thanking them for their work. Male-dominated church history ignores these women, but the text unapologetically supports their presence.

18 אֲנִי֙ נוֹתַ֣רְתִּי שָׁ֔ם אֵ֖צֶל מַלְכֵ֥י פָרָֽס

19 See chap. 13, "Prepared for Battle: Daniel 10:1–11:1," in Duguid, *Daniel*; chap. 10, "Daniel's Final Vision," in S. Miller, *Daniel*; Towner, *Daniel*, 150.

20 Breed argues this is the same Michael mentioned in 1 Enoch (Newsom, *Daniel*, 332–33). This argument is inconsistent with the descriptors given to Michael in Daniel 10. There may be an angelic figure outside of Daniel named Michael, but in Daniel he is just a man. Collins and Seow argue Michael is akin to a celestial patron, making him a divine protector of Israel (Seow, *Daniel*, 158–62; J. Collins, *Daniel*, 374–75). Like Breed's argument, their readings neglect the expressed human language used to describe Michael.

21 There is an entire cottage industry in Christian publishing dedicated to telling people how to be Christian men, the considerable majority of which reinforce toxic hegemonic masculinity. For example, in Michael Foster and Dominic Tennant's *It's Good to Be a Man:*

A Handbook for Godly Masculinity (Moscow, Idaho: Canon Press, 2022), the authors write, "Men were made to rule. They always have and always will. Nothing can change that. Nothing will. It is not a question of whether men will be ruling, but which ones and how." They also argue that proper biblical men are independent with aggressive instincts given by God. Daniel argues the opposite.

22 S. Miller, *Daniel*, 298.

23 See Tanner, Sprinkle, and Goldingay, to name a few.

24 Jerome, *JCD* 10:20–21; Mayer, *Commentary*, 560–61.

25 Zachary Mettler, "Christians, Be Not Afraid: You're Right to Believe in Two Genders and Preborn Life," *Daily Citizen*, April 21, 2021, https://dailycitizen.focusonthefamily.com/christians-be-not-afraid-youre-right-to-believe-in-two-genders-and-preborn-life/.

26 S. Miller, *Daniel*, 292.

27 William Wolfe, "Yes, Christians Are Being Persecuted in America: Here's How We Can Respond," *Christian Post*, July 18, 2022, https://www.christianpost.com/voices/yes-christians-are-being-persecuted-in-america.html.

28 Elena Kagan practices Judaism.

29 Callista Gingrich, "Persecution of Christians Skyrockets Worldwide as 360 Million Oppressed. We Must Stand for Religious Freedom," *Fox News*, February 4, 2023, https://www.foxnews.com/opinion/persecution-christians-skyrockets-worldwide-360-million-oppressed-we-must-stand-religious-freedom.

11 Daniel 11 Reconsidered

1 The NRSV reads, "He shall stir up all against the kingdom of Greece." The Hebrew is יָעִיר הַכֹּל אֵת מַלְכוּת יָוָן and is the source of much interpretive controversy (see Goldingay, *Daniel*, p. 503). This translation hinges on my rendering הַכֹּל as "the entirety" and using the אֵת as the standard marker of the direct object, which here is מַלְכוּת יָוָן, "the kingdom of Yavan."

2 A settlement located on the eastern coast of modern-day Cyprus.

3 J. Collins, *Daniel*, 377.

4 Newsom describes it as "the despair of commentators since they seem to be a jumble of ideas." See *Daniel*, 334.

5 וַאֲנִי בִּשְׁנַת אַחַת לְדָרְיָוֶשׁ הַמָּדִי

6 καὶ ἐν τῷ ἐνιαυτῷ τῷ πρώτῳ Κύρου τοῦ βασιλέως. θ Daniel agrees with OG Daniel: καὶ ἐγὼ ἐν ἔτει πρώτῳ Κύρου ἔστην εἰς κράτος καὶ ἰσχύν ("And, as for me, in the first year of Cyrus, I stood for power and strength").

7 Sprinkle, *Daniel*, 287.

8 Hartman and Di Lella, *Daniel*, 285; J. Collins, *Daniel*, 376.

9 Tanner goes so far as to say, "A better chapter break is after 11:1" (see *Daniel*, 638). See also J. Collins, *Daniel*, 362–63; Hartman and Di Lella, *Daniel*, 286; Towner, *Daniel*, 151; Seow, *Daniel*, 167–68. Goldingay takes a different approach and breaks 11:2 into 11:2a and 11:2b (*Daniel*, 528).

10 J. Collins' acceptance of this interpretive trend stands out as odd, as he cites chapter 11's unity from 4QDan-C to support the Darius the Mede reading not being a later gloss. 4QDan-C presents chapter 11 beginning at v. 1 and chapter 10 ending at v. 21.

11 Cyrus (539–530 BCE), Cambyses (530–522), Smerdis (522), Darius I (522–486), Xerxes I (486–465), Artaxerxes I (465–424), Xerxes II (424), Sogdianos (424–423), Darius II (423–404), Artaxerxes II (404–358), Artaxerxes III (358–338), Arses (338–336), and Darius III (336–331).

12 J. Collins, *Daniel*, 381.

13 In a highly supersessionist move, Christopher Watkin says all biblical prophecy "is to be read in terms of three cumulative peaks of fulfillment": (1) "fulfillment in the biblical history of Israel," (2) "a greater fulfillment in the incarnation, ministry, death, and resurrection of Christ," and (3) "their ultimate fulfillment in Christ's second coming and the advent of the new heaven and the new earth." Christopher Watkin and Timothy Keller, *Biblical Critical Theory: How the Bible's Unfolding Story Makes Sense of Modern Life and Culture* (Grand Rapids: Zondervan Academic, 2022), 301.

14 One need not look far to find this strict dichotomy in evangelical work. One recent example comes from Hugh Gauch, Robert Newman, and John Bloom, "Prophecy Arguments in Apostolic and Contemporary Times," *JETS* 65, no. 1 (2022): 37–46. Their argument is so deeply entrenched in this either/or paradigm that they make "atheism" one of the key words to their article, in which they say erroneously that any argument against prophetic historicity is atheism.

15 Lester Grabbe, "A Dan(iel) for All Seasons: For Whom Was Daniel Important?," in *The Book of Daniel: Composition and Reception*, ed. John J. Collins and Peter W. Flint (Leiden: Brill, 2001), 231. John Collins, *Daniel with an Introduction to Apocalyptic Literature* (Michigan: Eerdmans, 1984), 9

16 J. Collins, *Daniel* (1984), 12.

17 Shalom Paul, "The Mesopotamian Background of Daniel 1–6," in Collins and Flint, *Book of Daniel*, 63–64, n. 55.

18 J. Collins, *Daniel* (1984), 12.

19 J. Collins, *Daniel* (1984), 11.

20 Sharon Pace seems to support the speaker as Michael, but even that is unclear. See Pace, *Daniel* (Georgia: Smyth and Helwys, 2008), 316.

21 Sprinkle, *Daniel*, 287.
22 τὸ βδέλυγμα τῆς ἐρημώσεως.
23 One could argue the phrase appears at Dan 9:27, but this is contested.
24 David Wenham, "Abomination of Desolation," in *ABD*, 1:28–29.
25 Wenham, "Abomination of Desolation," in *ABD*, 1:28–29.
26 Gauch, Newman, and Bloom, "Prophecy Arguments," 46.
27 Peter Hodgson, *Winds of the Spirit* (Kentucky: Westminster John Knox, 1994), 289–90.
28 Michael Foust, "Mohler: Christians Should Support Israel yet Hold It Accountable," Baptist Press, April 25, 2002, accessed October 30, 2023, https://www.baptistpress.com/resource-library/news/mohler-christians-should-support-israel-yet-hold-it-accountable/.

12 Daniel 12 Reconsidered

1 This is not a typo; the Hebrew uses the exact shame phrase in succession (אֶחָד הֵנָּה לִשְׂפַת הַיְאֹר וְאֶחָד הֵנָּה לִשְׂפַת הַיְאֹר).
2 They cite Jacob being known as Israel (Gen 49:1) and Peter being Simon (Matt 10:2).
3 Don Stewart, "Is It Possible to Identify Michael the Archangel with Jesus?," Blue Letter Bible, accessed October 30, 2023, https://www.blueletterbible.org/faq/don_stewart/don_stewart_24.cfm; Catholic Answers, "Are Michael the Archangel and Jesus the Same Person?," March 3, 2020, https://www.catholic.com/qa/is-it-true-jehovahs-witnesses-believe-that-michael-the-archangel-and-jesus-are-the-same-person.
4 Hartman and Di Lella, *Daniel*, 306; Towner, *Daniel*, 165.
5 Owens, "Daniel," 456.
6 Tanner, *Daniel*, 728.
7 Hippolytus, *Scholia on Daniel* 12.1.
8 Wigand, *Brief Exposition*, 447; Calvin, *CO* 19:286.
9 Dan 12:1 uses בַּסֵּפֶר, meaning "in the book." Dan 10:21 reads, בִּכְתָב אֱמֶת ("book of truth" or "truthful book"), which puts the Hebrew for "book" in the construct form, possibly denoting a title or designation.
10 Exod 32:32–33; Ps 69:28; Isa 4:3.
11 Emphasis is mine. In the Hebrew, "will be delivered" is יִמָּלֵט, and "is found" is הַנִּמְצָא.
12 S. Miller, *Daniel*, 323; Tanner, *Daniel*, 734. Tanner boldly claims, "Israel must first repent and embrace the Lord Jesus as her Messiah."
13 Sprinkle, *Daniel*, 332.
14 For more examples for sleep as a death metaphor, see 2 Kgs 4:31, 13:21; Isa 26:19; Jer 51:39, 57; Job 14:12.

15 Frances Knight, "Cremation and Christianity: English Anglican and Roman Catholic Attitudes to Cremation since 1885," *Mortality* 23, no. 4 (2018): 301–19.

16 Billy Graham Evangelistic Association Staff, "Answers," Billy Graham Evangelistic Association, June 1, 2004, https://billygraham.org/answer/when-a-christian-dies-is-it-all-right-to-cremate-the-body/.

17 Gen 22:17, 26:4, 37:9; Exod 32:13; Deut 1:10, 1:22, 28:62; 1 Chr 27:23; Neh 9:23. Goldingay provides a brief overview of theories about these stars (see *Daniel*, 549).

18 See Isa 8:6 and 29:11–12. It also is like 4 Ezra 14:45–46 and Ezra's instruction to make some writings public but keep others secret.

19 Newsom, J. Collins, Hartman and Di Lella, Seow, and many other scholars support discussion around the theory, if not the theory itself.

20 הִנֵּה

21 The word is יד; the NRSV renders it as "power" at 1:2, which, despite conveying the symbolic meaning, robs the text of the actual "hand" metaphor.

22 Exod 6:1, 15:6; Deut 7:8; Pss 10:12, 89:13–15, 136:12–13; Isa 41:10, 48:13; Ezek 20:34; Job 12:9–10; 2 Chr 30:12.

23 Duguid, *Daniel*, at Dan 12:4–13, "How Will the End Come?"

24 Duguid, *Daniel*, at Dan 12:4–13, "How Will the End Come?"

25 Marc Swearingen, "The 1260, 1290, and 1335 Days: A Response to Futurist Interpretations of Daniel 12," *Journal of Interdisciplinary Graduate Research* 1 (2015): 28.

26 Jerome, *JCD* 12.11.

27 S. Miller, *Daniel*, 333.

28 For one example, see Hamilton and Carson, *With the Clouds of Heaven*, 53–54.

29 Pick any evangelical Christian reader cited in this book, and they will make the connection to hell and the "Lake of Fire" with expediency. Further, the concept of "hell" never appears in the Hebrew Bible or New Testament, but that is another argument for another book.

30 Duguid, *Daniel*, at Dan 12:4–13, "How Then Shall We Live?"

31 See Calvin and Towner.

32 Angela Davis, *Are Prisons Obsolete?* (New York: Seven Stories, 2003), 107.

Conclusion

1 Paul Griffin, "Protestantism and Racism," in *The Blackwell Companion to Protestantism* (New Jersey: Wiley-Blackwell, 2004), 360.

2 Phyllis Trible, "Eve and Adam: Genesis 2–3 Reread," *Andover Newton Quarterly* 13 (1973): 74–83.

3 Herbert Marbury, *Pillars of Cloud and Fire: The Politics of Exodus in African American Biblical Interpretation* (New York: New York University Press, 2015), 1.

4 Ultimate Daniel Fast, "Daniel Fast Food List," accessed October 19, 2023, https://ultimatedanielfast.com/ultimate-daniel-fast-food-guidelines/.

5 Ultimate Daniel Fast, "Daniel Fast Food List."

6 Hannah Jeon, "What Is the Daniel Fast and Is It Healthy? Experts Weigh In," *Good Housekeeping*, November 4, 2022, https://www.goodhousekeeping.com/health/diet-nutrition/a41723352/daniel-fast-diet/.

7 Merrill Willis, *Dissonance*, 181–95.

Bibliography

Aichele, George and the Bible and Culture Collective. *The Postmodern Bible.* New Haven: Yale University Press, 1995.

Allen, Clifton J, James Leo Green, Robert B Laurin, John T Bunn, and John Joseph Owens. *The Broadman Bible Commentary: Volume 6.* Nashville, Tennessee: Broadman Press, 1971.

Azzoni, Annalisa. "Betraying the Text: Creation Narratives in Their and Our Context." Pages 83–91 in *Focusing Biblical Studies: The Crucial Nature of the Persian and Hellenistic Period; Essays in Honor of Douglas A. Knight.* Edited by Jon Berquist and Alice Hunt. New York: T&T Clark International, 2012.

Bae, Chul-hyun. "Aramaic as a Lingua Franca during the Persian Empire (538–333 B.C.E.)." *Journal of Universal Language* 5, no. 1 (2004): 1–20.

Barton, John, and John Muddiman, eds. *The Oxford Bible Commentary.* Oxford: Oxford University Press, 2001.

Baumgartner, Frederic. *Longing for the End.* New York: Palgrave, 1999.

Beers, V. Gilbert. *The Early Reader's Bible.* Grand Rapids: Zondervan, 2001.

Bella, Timothy. "Pat Robertson Says Putin Was 'Compelled by God' to Invade Ukraine to Fulfill Armageddon Prophecy." *Washington Post,* March 1, 2022. https://www.washingtonpost.com/world/2022/03/01/pat-robertson-putin-god-russia-ukraine/.

Billy Graham Evangelistic Association Staff. "Answers." Billy Graham Evangelistic Association, June 1, 2004. https://billygraham.org/answer/when-a-christian-dies-is-it-all-right-to-cremate-the-body/.

Borger, Julian. "Fleeing a Hell the US Helped Create: Why Central Americans Journey North." *Guardian,* December 19, 2018. https://www.theguardian.com/us-news/2018/dec/19/central-america-migrants-us-foreign-policy.

Bretschneide, Joachim. "Life and Death in Nabada." *Scientific American,* January 1, 2005. https://www.scientificamerican.com/article/life-and-death-in-nabada/.

British Museum. "Object: The Cyrus Cylinder." Accessed October 30, 2023. https://www.britishmuseum.org/collection/object/W_1880-0617-1941.

Brown University. "Costs of the 20-Year War on Terror: $8 Trillion and 900,000 Deaths." September 29, 2023. https://www.brown.edu/news/2021-09-01/costsofwar.

Bullinger, Heinrich. *Daniel Sapientissimus Dei Propheta*. Zurich: C. Froschouerus, 1576.

Burke, Daniel. "Rick Perry Says Trump (and Obama) Were 'Ordained by God' to Be President." *CNN*, November 25, 2019. https://www.cnn.com/2019/11/25/politics/rick-perry-donald-trump-god/index.html.

Butler, S. A. L. *Mesopotamian Conceptions of Dreams and Dream Rituals*. Münster: Ugarit- Verlag, 1998.

Calvin, John. *Calvin's Commentaries*. Calvin Translation Society. 46 vols. Edinburgh, 1843–1855.

———. *Commentaries on the Book of the Prophet Daniel*. Translated by Jean Calvin and Thomas Myers. Grand Rapids: Eerdmans, 1948.

———. *Ioannis Calvini Opera Quae Supersunt Omnia*. Edited by G. Baum, E. Cunitz, and E. Reuss. 59 vols. Corpus Reformatorum 29–88. Brunswick and Berlin, 1863–1900.

Casper, Jayson. "The Wartime Prayers of Ukraine's Evangelicals." *Christianity Today*, March 11, 2022. https://www.christianitytoday.com/ct/2022/march-web-only/ukraine-prayer-bible-help-evangelical-christians-russia-war.html.

Catholic Answers. "Are Michael the Archangel and Jesus the Same Person?" March 3, 2020. https://www.catholic.com/qa/is-it-true-jehovahs-witnesses-believe-that-michael-the-archangel-and-jesus-are-the-same-person.

Clines, David J. A. *On the Way to the Postmodern: Old Testament Essays 1967–1998*. Vol. 1. London, United Kingdom: Sheffield Academic Press, 1998.

CNN. "Pat Robertson Says Haiti Paying for 'Pact to the Devil.'" January 13, 2010. http://www.cnn.com/2010/US/01/13/haiti.pat.robertson/index.html.

Collins, Adela Yarbro. "The Influence of Daniel on the New Testament." Pages 90–123 in *Daniel*, by John Collins. Minneapolis: Fortress, 1993.

Collins, John. *The Apocalyptic Imagination*. 3rd ed. Grand Rapids, Michigan: Eerdmans, 2016.

———. *The Apocalyptic Vision of the Book of Daniel*. Missoula, Montana. Scholars Press for Harvard Semitic Museum, 1977.

———. *Daniel*. Minneapolis: Fortress, 1993.

———. *Daniel with an Introduction to Apocalyptic Literature*. Grand Rapids, Michigan: Eerdmans, 1984.

———. *Introduction to the Hebrew Bible*. Minneapolis: Fortress, 2004.

Cone, James. *A Black Theology of Liberation: Fortieth Anniversary Edition*. New York: Orbis Books, 2011.

Connell, R. W. *Masculinities*. Oakland, California: University of California Press, 2005.

Cook, David. *The Action Bible*. Colorado Springs, Colorado: David C. Cook, 2010.
Corpus Scriptorum Christianorum Orientalium. Louvain, Belgium, 1903–.
Craigie, Peter, Page Kelley, and Joel Drinkard. *Jeremiah 1–25*. Dallas: Word Books, 1991.
Curchin, Leonard. "Old Age in Sumer: Life Expectancy and Social Status of the Elderly." *Florilegium* 2 (1980): 61–70.
Cyril of Jerusalem. "Catechetical Lectures." Pages 64–192 in *Cyril of Jerusalem and Nemesius of Emesa*. Translated by William Telfer. LCC 4. Philadelphia: Westminster, 1955.
Darr, Katheryn Pfisterer. "Ezekiel." Pages 1073–1607 in *The New Interpreter's Bible Commentary*, volume 6. Nashville: Abingdon, 1996.
Davidson, Benjamin. *The Analytical Hebrew and Chaldee Lexicon*. Grand Rapids: Zondervan, 1993.
Davis, Angela. *Are Prisons Obsolete?* New York: Seven Stories, 2003.
Davis, Dale Ralph. *The Message of Daniel*. Westmont, Illinois: IVP Academic, 2013.
Day, John. "The Daniel of Ugarit and Ezekiel and the Hero of the Book of Daniel." *Vetus Testamentum* 30, no. 2 (1980): 174–84.
De Graaf, Anne. *The Children's Bible*. Copenhagen, Denmark: Scandinavia Publishing House / Casscom Media, 2017.
Diodati, Giovanni. *Pious Annotations upon the Holy Bible*. London, United Kingdom: British Museum, 1651.
Diodorus Siculus. *The Library of History*. Vol. 2. Translated by C. H. Oldfather. Loeb Classical Library. Cambridge, Massachusetts: Harvard University Press, 2004.
Duguid, Iain. *Daniel*. Phillipsburg, New Jersey: P & R Publishing, 2008.
Dunbar-Ortiz, Roxanne. *An Indigenous Peoples' History of the United States*. Boston: Beacon, 2014.
Ephrem the Syrian. "In Danielem." Pages 203–33 in vol. 2 of ESSO.
———. *Sancti patris nostri Ephraem Syri Opera omnia*. Edited by J. A. Assemani. Rome, 1737.
Ferch, Arthur J. "The Book of Daniel and the 'Maccabean Thesis.'" *Andrews University Seminary Studies* 21, no. 2 (1983): 129–41.
Ferguson, Sinclair. *The Preacher's Commentary: Daniel*. Nashville: Thomas Nelson, 2002.
Ferguson, Sinclair, and Lloyd John Ogilvie. *Daniel*. Nashville: Thomas Nelson, 1988.
Fewell, Danna Nolan. *The Children of Israel: Reading the Bible for the Sake of Our Children*. Nashville: Abingdon, 2003.
———. *Circle of Sovereignty: Plotting Politics in the Book of Daniel*. Nashville: Abingdon, 1991.

Finkelstein, Israel, and Neil Asher Silberman. *The Bible Unearthed: Archaeology's New Vision of Ancient Israel and the Origin of Its Sacred Texts*. New York: Touchstone, 2001.

Foster, Michael, and Dominic Tennant. *It's Good to Be a Man: A Handbook for Godly Masculinity*. Moscow, Idaho: Canon Press, 2022.

Foust, Michael. "Mohler: Christians Should Support Israel yet Hold It Accountable." Baptist Press, April 25, 2002. Accessed October 30, 2023. https://www.baptistpress.com/resource-library/news/mohler-christians-should-support-israel-yet-hold-it-accountable/.

Freedman, David Noel, ed. *Anchor Bible Dictionary*. 6 vols. New York: Doubleday, 1992.

Gauch, Hugh, Robert Newman, and John Bloom. "Prophecy Arguments in Apostolic and Contemporary Times." Pages 37–46 in *JETS* 65, no. 1 (2022).

Gerhard, Johann. *Postilla: An Explanation of the Sunday and Most Important Festival Gospels for the Whole Year*. Vol. 1, *Sermons for the Church from Advent through Pentecost*. Malone, Texas: Center for the Study of Lutheran Orthodoxy, 2003.

Gifford, Edwin Hamilton. *From Nicene and Post-Nicene Fathers*. Second Series, vol. 7. Edited by Philip Schaff and Henry Wace. Buffalo, N.Y.: Christian Literature Publishing, 1894.

Gingrich, Callista. "Persecution of Christians Skyrockets Worldwide as 360 Million Oppressed. We Must Stand for Religious Freedom." *Fox News*, February 4, 2023. https://www.foxnews.com/opinion/persecution-christians-skyrockets-worldwide-360-million-oppressed-we-must-stand-religious-freedom.

Goldingay, John. *Daniel*. Grand Rapids: Zondervan Academic, 2019.

Grabbe, Lester. "A Dan(iel) for All Seasons: For Whom Was Daniel Important?" Pages 229–46 in *The Book of Daniel: Composition and Reception*. Edited by John J. Collins and Peter W. Flint. Leiden: Brill, 2001.

Graham, Billy. "The Rise of the Antichrist." *Hour of Decision*, September 16, 1972. https://billygraham.org/audio/the-rise-of-the-antichrist/.

Graham, Ruth. "Southern Baptists to Release List of Ministers Accused of Sexual Abuse." *New York Times*, May 24, 2022. https://www.nytimes.com/2022/05/24/us/southern-baptist-sexual-abuse.html.

Grayson, A. K. *Assyrian and Babylonian Chronicles*. TCS 5. University Park, Pennsylvania: Eisenbrauns, 1975.

Griffin, Paul. "Protestantism and Racism." Pages 357–71 in *The Blackwell Companion to Protestantism*. Hoboken, New Jersey: Wiley-Blackwell, 2004.

Hamilton, James, and D. A. Carson. *With the Clouds of Heaven: The Book of Daniel in Biblical Theology*. Westmont, Illinois: IVP Academic, 2014.

Hartman, Louis, and Alexander A. Di Lella. *The Book of Daniel*. Garden City, N.Y.: Doubleday, 1977.

Hartwig, Melinda K., ed. *A Companion to Ancient Egyptian Art*. Chichester, U.K.: Wiley Blackwell, 2015.

Herodotus. *Herodotus: Volume I*. Translated by A. D. Godley. Loeb Classical Library ed. London: William Heinemann, 1920.

Hippolytus. *Commentaire sur Daniel*. Vol. 14. Translated by Maurice Lefevre. Introduction by Gustave Bardy. Paris: Editions du Cerf, 1947.

———. *Kommentar zu Daniel*. Translated by Georg Nathanael Bonwetsch. Berlin: Akadamie Verlag, 2000.

———. "Scholia on Daniel." Orig. 3rd century CE. Translated by A. Mai; *Script Vetum Nova Collectio*. I.iii. 29–56.

Hodgson, Peter. *Winds of the Spirit*. Louisville, Kentucky: Westminster John Knox, 1994.

Hölscher, Gustav. "Die Entstehung des Buches Daniel." *Theologische Studien Kritiken* 92 (1919): 113–38.

House, Paul. *Daniel*. Westmont, Illinois: IVP Academic, 2018.

Irenaeus. *Adversus haereses*. Cambridge: Typis Academicis, 1857.

Irvine, Stuart. *Isaiah, Ahaz, and the Syro-Ephraimitic Crisis*. SBLDS 123. Atlanta: Scholars Press, 1990.

Isho'dad of Merv. "Commentarii in Danielem." Pages 101–35 in *Commentaire d'Iso'dad de Merv sur l'Ancien Testament, V. Jérémie, Ezécchiel, Daniel*. Edited by C. Van den Eynde. CSCO 328 (Scriptores Syri 146). Turnhout, Belgium: Brepols, 1972.

Jahn, Gustav. *Das Buch Daniel nach der Septuaginta hergestellt, übersetzt und kritisch erklärt*. Leipzig: Eduard Pfeiffer, 1904.

Jeon, Hannah. "What Is the Daniel Fast and Is It Healthy? Experts Weigh In." *Good Housekeeping*, November 4, 2022. https://www.goodhousekeeping.com/health/diet-nutrition/a41723352/daniel-fast-diet/.

Jeffress, Robert. "Pastor Robert Jeffress: Biden Is President-Elect—How Should Christians Respond?" *Fox News*, November 7, 2020. https://www.foxnews.com/opinion/biden-elected-christians-response-robert-jeffress.

Jerome. *Commentary on Daniel*. Translated by Gleason Archer. Grand Rapids: Baker Book House, 1958.

Jones, Dennis G. *Read with Me Bible: An NIV Story Bible for Children*. Grand Rapids: Zondervan, 1993.

Keck, Leander, ed. *The New Interpreter's Bible: General Articles & Introduction Commentary & Reflections for Each Book of the Bible including the Apocryphal*. Nashville: Abingdon, 1994.

Knight, Frances. "Cremation and Christianity: English Anglican and Roman Catholic Attitudes to Cremation since 1885." Pages 301–19 in *Mortality* 23, no. 4 (2018).

Knoll, Mark. *A History of Christianity in the United States and Canada*. Grand Rapids: Eerdmans, 1992.

Koch, Alexander, Chris Brierley, Mark M. Maslin, and Simon L. Lewis. "Earth System Impacts of the European Arrival and Great Dying in the Americas after 1492." *Quaternary Science Reviews* 207 (2019): 13–36.

Koch, Klaus. *Daniel: Biblischer Kommentar; No. 1–6*. Duisburg, Germany: Neukirchener Verlag des Erziehungsvereins, 1986.

Kvanvig, Helge S. *Roots of Apocalyptic: The Mesopotamian Background of the Enoch Figure and of the Son of Man*. Duisburg, Germany Neukirchener Verlag des Erziehungsvereins, 1988.

LaCocque, André. *The Book of Daniel*. Eugene, Oregon: Wipf and Stock, 2015.

Leprohon, Ronald, "Ideology and Propaganda." Pages 307–27 in *A Companion to Ancient Egyptian Art*. Chichester, U.K.: Wiley Blackwell, 2015.

Lindvall, Terry. *God Mocks: A History of Religious Satire from the Hebrew Prophets to Stephen Colbert*. New York: New York University Press, 2015.

Longman, Tremper, III. *The NIV Application Commentary: Daniel*. Grand Rapids: Zondervan, 2002.

Luther, Martin. *D. Martin Luther's Werke: Kritische Gesamtausgabe (Weimarer Ausgabe)*. Weimar: H. Böhlaus Nachfolger, 1883.

Luther, Martin, and Jaroslav Jan Pelikan. *Luther's Works*. Edited by Jaroslav Pelikan, Hilton C. Oswald, Helmut T. Lehmann, Christopher Boyd Brown, Benjamin T. G Mayes, and James Langebartels. American ed. St. Louis: Concordia, 1955.

Mann, Charles C. *1491: New Revelations of the Americas before Columbus*. New York: Vintage Books, 2005.

Mansfield, Stephen. *The Faith of George W. Bush*. New York: TarcherPerigee, 2003.

Marbury, Herbert. *Pillars of Cloud and Fire: The Politics of Exodus in African American Biblical Interpretation*. New York: New York University Press, 2015.

Marcus, David. "It's Time to Bring Back Prayer in Public Schools." *Federalist*, June 4, 2021. https://thefederalist.com/2021/06/04/its-time-to-bring-back-prayer-in-public-schools/.

Marti, Karl. *Das Buch Daniel*. HKAT 18. Tübingen: Mohr, 1901.

Martyr, Justin. *Dialogue with Trypho*. Translated by Thomas Falls. Washington, D.C.: Catholic University of America Press, 2003.

Mayer, John. *Commentary upon All the Prophets*. London, England: Robert and William Leybourn, 1652.

McGough, Matt, Krutika Amin, Nirmita Panchal, and Cynthia Cox. "Child and Teen Firearm Mortality in the U.S. and Peer Countries." KFF. July 18,

2023. https://www.kff.org/global-health-policy/issue-brief/child-and-teen-firearm-mortality-in-the-u-s-and-peer-countries/.

Mede, Joseph. *Daniels Weekes: An Interpretation of Part of the Prophecy of Daniel.* London, 1643.

Meinhold, Johannes. *Die Composition des Buches Daniel.* Greifswald, Germany: Julius Abel, 1884.

Melanchthon, Philippus. *Commentaire de Philippe Melanchthon sur le livre des révélations du prophète Daniel: Item les explications de Martin Luther sur le mesme prophète adjoutées à la fin, le tout nouvellement traduict. [Précédé de l'Argument du livre des révélations du prophète Daniel, par Jean Calvin].* Geneva: J. Crespin, 1555.

Merrill Willis, Amy C. *Dissonance and the Drama of Divine Sovereignty in the Book of Daniel.* London: T&T Clark, 2010.

Mettler, Zachary. "Christians, Be Not Afraid: You're Right to Believe in Two Genders and Preborn Life." *Daily Citizen*, April 21, 2021. https://dailycitizen.focusonthefamily.com/christians-be-not-afraid-youre-right-to-believe-in-two-genders-and-preborn-life/.

Migne, Jacques Paul. *Patrologiae Cursus Completus.* Alexandria, Virginia: Patrologia Latina Database, 1996.

Miller, Dave. "Did God Choose Barack Obama as President?" *SBC Voices*, November 8, 2012. https://sbcvoices.com/did-god-choose-barack-obama-as-president/.

Miller, Patrick. "Jeremiah." Pages in 983–1010 in *The New Interpreter's Bible*, volume 6. Nashville: Abingdon, 1994.

Miller, Stephen R. *The New American Commentary: Daniel.* Nashville: Broadman & Holman, 1994.

Mineo, Liz. "Racial Wealth Gap May Be a Key to Other Inequities." *Harvard Gazette*, June 17, 2021. https://news.harvard.edu/gazette/story/2021/06/racial-wealth-gap-may-be-a-key-to-other-inequities/.

Moody, Chris. "How US Right-Wing Views Putin amid Russian War on Ukraine." *Al Jazeera*, March 4, 2022. https://www.aljazeera.com/news/2022/3/4/how-us-right-wing-views-putin-amid-russian-attack-on-ukraine.

Moore, Megan Bishop, and Brad E. Kelle. *Biblical History and Israel's Past: The Changing Study of the Bible and History.* Grand Rapids: Eerdmans, 2011.

Murphy, Kevin. "Kansas Lawmaker Suggests Immigrants Be Shot like Hogs." *Reuters*, March 25, 2011. https://www.reuters.com/article/us-immigration-kansas/kansas-lawmaker-suggests-immigrants-be-shot-like-hogs-idUSTRE72O71H20110325.

Newsom, Carol. *Daniel.* Louisville: Westminster John Knox, 2014.

Noegel, Scott. "On the Wings of the Winds: Towards an Understanding of Winged *Mischwesen* in the Ancient Near East." *Kaskal* 14 (2017): 15–54.

Olander, Olivia. "Trump: 'God Made the Decision' Overturning Roe." *POLITICO*, June 24, 2022. https://www.politico.com/news/2022/06/24/trump-to-fox-god-made-the-decision-overturning-roe-00042284.

Orr, Avigdor. "The Seventy Years of Babylon." Pages 191–235 in *Vetus Testamentum* 6, no. 3 (1956).

O'Sullivan, John. "Annexation." Pages 5–10 in *Democratic Review* 17 (July–August 1845).

Owens, John. "Daniel." Pages 373–460 in *The Broadman Bible Commentary: Volume 6*. Edited by Clifton Allen. Nashville, Tennessee: Broadman Press, 1971.

Pace, Sharon. *Daniel*. Macon, Georgia: Smyth and Helwys, 2008.

Paul, Shalom. "The Mesopotamian Background of Daniel 1–6." Pages 55–68 in *The Book of Daniel: Composition and Reception*. Edited by John J. Collins and Peter W. Flint. Leiden: Brill, 2001.

Peterson, Eugene. *Reversed Thunder: The Revelation of John and the Praying Imagination*. San Francisco: Harper & Row, 1988.

Portier-Young, Anathea. *Apocalypse against Empire: Theologies of Resistance in Early Judaism*. Grand Rapids: Eerdmans, 2011.

Primasius of Hadrumetum. *Commentary on the Apocalypse*. CCSL 92. Turnhout, Belgium: Brepols, 1985.

Rendell, Ed. "No More 'Thoughts and Prayers'—Pass the Gun Laws America Needs." *Hill*, March 28, 2023. https://thehill.com/opinion/criminal-justice/3922561-no-more-thoughts-and-prayers-pass-the-gun-laws-america-needs/.

Retief, F. P., J. F. G. Cilliers, and S. P. J. K. Riekert. "Eunuchs in the Bible." Pages 247–58 in *Acta Theologica Supplementum* 26, no. 2 (2006).

Roberts, A., and J. Donaldson, eds. *Ante-Nicene Fathers*. 10 vols. Buffalo, N.Y.: Christian Literature, 1885–1896. Reprint, Grand Rapids: Eerdmans, 1951–1956. Reprint, Peabody, Mass.: Hendrickson, 1994.

Sasson, Jack M. *Civilizations of the Ancient Near East*. New York: Charles Scribner's Sons, 1995.

Schaff, P., et al., eds. *A Select Library of the Nicene and Post-Nicene Fathers of the Christian Church*. Buffalo, N.Y.: Christian Literature, 1887–1894. Reprint, Grand Rapids: Eerdmans, 1952–1956. Reprint, Peabody, Mass.: Hendrickson, 1994.

Seow, C. L. *Daniel*. Louisville: Westminster John Knox, 2003.

Shabo, Magedah. *Techniques of Propaganda and Persuasion*. Smyrna, Delaware: Prestwick House, 2008.

Smietana, Bob. "When Abuse Victims Are Adults, They're Often Treated as 'Sinners,' Threats to Churches." *Word and Way*, July 8, 2022. https://wordandway.org/2022/07/06/when-abuse-victims-are-adults-theyre-often-treated-as-sinners-threats-to-churches/.

Smith, Gregory A. "About a Third in U.S. See God's Hand in Presidential Elections, but Fewer Say God Picks Winners Based on Policies." Pew Research

Center, March 12, 2020. https://www.pewresearch.org/fact-tank/2020/03/12/about-a-third-in-u-s-see-gods-hand-in-presidential-elections-but-fewer-say-god-picks-winners-based-on-policies/.

Smith, Jonathan Z. "'Narratives into Problems': The College Introductory Course and the Study of Religion." Pages 727–39 in *JAAR* 56 (1988).

Smith, Mark. *The Origins of Biblical Monotheism: Israel's Polytheistic Background and the Ugaritic Texts*. New York, New York: Oxford University Press, 2003.

Smith, Uriah. *The Prophecies of Daniel and the Revelation*. Battle Creek, Michigan: Review and Herald, 1904.

Smith-Christopher, Daniel. *Daniel*. Nashville: Abingdon, 1996.

Sprinkle, Joe. *Daniel*. Bellingham, Washington: Lexham Press, 2021.

Steinmann, Andrew. *Daniel*. St. Louis, Missouri: Concordia, 2008.

Stanley, Jason. *How Propaganda Works*. Princeton, New Jersey: Princeton University Press, 2015.

Stewart, Don. "Is It Possible to Identify Michael the Archangel with Jesus?" Blue Letter Bible. Accessed October 30, 2023. https://www.blueletterbible.org/faq/don_stewart/don_stewart_24.cfm.

Swarns, Rachel L. "My Research into the History of Catholic Slaveholding Transformed My Understanding of My Church." *New York Times*, March 16, 2021. https://www.nytimes.com/2021/03/16/us/catholic-church-enslavement.html.

Swearingen, Marc. "The 1260, 1290, and 1335 Days: A Response to Futurist Interpretations of Daniel 12." Pages 1–32 in *Journal of Interdisciplinary Graduate Research* 1 (2015).

Swim, Roy. "Daniel." Edited by A.F. Harper and W.T. Purkiser. Pages 537–600 in vol. 4 of *Beacon Bible Commentary*. Kansas City: Beacon Hill Press, 1966.

Swindoll, Charles. *Daniel, Volume 1: God's Man for the Moment*. Frisco, Texas: IFL Publishing House, 2008.

Tagholm, Sally, et al. *Children's Bible Stories: Share the Greatest Stories Ever Told*. London: DK Publishing, 2021.

Tanner, J. Paul. *Daniel*. Bellingham, Washington: Lexham Press, 2021.

Team ENOUGH. "Gun Violence Statistics." Accessed October 30, 2023. https://www.teamenough.org/gun-violence-statistics.

Tertullian. *Against Marcion*. Translated by Peter Holmes. Edinburgh: T&T Clark, 1909.

———. *An Answer to the Jews*. Available at https://www.newadvent.org/fathers/0308.htm. Accessed July 24, 2023.

Theodoret of Cyrus. *Commentary on Daniel*. Translated by Robert Hill. Boston: Brill, 2006.

Thomas, Hugh. *The Slave Trade: The Story of the Atlantic Slave Trade, 1440–1870*. New York: Simon & Schuster, 1997.

Towner, W. Sibley. *Daniel*. Louisville: Westminster John Knox, 1984.

Trible, Phyllis. "Eve and Adam: Genesis 2–3 Reread." Pages 251–58 in *Andover Newton Quarterly* 13 (March 1973).

Ultimate Daniel Fast. "Daniel Fast Food List." Accessed October 19, 2023. https://ultimatedanielfast.com/ultimate-daniel-fast-food-guidelines/.

United Nations. "Slave Trade." Accessed October 29, 2023. https://www.un.org/en/observances/decade-people-african-descent/slave-trade.

Van der Toorn, Karel, Bob Becking, and Pieter Willem van der Horst. *Dictionary of Deities and Demons in the Bible*. Boston, Massachusetts: Eerdmans, 1999.

VBS Curriculum. *Knights of the North Castle*. Nashville: Cokesbury, 2020.

Waltke, Bruce and Michael Patrick O'Connor. *An Introduction to Biblical Hebrew Syntax*. Winona Lake, Ind.: Eisenbrauns, 1990.

Warrior, Robert Allen. "Canaanites, Cowboys, and Indians." Pages 93–105 in *Native and Christian: Indigenous Voices on Religious Identity in the United States and Canada*. Edited by James Treat. New York: Routledge, 1996.

Watkin, Christopher, and Timothy Keller. *Biblical Critical Theory: How the Bible's Unfolding Story Makes Sense of Modern Life and Culture*. Grand Rapids: Zondervan Academic, 2022.

Weems, Renita. *Battered Love: Marriage, Sex, and Violence in the Hebrew Prophets*. Minneapolis: Fortress, 1995.

Wenger, Tisa. *Religious Freedom: The Contested History of an American Ideal*. Chapel Hill: University of North Carolina Press, 2017.

Wesley, Fiona. *Bible for Kids: A Collection of Bible Stories for Children*. Independent Publication, 2014.

Whitley, C. F. "The Seventy Years Desolation: A Rejoinder." Pages 416–18 in *Vetus Testamentum* 7 (1957).

Wigand, Johann. *Brief Exposition of the Prophet Daniel*. Jena, Germany: Guntherus Huttichius, 1571.

Wiseman, D. J. Nebuchadnezzar and Babylon. New York: Oxford University Press, 1985.

Wolfe, William. "Yes, Christians Are Being Persecuted in America: Here's How We Can Respond." *Christian Post*, July 18, 2022. https://www.christianpost.com/voices/yes-christians-are-being-persecuted-in-america.html.

World Population Review. "Incarceration Rates by Country 2023." Accessed October 30, 2023. https://worldpopulationreview.com/country-rankings/incarceration-rates-by-country.

Writings from the Greco-Roman World. Atlanta, Georgia: Society of Biblical Literature, 2001–.

Xenophon. *Cyropaedia*. Translated by Walter Miller. New York: Macmillan, 1918.

Zerafa, P. "The Old Testament Life Span." *Angelicum* 65, no. 1 (1988): 99–116.

Zinn, Howard. *A People's History of the United States*. New York: Harper Perennial, 2015.

Index